D1739870

DOWN TO THE CROSSROADS

Guy Rundle is currently *Crikey's* global correspondent-at-large. Born in Melbourne, he was a co-founding editor of *Arena Magazine* and has worked with the Arena publishing group for twenty years. A frequent contributor to *The Age, Sydney Morning Herald, The Australian, Spiked* and many other publications, his books include *The Opportunist: John Howard and the Triumph of Reaction* and half of *The Happy Phrase* (with Shane Maloney). He has written for and produced a wide variety of TV programs, and co-devised *Comedy Inc, Shark Bay* and worse. He has written three hit stage shows with and for Max Gillies, with a fourth, *Godzone*, to premiere in 2009. At the time of writing he lives in New York.

DOWN TO THE CROSSROADS

ON THE TRAIL OF THE 2008 US ELECTION

★ ★ ★ ★ ★

GUY RUNDLE

Penguin Books

PENGUIN BOOKS

Published by the Penguin Group
Penguin Group (Australia)
250 Camberwell Road, Camberwell, Victoria 3124, Australia
(a division of Pearson Australia Group Pty Ltd)
Penguin Group (USA) Inc.
375 Hudson Street, New York, New York 10014, USA
Penguin Group (Canada)
90 Eglinton Avenue East, Suite 700, Toronto, Canada ON M4P 2Y3
(a division of Pearson Penguin Canada Inc.)
Penguin Books Ltd
80 Strand, London WC2R 0RL England
Penguin Ireland
25 St Stephen's Green, Dublin 2, Ireland
(a division of Penguin Books Ltd)
Penguin Books India Pvt Ltd
11 Community Centre, Panchsheel Park, New Delhi – 110 017, India
Penguin Group (NZ)
67 Apollo Drive, Rosedale, North Shore 0632, New Zealand
(a division of Pearson New Zealand Ltd)
Penguin Books (South Africa) (Pty) Ltd
24 Sturdee Avenue, Rosebank, Johannesburg 2196, South Africa

Penguin Books Ltd, Registered Offices: 80 Strand, London, WC2R 0RL, England

First published by Penguin Group (Australia), 2008

10 9 8 7 6 5 4 3 2 1

Text copyright © Guy Rundle 2008

Hillary image: Robyn Beck/AFP/Getty Images, John McCain image by William Thomas Cain/Getty Images, Barack Obama image by Bill Pugliano/Getty Images, Sarah Palin image: Robyn Beck/AFP/Getty Images

The moral right of the author has been asserted

All rights reserved. Without limiting the rights under copyright reserved above, no part of this publication may be reproduced, stored in or introduced into a retrieval system, or transmitted, in any form or by any means (electronic, mechanical, photocopying, recording or otherwise), without the prior written permission of both the copyright owner and the above publisher of this book.

Cover design by Daniel New © Penguin Group (Australia)
Text design by Tony Palmer © Penguin Group (Australia)
Typeset in 11.5/17pt Adobe Garamond by Post Pre-Press Group, Brisbane, Queensland
Printed and bound in Australia by McPherson's Printing Group, Maryborough, Victoria

National Library of Australia
Cataloguing-in-Publication data:

Rundle, Guy.

Down to the crossroads : on the trail of the 2008
presidential election / Guy Rundle.

ISBN: 9780143010425 (pbk.)

Elections–United States.
Presidents–United States–Election–2008.
United States–Politics and government–21st century.

324.973

penguin.com.au

To my mother, who went back to school then university
during the Whitlam years, and then much more,
and in memory of my father, who voted for Gough Whitlam
five times (or claimed to) – both early and most important
lessons in being the change you want to see in the world.

Barnaby,
belated happy
birthday. Hope
all is well.
With love +
apologies for being
such a vindictive
ass. Oli.

To dare is to lose one's footing momentarily.
Not to dare is to lose oneself.
Kierkegaard

Rather than it should have failed,
I would have seen half the earth desolated.
Thomas Jefferson, on the French Revolution

Like a bunch of junkies building a rocket to the moon,
to check out a rumour the craters were full of smack.
Hunter S. Thompson, on a failed campaign

Contents

INTRODUCTION

On Friday the seventh of November, the year of our Lord two thousand and eight, the President-elect of the United States, Barack Hussein Obama gave his first post-victory press conference. That morning, another disastrous series of economic results had been released, with the US losing 159 000 jobs in the month of September, for a total of 760 000 for the year. With a phalanx of twenty or so of his transition-team economic advisors behind him, the man who would take power in January 2009 addressed the pressing questions of the time: a stimulus package for the economy, relations with Iran and the choice criteria for the new White House puppy. He was low-key, he was focused, he was precise – which was a change in itself after the previous eight years.

Whatever people may, in the back of their minds, have expected from the first black president – a Martin Luther King-style piece of soaring oratory, a Jesse Jackson burst of thumping anger – they didn't get it. This thin, young-looking man speaking from the podium sounded more like a precise European prime minister or chancellor, one of the interchangeable technocrats of the Nordic countries, than an occupier of the office of Jefferson, of Lincoln, of FDR, of Reagan. All straightforward, all very matter-of-fact.

Yet watching it on CNN in the debris of a destroyed motel room, through the exhaustion of a week, a month, ten months, of being witness to a presidential campaign, it was still impossible to believe. It was that literal point between dream and reality, the *nomos*-land between waking and sleep, when real figures commingle in fantasy situations, when the blasts of a horn turn out to be the digital clock's alarm . . . Over the days after the evening at Grant Park, Chicago, where President-elect Obama had claimed victory, one had kept forgetting it had occurred, and then remembering and feeling that extraordinary rush of emotions all over again, the joy, the ecstasy, the sudden realisation of how much you had wanted, needed, this to happen.

What was there in that press conference, in those first days, was a sudden realisation not merely of what was beginning, but of what had ended – and, most importantly, what had been avoided. In the final eight weeks of the campaign, the Republican candidate John McCain – a half-decent man whose decency had nevertheless been overrated by liberals eager to find wholesome people on the right – had, in desperation, launched a campaign of suspicion and fear, leaning heavily on Obama's fairly brief associations with members of the Chicago and New York post–new left, to segue to a notion of 'un-Americanism' at the heart of his campaign.

Though McCain never revisited the attacks on Obama's one-time pastor Jeremiah Wright and his black liberationist theology – attacks that had largely been mounted by Hillary Clinton – it seems likely this was because poll after poll showed it was of little import to the electorate in the wake of the September economic meltdown. For the rest of it, the politician who had begun spruiking his 'Straight Talk Express' and a clean campaign had employed the bulk of the Republican political operatives who had smeared him during the 2000 primary season, and was, in desperation, throwing the sink at Obama.

Though it threw a wobble into even the most optimistic Obama supporter at the time, John McCain's negative campaign may well prove to be one of his great, albeit inadvertent, contributions to America – for on 4 November 2008, the American people rejected not only an unambiguous view of American exceptionalism, and a harsh and exhausted punitive economics, they rejected an appeal to the darker side of American history and personality, to fears old and new, to a limited notion of human and national possibility.

It was only in the final weeks of the campaign that those of us who believed that American was facing something more than a trivial choice began to get seriously worried – and eventually, cripplingly anxious – about what the American people would choose. Even though the polls had been trending up for Obama ever since the September meltdown, the relentless echo chamber of the 24-hour news media couldn't but have you spooked by various phantoms. The 'Bradley effect' – the idea that white people would not honestly tell opinion pollsters that they wouldn't vote for a black person – was marshalled incessantly, as was the idea of a 'late tightening', of people 'stepping into the ballot box and coming to their senses' [sic].

So when, in the end, none of that came to pass, and the victory of Barack Obama and the Democratic Party arrived almost exactly as the polls said it would, the emotion was overwhelming, multiple, manifold. It was not merely a hope, for anyone who knew the USA, that this country might start to address its hallucinatory foreign policy, its murderous and cruel health system, its failed schools, its poverty and want of opportunity along lines of class, race and gender. It was a deep resolving sense that the worst could be surrounded and defeated by the best in a society. That it was now possible to surrender a suspicion, an occult belief, that the worst would out.

When Illinois Senator Barack Obama announced his candidacy in 2007, after much anticipation, it was greeted by almost everyone as a long shot, a first excursion into the field of presidential politics, to test the water. Hillary Clinton was, after all, the presumed candidate at a time when George Bush and the Republican Party had fallen to record lows of public support. Obama was forty-six; in four of eight years he would be in his fifties and, whether Hillary won or lost, more in a position to launch a credible campaign to become – wow, imagine it – the first black president.

But for those observing it, it quickly became clear that Obama meant it, this time round, like, now. He had marshalled an impressive and innovative grassroots campaign, combining his experience as a Chicago community organiser with the internet-based techniques pioneered by Howard Dean in the 2004 race. He was oracular without being bombastic, tight on policy without being wonkish. He had a loose style that could suddenly become electric. He was a player. This was the real thing. This was not a drill, baby, this was not a drill.

When *Crikey* editor Jonathan Green suggested I go to the US and spend the full year covering the US elections – a departure not only for Crikey, but for niche news websites in general – I was living in Sweden, pursuing a master's degree in European culture and politics, and wondering, notwithstanding the excellence of the course, why I had projected myself back into the straitjacket of formal study.

Everyone else wondered why I had projected myself into Sweden – not least Swedes – and especially Uppsala, Scandinavia's Oxford, an hour north of Stockholm. For Swedes, the comment was part of an ingrained self-deprecation that masked a (not unrealistic) belief that they were the smartest guys on the planet, and should probably be left to run stuff.

'Oh, we're so boring,' they would say, inaccurately, of a culture where passion and reserve are simply assembled differently than elsewhere, but one knew what they meant. For the truth was that Sweden, notwithstanding the occasional reversal, had got it right. It was rich but it was reasonably equal; it had virtually abolished poverty but people were energetic and entrepreneurial; it had high wages but it had managed to renovate and revolutionise its industrial base so that it still made things and had a real economy.

Its health system was both universal yet less sclerotic than, say, the UK; it was on the way towards a 70–80 per cent uptake of higher education; it had child care and 400+ days of paid parental care; its Nordic and monocultural society had extended a hand to refugees from across the world and never drawn it back. In 2006, the US had taken 700 Iraqi refugees; Sweden, despite the fact that every one of its political parties had opposed the US invasion, had taken 15 000. In Uppsala, they opened candy stores and tobacco shops, adding themselves to earlier waves – Iranians, Somalians, Kurds, Palestinians and, back in the '50s and '60s, black Deep South Americans; anyone who faced, in their own country, a choice between silence and the noose – who had enlivened the place decade on decade. Swedes were wont to lament how much the 'folkshuset', the people's home of the welfare state, had drawn in since the 1970s, but they only needed a little goading to reassert that they knew that, in some way, they had got things right.

The problem that many people identified with Sweden was that there was a certain ennui to it, a slightly depressive quality. As loyal viewers of Bergman movies may have noted, this is a reasonably deep-seated thing, but it was easy for people to attribute this to some deadening quality of the Nordic social system. In fact, if Sweden had a problem, it was that it didn't have a problem – it had burst the tape, into the realm of a fully completed modernity, a system in which the equal development of each had some significant relationship to the equal development of all. What many saw as boredom or ennui was in fact the next historical challenge – when the old struggles are substantially over, what do you do then? How do you define yourself, your civic identity, the meaning of your effort, in a post-historical space?

These were the thoughts that were going through my head as winter came on in the frozen north. I remember one signal moment in Uppsala, just beneath the historic castle, when a dozen bedraggled Swedish neo-Nazis staged a demonstration to defend Viking values. The ten-person police contingent sent along to supervise was 60 per cent female and the other four were two Kurds, a second-generation Chilean–Swede, and one single central-casting Nordic blond male. God, it was so obvious what had been intended. God, it was funny.

But it was all a great background to an American gig, because, in all aspects of modernity, all conceivable measures, Sweden had succeeded and the US had failed. I knew this from previous visits to the latter. It was exciting, it was various – though less various than its parochial population thought it was – but the bulk of its colour and motion was a product of the hardscrabble lives that more than a hundred million American people lived. Through forty years of the cheap junk of exceptionalism – 'We're Americans! We're the best in the world!' – the expectations of Americans had been gradually lowered until they would accept almost any conditions foisted on them, conditions that would cause riots in any other modern society.

Michael Moore's *Fahrenheit 9/11* began with a George Bush vox pop in which he was speaking to a woman who held down three jobs to keep up her mortgage. 'Three jobs . . .' Dubya said. 'Only in America!' he added approvingly. The line got full-bodied laughter in European cinemas, tentative giggles in middle-America. Why the latter? Because the belief that this martyrdom to wage-labour was somehow a mark of inner virtue dies hard in a puritan society.

So the American gig was always going to be an adventure. But Sweden served as a sort of prelude, a question which America could answer one way or t'other – either a frank facing of their deep-seated problems or a further retreat into self-reassurance and denial. Fair to say, though, that most of those who hoped the country could measure up to its challenges presumed that they would have to accept the dynastic elevation of Hillary Clinton in order for it to occur.

Most people will deny it now, but for the first couple of months it seemed obvious to many that however good a run Barack Obama had, it would be only a matter of time before Hillary Clinton prevailed and became the nominee – at which point everyone could then look back on what an amazing run (unprecedented, etcetera) Obama had enjoyed and how it stood him in good stead for 2016, etcetera etcetera.

To a degree there was also a hope among many hard-bitten Democrats that this would be the case. The past thirty years had seen so many occasions in which the liberal wing of the party had succeeded in selecting a candidate too leftish, big city and/ or northeastern for the majority of the country – McGovern, Dukakis, Kerry – to win, that it was beginning to seem like there was a death wish in the party. Now, with a regime commonly agreed to be among the worst in America's history, and with a mainstream candidate – Hillary – who had hitherto been thought of as the left candidate, the grandees of the party were about to be swamped by a campaign for a figure who was out of the post-modern left, the Chicago machine, and was . . . black.

Like many people sympathetic to the Democrats – from far to the left, in my case – I was torn between the two scenarios. The Obama campaign was so audacious, so historic that the idea of it was hard to resist. But the possibility that, through over-reaching, the Democrats might allow the Republicans to get further along the way to their 'permanent majority' was too awful to contemplate. There seemed little doubt that John McCain or Mitt Romney would run a better administration than the chaotic Bush regime, and thus re-establish the idea that Republicans were competent and the Democrats hopeless dreamers, a result that might have consequences for decades.

Personally, I had no great investment in a Democratic victory per se. Indeed, if the Republicans had by some miracle continued to control Congress – they lost it in 2006 – I would have been hopeful of a McCain presidency, on the grounds that its prosecution of an infantile idea of American supremacy and virtue would have done more to push the world into multiple conflicts (all of them, in the long run, benefiting the post-colonial world) and the decline of American power than anything else could.

But once the Democrats had taken control of the House, it was clear that the choice of a Republican president would just serve up a boring gridlocked, ineffectual mishmash. A Democratic president and Congress working together would at least be able to address some of the grievous social problems that cause so much unnecessary suffering in the United States. From previous trips I had become acquainted – as only the most blinkered could not – with the slow disaster that had befallen many average wage earners and workers in the US, the slow leaching away of hope and possibility.

My first months in the US would only confirm that impression and deepen it. Compared to, well, Sweden, the everyday decay of large parts of the US was pitiful to behold, and some attempt to give an account of it is a part of the pages that follow. Politically, though, the principal result was a hope that a Democrat, any Democrat, could take the White House and mitigate some of the suffering, and for quite a while that seemed like Hillary Clinton.

But as the year and the primary campaign progressed, it became clear that something else was going on. As Hillary's campaign became more desperate, she reached into the lower depths of a populist tradition, at one point talking about her desire to represent 'hard-working white people'.

Simultaneously it became clear that Obama's campaign was no flash-in-the-pan, no exploratory effort – it was indeed a synthesis of grassroots action, the Chicago machine, cutting-edge online techniques and, above all, a deeply thoughtful reconsideration of the American mood crafted by the candidate himself, a veteran of the postmodern left, and someone who had at some point stopped to think a few things through.

A confrontation between Hillary and John McCain – who was by then pulling ahead in the Republican primaries – would have been a choice between two versions of something similar – white political professionalism, slanted towards the centre. But it was becoming clear that McCain would be lining up against Obama, and a very different choice was emerging.

Not for the first time in those months, the myth of the crossroads came to me. You know the story, told in many cultures, but in the US, most recently about the old blues guitarist Robert Johnson. Effectively the founder of rock'n'roll, Johnson took slow country blues and turned it into the urgent, urban, industrial rhythms of what would become electric music – but he did it all on an acoustic guitar, making, in the recordings we have of him, that single instrument yell, moan and sing like something was trying to escape from it.

Johnson was a country boy, a criminal, a bit of everything, who'd shown no great chops as a guitarist – until he went away for a while and came back one of the greats. People around said there was no mystery about it – he'd gone down to the crossroads and sold his soul to the devil in exchange for his talent.

For a while, after Obama's victory in the primaries, and before the first debates, the strange dog days of the election, I tried that story on a few people as a metaphor for the whole thing. But I soon stopped because I realised that people were misinterpreting me, wilfully and otherwise. In retrospect it seemed obvious that people would presume I was equating Barack Obama with Robert Johnston, the man who ascended to a height beyond anything hitherto dreamt of – but only by making the Faustian bargain.

Once that equation was made, I realised how liable it was to being understood other than in the way I had dreamt it. Liberals greeted the idea as a racist horror – that the rise of a black man could only be considered as the victory of evil – but even worse was the response of some Republicans, who took it up enthusiastically. They were only too eager to fit Barack Obama's passage through the trailing caravans of the new left in '80s New York and Chicago (the encounters with old radicals like Bill Ayers, and Palestinian advocates such as Rashid Khalidi) into the metaphor, and thereby forecast the coming death of America at the hands of this tempted and fallen trickster.

But I had never thought of it like that. It had always seemed to me, duh, that America was Johnston, and Obama the crossroads, or one direction away from them, in any case. That it was a nation tempted, and capable of being almost endlessly tempted, by satanic (in the original Judaic sense of the word as adversarial, contrary to life and hope) thoughts of a special, invulnerable role in the world, of protection from its own inimical habits, and of an endless search for enemies requiring torment, both within and without its borders.

Yeah, it was a hallucinatory sort of notion, but it was one borne of hope – hope for the world, that the US, in its inevitable process of decline from superpower to one among a multipolar world, would choose a president who had a reflexive wisdom about the aspirations of the other nineteen-twentieths of the earth, and how their understanding of recent history differed pretty fundamentally from that of the conservative think-tank commanders.

But it was also borne of a hope for the hundreds, the thousands of Americans – and the tens of millions they represented – that I had met along the way through writing these reports, in cheap motels, in dingy taverns, in Greyhound stations, in all the places you never see on the package tours or in the sitcoms. It is the American world of needless suffering, of lives blighted. Not merely those in absolute poverty, but the pinched existences of the working poor and the desperate middle class: one bad bill, one illness away from penury. It is the America true patriots like Michael Moore turn their attention to, and the one to which conservative foreign policy Americophiles in Australia and the UK show utter indifference.

It is the America that, if you develop any love for this country, as I have after nearly a year here, you cannot ignore, because it is the America that results from a broken promise, from a failure of moral and political will. Australia, Sweden, elsewhere – we have a ways to go on the road to equality and opportunity for all, but nowhere have we turned the machinery of the state and the economy against the population so relentlessly as has occurred in the US, from the election of Ronald Reagan – and with barely a respite in the Clinton years – onwards.

To believe that the election of Barack Obama, this inner-city leftist who has triumphed only by understanding the limits within which someone seeking executive power in the US must work, is of itself some sort of deliverance from and defeat of that would be foolish. To believe that it was not a categorical moment of change for America and the world is to fall into a cynicism that is ultimately naive, because it believes that everything is ultimately as it appears, that nothing changes, that nothing ever happens or is made.

Working through the record that follows, the reader will find something that is far from an exhaustive record of the blow-by-blow events of the campaign – though looking over it, I was pleasantly surprised by how much it had touched on. It rapidly became clear in the reporting that there was no point in simply relating the events that every other Australian correspondent was lifting and rehashing ad nauseum – uselessly, in a world where every newspaper in the world (you know, all the ones Sarah Palin reads) is a Google away. Instead it was an attempt to record the feel of the campaign and the character of the country, the hopes, bewilderments and sloughs of despond of a correspondent who never made any secret of his loyalties.

Some of the day-to-day judgements will jar with what is becoming the official version of the Obama campaign – that it was a flawless and expert takeover and transformation of American politics. Yet I stand by much of the hair-tearing that you will read in the sections covering July and August especially. There's no doubt in my mind that following the primaries, the Obama campaign was thoroughly outclassed by John McCain's punchy, feisty attacks on foreign policy, experience, character and so on, and was as ineffective as any previous Democratic campaign – the nightmare memories of Dukakis and Kerry – in hitting back. It was a period when I introduced to selected US interlocutors the indispensable phrase 'stunned mullet'.

Then the Democrats caught a break. McCain inexplicably picked – or was convinced to pick – Sarah Palin as a running mate, and the 'experience' angle went out the window. The financial system collapsed and the old Navy pilot decided to crash one last plane on the carrier deck, coming off as erratic and inexperienced. To their credit, the Obama campaign was, in the old ward heeler saying 'willing to be lucky', and after the crash they never put a foot wrong. But it was a damn close-run thing. Had Hank Paulson bailed out Lehman Brothers and staved off collapse for a few months the final result might have been very historically different. On that stuff I was spot on. On some of my other helpful advice to the campaign, not so much – possibly why they're in the White House and I'm wrangling this into shape in a fifty-dollar-a-night motel on the Chesapeake Bay. But for good or ill, I've left it all in.

At midnight, at the crossroads, the American people took the way that, even many of John McCain's supporters would agree, had a reasonable chance of getting them back on the path of righteousness. Sweden – Europe – was always the fear that conservatives brandished against Obama in the campaign – that America would lose its soul to alien ideas, to 'socialism'. Their fear should now be that he may usher in just enough for people to get to like it. For the waitresses on the swing shift, the laid-off workers of Ohio, the Hispanic families in the hospital emergency room, the couple living in room eight of the Motel Six, the bankrupted and foreclosed on, the cast of the American nightmare, one can but hope.

In the days between Obama's victory and that first press conference, I and millions of others floated in a period of lightness, of joy whose exact qualities I have rarely experienced as a mass and political phenomenon. Everyone remarked on it, the sudden kindness and courtesies, the sense of shared possibility and hope, that whatever the compromises, disappointments and clashes to come, the struggle would occur in a spirit of reason and collective possibility, not of division and fabricated hate. That they could cleave to the best, not the worst, in their shared traditions. Well, we can but hope, as the man says. And now this book has to be finished and this copy sent. And now dawn is coming up across the car park, the diner, the grey bay and the ocean beyond . . .

Havre de Grace, Maryland, November 2008

PART ONE

THE
PRIMARIES &
CONVENTIONS

I

AN EXTENDED STAY IN THE PRIMARY PROCESS

From Iowa to Florida

ORANGEBURG, SOUTH CAROLINA: SATURDAY, 19 JANUARY

It's twilight in Orangeburg. You can see the queue from half a mile away, snaking through the grounds of South Carolina State University towards the athletics arena – the Smith Hammond Middleton Memorial Center, named for three young black men killed in the 1968 'Orangeburg Massacre', when police fired on a crowd demonstrating to desegregate a local bowling alley. Closer to the arena, the queue's been split into four to get them through different doors, the pace slowed by searches and metal detectors.

'Excuse me, sir, are you going to the Obama rally?'

A reporter, pad out, everything but the fedora with 'Press' in the band, gloms on to me because . . . well, obviously because I'm white and I appear to be the only one among thousands of people here, the only media rep going into the general audience rather than the roped-off media section. The journo, from *The New York Times*, was desperate for a story and here it was – White Southerner at Obama Rally.

'You're going where?' the white cab driver had asked a half hour earlier, as I directed him towards the college. There was no malice in his voice, simply a bewilderment at the concept, as if I'd suggested I was going to the aquarium to skydive.

Inside the large sports hall – bleachers on all four sides and a large square scoreboard and clock display hanging in the centre – a Methodist choir is filling the space with a cappella gospel, a bank of about fifteen people in white and purple robes, swaying with the music. The hall keeps on filling and filling. The place is one of the South's leading black universities. There is, of course, no official colour designation in the US college system, but you can still find an all-black or all-white one if you want. The kids here are all black middle class, a matter of the bling and sports gear being worn with a touch of irony. Barack Obama has supporters in every social sector of the US, but if there's one group running close to 100 to zero in favour of him, it's got to be black youth.

The kids' chatter is building up as more stream in. It's starting to overwhelm the noise of the choir, and the waiting is just starting to annoy, when there's a cheer from down below as the preliminary entourage come in and walk up onto the central stage. Actress Kerry Washington and rapper Usher (the nice safe type, not the nasty gangsta type) do a bit of a warm-up, leaning heavily on the 'get out the vote, donate your money and your time and your money', and then there's a murmur and everyone rushes to the edge of the balcony as Barack Obama emerges into the auditorium.

Like all celebrities, at first sight the real Barack Obama is different from the endlessly circulated image on TV – smaller, but also more substantial than the whippet-thin cool jazz muso he appears to be on CNN. He's quick on his feet, but there's more of a force to him as he comes through the . . . well, the stadium race between the seating banks, touching hands extended to brush against his, taking small gifts and passing them back to his minders, and with his secret service detail (including a bald, chunky man so alabaster-white that he must have been chosen as some sort of gag) moving in lattice formation around him. Forty-six is young to be tilting for the presidency but this guy looks so young – he looks twenty-five, a thoughtful-student-who's-lingered-a-year-too-long-on-his-PhD type of young. The idea that he could run the world's largest nuclear arsenal seems absurd and not a little frightening.

For many people – let's be honest, for *everyone* – it is still hard to believe that we are here, listening to a speech by a candidate for the Democratic presidential nomination who is black, and who is also now the frontrunner, or close to being so. And not just black, but young, professional, urban and with little or no media visibility before 2004. Chosen to deliver a now-famous keynote speech at the ill-fated 2004 Convention nominating John Kerry, Obama had been spoken of as a possible presidential candidate ever since. The junior Senator from Illinois had hitherto said he wouldn't run for '08, after having spent no more than a year in Congress, but as the second Bush administration went from disaster to disaster, from Katrina to Anbar, it became clear to many that this was a year in which almost anyone with a Democratic brand would have a real chance of winning – and that the party rank and file might be willing to take a risk.

It was a measure of how battered and beaten the Democrats had been by the 2004 defeat that the party's de facto official candidate, Hillary Clinton, had seemed a hopelessly liberal choice at the time, with the party casting around for their usual go-to choice, a white-haired Southern governor. For all but the most starry-eyed Democratic pro, the only point of an Obama run would be to further establish – after Shirley Chisholm in 1972 and Jesse Jackson in the '80s – that it was possible to imagine a black president sometime in the future (both the TV series *24* and the asteroid disaster movie *Deep Impact* had cast black presidents, as a way of suggesting their futuristic character).

As Republican ratings sank through the floor in 2005 and 2006, Hillary gradually assumed the air of a frontrunner, and she had good reason to. In other circumstances, most of the thousands of kids in this auditorium would have dutifully lined up behind her. Though she could never be thought of as Bill was, in the words of Toni Morrison, the '[first] black president', she would have enough of the rub-off gloss to be going on with. Nor would she have been able to generate anything like the sheer feeling, the hum, the thickness of the air you can rub between your fingers, in this hall tonight.

It's nine-thirty and Obama's up on stage. He begins to speak and instantly you understand how he got this far and why so many people have invested their hopes in a man whose policies really differ little from those of Hillary, or any general Third Way program. His begins his stump speech – the standard address that all US politicians develop, with an unchanging spine and elements chosen to fit, a sort of Chinese dinner of discourse – with a few local refs and then gets into the main body.

'This election is about the past versus the future. It's about whether we settle for the same divisions and distractions and drama that passes for politics today, or whether we reach for a politics of common sense and innovation, a politics of shared sacrifice and shared prosperity.'

Everyone was focused on the New Hampshire primary, conducted first in the nation since 1924 and the arbiter of candidates since 1952, in the whitebread state with 1.3 per cent blacks and as many Hispanics as people need maids. How would it vote? Could Obama win it? For some unaccountable reason, no one paid much attention to the Iowa caucus, held a few days before New Hampshire, and a vote that has winked in and out of significance since it rose to attention in the 1970s. The Iowa caucus involved everyone in the state interested in selecting a Democratic (or Republican) candidate getting together on one snowy night in January and arguing about it in living rooms, school basketball courts, etcetera, until a vote was taken and a candidate selected.

Jimmy Carter had got on the road to a candidacy in 1976 by 'winning' the Iowa caucus, so it was kinda weird that the Clinton campaign had all but ignored it. The Obama campaign had been there since August 2007, at least, and day by day they had worked their way round the malls, the churches, the small towns, the endless minutiae of everyday life, and quietly, quietly persuaded the population that Obama was the man who would represent the values and aspirations. He won 37.5 per cent to 29.4 per cent, and suddenly Hillary was the underdog who had been the favourite. And she was up against someone who, it was becoming clear, was extraordinary.

Obama's voice is the first thing you notice. Maybe he's had some training, maybe not, but whatever the case, Obama has a voice like no other candidate. There's a deep base to it somewhere in the stomach, but it's not a low-tined voice. It's clear, but it's not thin or reedy. The best way to describe it is as two-layered, as subtle as a single malt, the ballast rising slowly within it. At once authoritative and talkative, portentous and personal.

'There are those who will continue to tell us that we can't do this, that we can't have what we're looking for, that we can't have what we want, that we're peddling false hopes. But here is what I know . . .'

The second thing you notice about an Obama speech is its prophetic quality. This is no shopping list of special interest special causes ticked off in exchange for a vote – it is not even recognisable as a speech of a traditional left or right sort of framework. It is addressed not to people as black or white, middle class or working class, but as humans, citizens within a society, trying to find a way to be part of its life.

'Don't tell me we can't change. Yes, we can. Yes, we can change. Yes, we can.'

Well, yeah, sort of. But days prior to this event, Hillary had surprised everyone by showing that yes, she could too. Campaigning hard in New Hampshire, from living room to diner to wherever, she broke down briefly when asked a question in a cafe about how she kept herself going day after day, letting a tear go and telling everyone how hard it was, but that she was fighting on because it was so important. The next day, the people of Dixville Notch went to vote at midnight on 8 January, with the rest of the State following during the day, and Hillary won New Hampshire with 39 per cent.

'Yes, we can heal this nation. Yes, we can seize our future. And we take this journey across this great country, a country we love, with the message we carry from the plains of Iowa to the hills of New Hampshire, from the Nevada desert to the South Carolina coast, the same message we had when we were up and when we were down, that out of many, we are one; that while we breathe, we will hope.'

It's the sort of speech Obama's been giving for six months or so now, the type he premiered at the Democratic Convention in 2004, the speech that drives his opponents wild because they can't get a handle on it. For months they've bitched about how general it is – how airy, how abstract, how much it shades into self-help, into general aspirationalism – failing to understand that in a country where so many people feel not only utterly alienated from the political process, but beaten down by day-to-day life, the simple notion that change is possible and that you can play a role in your own life becomes, by definition, a political thought. And a necessary one, prior to any more developed or complex ideas.

Obama gives them that and does it in an oratorical style drawing on every source of consolation and inspiration that have been available to the American people in the last half-century. He's as oracular as a travelling preacher, as individually focused as a motivational speaker, as radically political as a black power leader of old, as reasonable and conciliatory as a leader who's already been elected. And finally, he employs the call and return of the old blues, the backwoods gospel church, with the simple, mantra-like phrases: 'Yes, we can.'

'Yes, we can, yes, we can.' Then he's gone and the evening breaks. Then, as the crowd starts to move towards the exit, suddenly there are white faces – Obama campaign organisers, white college kids come down from the north, moving through the human stream with clipboards and cards, trying to sign people up.

COLUMBIA, SOUTH CAROLINA: MONDAY, 21 JANUARY

'This is what we are fighting for. This is what these things mean. For the schools in Bennettsville, in this state, with the holes in the ceilings and the walls, the kids without books, this is what we are still fighting for.'

It is Martin Luther King Day in Columbia, but if Hillary Clinton is intimidated by the obvious candidate of choice she isn't showing it. Standing before the mic, her hands in her winter coat pockets, she speaks hard into the late winter wind, defiant and proud and claiming her right to be there.

It's grey now, but earlier the morning sun was shining through the white stripes of the American flag on the dome of the South Carolina State House building. The crowd coming down Gervais Street is in cheap scarves and windbreakers. Nine out of ten black – and those whites there are scribbling in pads and snapping cameras – they file up towards the State House steps marching behind NAACP leaders. They're moving between stacks of speakers pouring out Martin Luther King's 'dream' speech, and maybe it's the disembodied nature of it, as though it's coming out of the ground, but dang, what a great speech it is, rolling and halting, then surging forward, lifting you up and taking you with it.

Another crowd is surging in from the side and the beefy white cops are trying, unnecessarily, to control flow. 'Keep moving back,' they're saying, a gesture which seems more atavistic than rational, a pantomime of the last fifty years of SC history. At the top of the steps, the university choir is warming up.

It's a carnival but it's also an insurgency. To get to the State House, the crowd has to come past the statues of the great and good whites of the State, not least 'Pitchfork Ben' Tillman, the political leader who disenfranchised blacks after the Civil War ('We of the South have never recognised the right of the negro to govern the white man, and we never will'). And, of course, flying above the assembled press is the Confederate flag, the 'stainless banner' – deposed from the State House flagpole, but flying still.

'South Carolina had never done right 'less we made it to,' NAACP Field Op director Reverend Nelson Rivers tells the crowd, as the best of the dozen or so speakers warming us up for the candidates. Fire-breathing, he gets the crowd in on a call and return. 'Fire it up!'

'Ready to go!' comes back from the crowd, as Rivers hammers home the truth of the state, the truth of the South, and of the nation – still divided, not by race per se, but by race as class, by the opportunities that attach to the colour of your skin, and the armies of the poor, overwhelmingly black, that clean the hotel rooms, pour the coffee, ride the buses.

Speaker after speaker keeps coming back to the flag, 'that racist red rag', white SC's provocation, its bitter last shot at a state remorselessly becoming black and brown. Is the anger righteous and energising, or needy, self-victimising? Would a confident movement just ignore the provocation or blow up the flagpole, or both? How will they set the agenda?

For this week is one when black South Carolina does get to set the agenda, providing more than 50 per cent of Democrat primary voters. So all three candidates are here, fired up, ready to go . . . to give their stump speech with a few minor variations. Preceded by speakers delivering unflinching attacks on the official self-image of the US as a place of fairness and opportunity, it was always likely that the actual candidates would come in from that edge. And given that it is the only time outside of televised debates that they would all be together, they were determined to keep it clean for the national audience. Least impressive, it has to be said, was John

Edwards, whose candidacy is looking increasingly irrelevant – not only because of his bad beating in Nevada, but also because both Barack Obama and Hillary are creeping into his territory, ratcheting up from their commitment to reform health care to Edwards' starker call for universal coverage. Faced with this, Edwards needed to come up with something distinctive, to go in harder on the 'two nations' rhetoric that has drawn so much Republican fire on him. Someone needs to be saying that America, as it stands, is a racket, a nation where the poor are exhausted, dragging themselves between two jobs, and the well-off are terrified that their lives will be destroyed by an illness that exhausts their insurance (50 per cent of all personal bankruptcies are caused by people paying for health care). American freedom is a fairly ghastly system of higher constraint, but no one has yet stepped up to the plate to really say this. Edwards has come closest, but he needed to say it loud and large here, and he flunked the opportunity.

He needed to do something, because he was following Obama, who was speaking to an overwhelmingly proBama crowd – which is to say, young and black. Obama's appearance on stage created a Beatlesesque wave of squealing through the crowd. You can't ignore the importance of his physicality – slight, elegant, dressed down, Obama doesn't look like the black activists/politicians of an earlier generation. And I suspect that much of his appeal is that he doesn't guilt-trip the young with the freighted language of the Civil Rights generation, the blood and sacrifice, the opposition that is – in some ways – easier to stand up to than the soft white power many face today. Obama speaks to that in his now famous abstractions – hope, change, audacity – a routine the criticism of which he has worked into his stump speech, a pretty magnificent piece of rhetoric, honed to an edge.

'There is a deficit in this country, but it's not an economic deficit . . .' He begins slow, quiet. 'It's a moral deficit, an empathy deficit, a failure to recognise ourselves in each other.' Meandering through various proposals before gathering the energy of the crowd and giving it back to them as he turns it up to eleven. 'They tease [tease?] me when I talk of hope . . . But I had to have hope to be standing here, we had to have hope to be here on the steps of the South Carolina State House . . .' and on and on, drawing the crowd to a roar.

God it was good, but it was also lacking of content, and it was that factor that Hillary, speaking last, supplied. If it was her stump speech, it was so transformed for the occasion as to be unrecognisable. She twisted through a tribute to King, to listening to the 'dream' speech, and then into an extended disquisition on the racist poverty of SC, of schools in Bennettsville with mould growing in the corridors, before getting into specific workplace disputes, and then a half-dozen biblical quotes that had the crowd shouting back. It was a performance of quiet, understated authority, tremendously impressive, undercut only by the deep-seated feeling that you can't trust a thing the Clintons say.

Though the morning had a ways to go, it pretty much fell apart from there, with the choir unable to hear their own foldback and the final benediction drifting off into the sharp air. You couldn't help but feel that this was the fate of much of the day's rhetoric. Though everyone celebrated the fact that a woman and a black man being up for the presidency was a vindication of King's dream, the sad truth is not only the degree to which progress had stalled in many ways, but that there seems no clear way forward, nowhere to march to, no next revolution in the cautious policies of the candidates. So in Columbia, so in America – a great disjuncture between the growing awareness of how deeply bogged down the country is (white and black), yet no clear sense of where it wants to go to. Hence candidates, whatever language they use, talk to the country's anxieties, rather than its real sense of possibility. And for very different reasons, white and black alike turn to a fight over an old defeated flag as a source of meaning anew in strange times.

And in the Starbucks where the press decamped to download photos, in a basket near the cash register, a new way to 'support our troops' – a 'coffeegram', a kilo of vanilla bean roast sent with a personalised message.

BENNETTSVILLE, SOUTH CAROLINA: WEDNESDAY, 23 JANUARY

'We got two nations in this country, don't make no doubt about that.'

In a small community centre, John Edwards, a lithe man with a wide smile and a sharp haircut (famously so, this working man's tonsure didn't leave him much change out of $400), is working a room of people one can't help but notice are considerably greyer, lumpier and rougher than he.

'We need a president of the United States who actually understands your life. It's one thing to fly into South Carolina from someplace else, give a speech, go to a debate and then fly back out. It is a very different thing to have lived here, to have grown up in this part of the country and to understand in a personal way what's happening in your lives.'

With a chunky, old-fashioned hand mic clasped tightly, Edwards is prowling the room, doing a Q and A as part of the opening leg of his 'Back Roads, Back Home Barnstorm' tour. Born in South Carolina, raised in North Carolina (a difference that looms significantly larger in most Carolinians' thinking), Edwards is hitting the back country towns hard. He knows he won't win this thing – he and Hillary will split the white vote – but all he needs to do is come a good second. Take second and Hillary ain't the only alternative to young prince Barack. Knocked back to third in South Carolina, she'll be running one for three, and Edwards will suddenly be credible. It's a long shot, but he doesn't have any short ones.

'We've seen what's happening here in South Carolina, with the unemployment rate going up, 6000 jobs lost last month, and then John McCain said just a few days ago that the economy actually is doing fine, that we're not headed into a recession, the fundamentals were strong and remain strong. He needs to come here and see what's actually happening in the real world – because out here in the real world people are struggling.'

Edwards doesn't do big meetings, and not only because he couldn't guarantee the turnout. It's also because his style works best in a smaller room of like-minded people, in places organised around working life – the union hall, the community centre of a mill town, the former site of a working factory. Of all the candidates in the race, he's the one most reliant on the oldest politics – unashamed appeals to working Americans in the context of a system that's ripped them off and stepped on their neck. Such politics is usually howled down with talk of 'class envy' and 'raising everyone up' and other such blather, but Edwards is gambling on the possibility that eight years of Bush have left people so badly off that they can now see through the blizzard of propaganda that bombards them from every corner, and that a more clear-sighted view of their own interests will help put Edwards into the nomination and then the White House. Can he really believe it's likely? No one could sustain the gruelling schedule, the mind-numbing repetition, the endless patience at questions by turns rambling, obscure or plain mad, if they did not think there was a chance that they might be able to come through the pack. If they were not, as the old party machine saying has it, 'willing to be lucky'. But Edwards is no fool – if nothing else, the campaign will serve to keep up his profile and bang the drum for the dispossessed.

'What we need is a middle-class revolution . . .'

Say what? Middle class? Surrounded by thick beards, Miller shirts and truckers' hats – and the men are even more formidable – what's this 'middle class' stuff?

It's down to one of the peculiarities of American political life in the 21st century, that even when you are pitching solely to working men and women, to manual and service workers, pointing to a small rich cabal and saying 'over there, there's the problem', you simply cannot refer to them as 'working class' – at least not more than a couple of times a week. For the simple fact is that though the signs, symbols and accoutrements of working-class life have not only persisted but even become exaggerated, the term 'working class' suggests to working people the class who are economically below them, i.e. the benefit-dependent underclass, for whom steady well-paid work is a rarity.

The paradoxical fact of American life over the last half-century has been a split in working-class fortunes, whereby those in the old industrial jobs – and the small amount of mill work that remains in these Carolina backwoods qualifies – were, relatively speaking, so well paid that their fortunes and lifestyles separated from those relying on service industry work, casual labour or the like. Until the 1970s, full employment and strong unions meant that a mill worker could draw in what would now be cashed out as around $80 000 a year, enough to buy a house, cars, maybe a boat, etcetera. Those jobs have been leaching away for a long time, as have their conditions and remuneration, but they remain a memory of American good times and they became a definition of what middle class is.

During his campaign Edwards has given every indication that he'd prefer to talk about 'working-class' people, and the term would certainly clarify the political relationships at hand, because 'middle class' gives the sense of individual striving, and virtue or vice, as if a mill worker with no high-school diploma had much control over their own job prospects in a post-industrial economy.

The questions begin. A woman gets up, large, super-chunky, like a fair few of the people here. She's got a question about the health system and Edwards' face brightens . . . and then readjusts itself as a rambling account begins of the woman's mother's attempt to negotiate the labyrinthine particulars of the South Carolina managed care system. Edwards is listening, but listening like a professional mnemonist, simultaneously getting the details, putting them in some sort of order and working out his next bit of shtick. Somewhere in there he needs to find a way to give some concrete advice before jumping off into a general discussion of health care, without making it sound like a pretext.

He gets a lot of these sort of questions, does Edwards, doing these Q and As up and down the country, and it's for the same reason as the success of Obama's motivational rhetoric. In a place like backwoods South Carolina, which relied for its unity and identity on a single industry (textiles) that has now departed, a sense of confidence has gone with it too. This region and industry, was, after all, the setting for *Norma Rae*, the great '70s movie about a Southern woman radicalised by a union organiser, who then unionises the mill where she works.

What has become an overwhelming public political emotion in American life is neither triumphalism nor anger, but bewilderment. Bewilderment at a contract broken – that a lifetime in full-time, tiring, dirty, boring and sometimes dangerous work would not be repaid with the secure ability to raise a family and live in modest comfort. Bewilderment that successive answers as to who the culprits were for this – from big corporations, to the elites, to gay marriage – have failed to make any substantial change in people's predicament. A sense of disconnect between system and life – invited to surrender old notions of class solidarity and class conflict, America's working—sorry, middle class have been given no genuine national 'fair deal' that would fill the gap.

Edwards, former trial lawyer, a rainmaker specialising in suits against corporate interests, a man who is the very image of the trickster, his real attitudes and interests hidden deep behind that wide smile, understands this. And much of his pitch is about reminding people of a few simple facts.

'If you don't think there are two Americas, let me share with you three facts. First, the typical CEO makes more by the end of lunch than an average wage worker makes all year – in fact, the income gap is wider than at any time since before the Depression.'

If it's courage rather than hucksterism – or at least more the first than the second – I admire it, not least because it seems such an uphill battle to convince people that their fall from prosperity to penury was because of nothing they did, to challenge this ingrained illusion that economic exploitation is somehow individual failure. I wonder if, in the depths of his eyes, there is a weariness there at such a Herculean task, at the lack of anger transmuting into politics. At the easy way in which a meeting like this breaks up, once the microphone's down and the applause has died away, into a backslapping, hoedown session, with the beer 'n' bumps flowing and country music on the juke, as though this here was the real life, earned after that political thang.

PALM BEACH, FLORIDA: THURSDAY, 24 JANUARY

'We don't want to do anything that would endanger American innovation in pharmaceuticals.'

It was inevitable that John McCain would talk about prescription drugs to this crowd, this gathering of sun-kissed retirees in a conference centre in the vast hinterland of Florida sprawl, a place whose sense of instantaneous history-less-ness makes Surfers' Paradise feel like Rome under the Medicis.

This 'town hall meeting' had already been moved once – a double booking with the launch of some self-help CD package called *A Woman's Journey* (lots of lilac and crystal). Now we were in the second-best hall, an enormous American flag draped behind the podium, with folks in muted Hawaiian shirts and white shorts drifting in from the mall opposite.

There's a McCain loyalist crowd here, upfront, dressed in Florida formal – white slacks, bling, skin that would have Bindi Irwin wrestling you to the ground – but they're scarcely in the majority, and the hall (half-)fills with the merely curious, the slightly bored and those attracted to the powerful airconditioning on a humid sub-tropical day.

McCain aides have already worked through the crowd, picking out a few pretty girls to put on the podium behind McCain (a curiously unabashed process, like Led Zep's coke roadies putting together the backstage party). As up-tempo white rock plays – Stevie Nicks, Tom Petty, Abba (Abba?) – we're wound up in the most perfunctory way and the candidate bounces in, glad-handing the room. Like everyone except 'Bama, he's sprier and livelier than on the small screen and thankfully, due to the heat, he's left the lucky jumper behind.

'I've got my Irish friend here,' he says, referring to the local contact. 'So let me tell you a joke.'

Oh God. Oh no, Uncle John, not your joke. Please. It's Christmas.

'. . . oh, it's just the O'Reilly twins getting drunk again.'

Cue laughter. It ain't a bad joke (which you'll have to reconstruct) but we're not far from Morning Melodies here. You can't really get around the fact – McCain's old. And spin aside, he's not carrying it as well as Reagan did. The man's done more than most people do in three lifetimes (including having already tilted at the prize once), and he sounds tired. And though it's unfair – cos the North Vietnamese done it to him – the bulging jaw and the stiff limbs remind me unshakeably of Wallace, without the Gromit ('Cracking toast, Dubya').

Once he gets beyond the flannel and into a real speech, he's on firmer ground. This is a Republican-only primary, and McCain and Romney are running close – 27 to 25 per cent in the polls, with Giuliani having fallen through the floor, running equal on 15s with Huckabee. McCain's leading with the war, endlessly pitching himself as the national security candidate.

'Remember, in November, you're electing the Commander-in-Chief, and nothing, nothing is more important than giving our troops the best leadership.'

Nothing? Really? This is what the North Koreans call 'army-led politics', in which society is seen as nothing other than a support system for the military. But of course, it's substantially rhetoric, and in part intended to shore up McCain's weakness on another topic dear to this audience – border security, on which, in GOP terms, McCain has a bad (i.e. vaguely liberal) record. It's a topic he never touches on in his main speech, but he's immediately bailed up in the Q&A.

'Will you build a wall?' asks one of many crackpots, referring to the idea that the whole Mexican–US border can be sealed off, Berlin-style. It's a measure of McCain's core sanity that he replies reasonably, pointing out that a wall is basically unbuildable and unpoliceable. (Howard and Ruddock would have promised not a only a wall but levitating machinegun posts and heads on spikes.) But it doesn't go over well and he shifts gear a little: 'But of course, in urban areas and border towns we need a wall. Maybe a double wall.' That gets applause. Double wall. That's twice as good.

But McCain already has these people up the front. It's those at the back he needs, and they want to talk about drugs. As one ageless female life form remarks, 'If sixty is the new fifty, then a lot of us around here are going to be around for quite a while, and it's a question of prices . . .' It's code for 'We're gonna live so long we're gonna outlast our pension'. The questions send McCain into a long political tango, lunging towards populism ('We've got to stop these companies from patenting clone drugs to keep generics off the market'), before shuffling back to a position that won't put him on the wrong side of Big Pharma. And then: 'I mean, if you've got to go to Canada to get prescriptions – I support that.'

'Scuse me? Unless I misheard, McCain is suggesting that the US should basically free-ride on a socialised universal health care system of a country a tenth of its size – so that it can preserve the illusion that its own system is still functional, and an expression of 'choice'.

'Did he just urge people to rip off Canada?' I asked the wire service journo next to me. He nodded, shrugged, a response that sums up much of the American media's attitude to the *Alice*-world of health care.

And then it was over. After a bit more glad-handing with some iconic guests – a bottle-blonde Cuban exile in a stars-and-stripes spangled top hat and holding a cardboard Liberty torch – he was out and away, further down the coast, from nowhere to nowhere.

In South Carolina, the Democrats are working every corner of the state for every last vote. Even Hillary flew back in. Unless the polls are dead wrong, again, the Clinton team are simply trying to rein in Obama's likely win. A more than 5 per cent victory would be bad for Team Clinton. Double figures (as the polls predict), a disaster.

But back in West Palm Beach, you'd be hard-pressed to believe anything was happening anywhere at all. The crowd spills out into Cityplace Mall, a faux Spanish-mission piazza, where one enormous building has been made to look like countless, slightly aged, Spanish-era row buildings.

Outside the Japanese steak house I catch up with two men who I saw at the McCain thing: Dan, in his eighties, and his comically identical son, Jerry – same baseball cap tilt, same pencil moustache. What did they think of McCain? 'Yew knawww, I'm unconvinced,' says Dan. What about Romney? 'I'm a Republican but I ain't convinced by any of 'em this year.' Dan's obviously retired, but what does Jerry do? He looks startled at the question. 'Well, I'm retired too.'

Thus Florida, so the future – for some. People living so long that they retire with their parents. And the golden days in the faux malls spread out forever. In such surrounds, McCain, trumpeting the threat of global Islamist terror, seems like a time traveller from the past. Who would blow up the Cityplace Mall? What possible difference would it make to anything?

CHARLESTON, SOUTH CAROLINA: SATURDAY, 26 JANUARY

The moment I saw the name – Extended Stay Hotel Charleston Airport – I knew I just had to stay here. Number 5125 on a street that didn't exist five years ago, on a row of chain hotels, a perfectly pleasant tilt-slab commuter chain hotel. The name is so honest, so perfectly . . . *Maoist*, in its expression of a civilisation now expressed largely through brands and chains, that I just couldn't resist. Across the featureless boulevard is the sprawling shopping centre – identikit buildings of identikit chains in low-rise buildings in a half-hearted pseudo-Southern style. Alienated isn't in it – the place makes Jeffrey Smart look like Grandma Moses.

I'm all for challenging postmodern landscapes, thrilling in their brutal emptiness, but this is ridiculous. Every town, every city seems to be like this, its old high street dilapidated and boarded up, its old shaded neighbourhoods of wooden houses under willows broken up by sporadic Subways and Pizza Huts, its shops and stores strung out along a highway that takes you past a place where the town used to be.

This is where America lives now, in these sub- and ex-urban tracts of housing disconnected from any centre, of megastores marooned in carparks, the whole thing tied together by cable, the web and the freeway. It's happening everywhere, but elsewhere there was more resistance from some notion of community, of place and history. Here, in a country that takes a pride in ripping it up and starting again, it all happened so fast that people never realised it was going on – and still have not. Yet everything that is happening, or not happening, in America, is a consequence of this great social self-deconstruction, the fact that the country has essentially fallen through a hole in itself.

What it means is that every candidate – save for Huckabee, with his united evangelical base – must talk to people as either individuals, or as individual members of the nation as a whole. The days of the intermediate group – of race, region, gender, and, above all, class – being spoken of, at least explicitly, are over. What must be appealed to in people is their inner goodness, their inner patriotism, their inner desire for 'hope' and 'change'. Even John Edwards, the closest thing the campaign has to an old-style politician, willing to use the 'c' word, is running on the idea of fixing something 'broken'.

No candidate can do what politicians used to do – give an account of how things work, whether that be class struggle, or king and country, or whatever, which connects to what should be done. 'There is poverty because . . . You are perpetually struggling because . . .' These are the things you need to say to arm people for the struggle. When you are talking to your constituency, hope and change, etcetera, leave them with little place to go.

It was voting day for the South Carolina primary, and of course Barack Obama had won it handily, 55.4 per cent to something. John Edwards had bravely kept on hacking away at it but Hillary had already left the state, moving briefly on to Florida, where she wasn't supposed to go because the candidates had agreed not to campaign there, and then to Nevada, another caucus state she suddenly realised she had to win. Watching three cable news networks covering the thing – one on the laptop and I had persuaded the Extended Stay to let me borrow a second TV – it seemed apparent that, in one sense, it would be truer and more accurate to watch the whole campaign from somewhere like this, right through to November.

The challenge faced by anyone wanting to get the place really moving is to make these more amorphous, less obviously immoral conditions visible – and to do so in conditions where the whole notion of gathering and place is slowly dissolving. True, Obama has built an impressive grassroots community-based organisation, which had helped him overtake Hillary in South Carolina and match her deeper war chest. But it's a movement of activist-professionals, switched-on kids, projecting the appearance of a mass movement. In face of that, Hills has left the state to Bill, who was right up and down the coast today, taking time off only to once again unload on the press.

The Republicans, of course, are not faced with these problems, because they're still dealing in fantasy – Mitt Romney peddling the idea that America can be re-industrialised by market forces alone, John McCain tapping into exceptionalist jingoism ('We are Americans and we never surrender'). Their pitch is barely to the 'people' at all, so much as to an audience – up and down Florida, ahead of the Tuesday 29 primary, they're talking to small groups of people, in delis and lobbies, their staff frantically ringing around to get a quorum. And if the economy continues to tank, their increasing delusional smiley rhetoric will lead them into electoral disaster.

Only Huckabee has a real organisation on the ground – and if he hadn't he would have been out of the race long ago – evangelical Christianity being the perfect counterpart to atomised life, the last source of social solidarity in concrete, anti-modern myth.

But Huckabee is on the clock. As is Edwards. It would be wildly wrong to say that there is no difference between McCain and Obama or Clinton – this contest has a greater left–right split than the recent Oz or UK elections. But nor does there seem to be anyone on the ground who can yet get people out of the mall or the Maccas and up on their feet to tear the joint apart.

It's not easy to see where the country is, but that problem is not unique to the view from Extended Stay Hotel No. 23. By the time I checked out to go to the Republican-only Florida primary, Obama had become, with 102.5 delegates to 80.5, a serious candidate.

JACKSONVILLE, FLORIDA: SUNDAY, 27 JANUARY

'Alright, shall we crank this thing up?'

Mike Huckabee is strapping on his battered old Fender bass and the band is tuning up. We're in Jacksonville, Florida and the Huck's just given his stump speech off a car park stage, full of stuff about abolishing income tax, putting the Ten Commandments into the Constitution ('It seems easier to change man's law to fit with God's law than the other way round'), and now it's dessert. The drummer counts them in and the band thumps its way through the opening chords and into 'Brown Eyed Girl'. The song hangs on its bass line, and Huckabee keeps it going. He's not the world's greatest bass player, and has that slight rustiness of someone who doesn't do it for a living, but he's no show pony. This isn't Bill Clinton playing a one-off sax solo on a talk show – the bass is a workhorse instrument and Huckabee's absorbed in it, totally with the music. It's a glimpse of someone with the mask off, just being.

And therefore one of the most contrived things in the whole campaign. Who hasn't played in a garage band, or wanted to? Playing a bit of rock'n'roll is to a postmodern political campaign what chowing down on ethnic food was twenty years ago, or driving in a railroad spike was to the 19th century – a testament that the candidate is one with the dominant spirit of the age. By common consent of the floating press corps, the Huckabee trail is the best of all the (now depleted) candidates on the primaries trail, and it's not just the because the music relieves the boredom. Despite the crackpot nature of the solutions he offers – the abolition of income tax, for example – Huckabee is the one who comes closest to talking straight sense about the problems the country faces. And he's certainly the only Republican whose rhetoric is not wreathed in clouds of cheer-squad enthusiasm about the capacity of Americans to innovate, come through, not surrender, etcetera etcetera. His sense of humour is unforced, and he's unfazed by tripwires of political correctness – he let Keith Richard slip a drugs charge in Arkansas, not because of a legal technicality, he said, but because he's a damn good guitarist.

But therein lies the problem for the Huckabee and a clue to the deeply schizoid nature of the whole Republican campaign. For Huckabee is trying to play both sides of the street. He's been trying to appeal to the evangelical voters, but he can't resist strapping on the bass and getting down with the crowd. But you can't do both, by the very nature of the politics involved. The preacher who goes into politics gets his earthly charisma from the same place as he gets his religious power – from giving off an expression of being the impersonal, and slightly distanced, vessel of God, set apart from man. You can't imagine Ian Paisley or Pat Robertson strapping on a bass and cranking out some riffs, and if they did they'd be out of business pretty quickly. The preacher–politician is meant to act as a rock upon which followers can build their wavering faith, their sense of a one true path in a cosmopolitanised and pluralist world. When your preacher–leader starts praising the man who cranked out 'Sympathy for the Devil' then, consciously or otherwise, many would think that he's been tempted and fallen. Huckabee was being flippant about the Keith Richards thing, but any real preacher would put a rock-solid barrier between himself and that satanic music. Huckabee can't bear to. He likes rock'n'roll too much. He is, after all, the same age as Johnny Rotten.

Huckabee's early success in Iowa was largely due to this personal folkiness and to the bewildered disarray of the more mainstream candidates. His subsequent failure to win a second primary has been due to his inability to unite the evangelical vote into a solid bloc. Deep down they don't think he's serious.

Huckabee's roadshow is about to hit the wall of Super Tuesday, when twenty states hold their primaries and massive amounts of highly expensive TV advertising set the agenda. Yet the truly weird thing about Huckabee's campaign is that it resembles not so much an old fashioned revivalist caravan, as a latter day version of Ken Kesey's Merry Pranksters, taking the electric Kool-Aid acid test bus across the country. The people willing to stump for Huckabee are a self-selecting crowd, with a measure of life to them – folks you can talk to, as long as you don't let the issue of abortion or speciation come up. They are the type of evangelicals capable of cutting a bit loose because they 'know who they are', a phrase that has come up more than once. Their faith is solid, so they can relax about the occasional gag. Indeed one of Huckabee's campaign ads focuses on his faith in instrumental terms. 'I don't have to get up in the morning and think about who I am,' his voice intones over scenic landscapes. 'I know who I am and that means I can get to work straightaway.' In a political context where people have had many of their beliefs sorely tested – in unending prosperity, in America's unquestioned military might – a secure belief system can be offered not in terms of its content ('this is the truth'), but in terms of its form, as an instrumental aid to efficient govern-ance. It is the de facto justification for a literalist belief system in a pluralist and atomised society.

Mike Huckabee's unlikely survival is a testament to the US primary system, but not for the reasons its supporters put for-ward. This all-involving political carnivale, which may or may not be/have been effectively concluded by the Super Tuesday vote, is taken as a measure of American democracy, some origi-nal spirit passed down from the founding fathers. These days the midnight primary ceremonies of Dixville Notch and Hart's Location are attended by the world's media, and the minutaie of the vote – separate booths, the immediate tally – take on the sacramental role of sacred objects in a civil religion. The caucuses where people come in person to select a candidate in open face-to-face votes over several rounds are taken as a guarantee that however much the US may become a zone of intersecting commercial, military and hi-tech systems, it has somehow preserved the spirit of the 1776 agrarian republic.

The only contender with a genuinely different politics, with a program – the Huckabee, preacher, champion dieter, rock star – is putting away his bass as the roadies strike the stage and what can only be described as Christian groupies gather around.

'He's great,' says the young photographer beside me, snapping for a Baptist university student newspaper.

'Will you vote for him?'

'Well, I was thinking of it, but I'm leaning towards Obama. He's really inspiring.'

LAKELAND, FLORIDA: MONDAY, 28 JANUARY

Stay on the surface and Mitt Romney is a bland cipher. But dig deeper and he's not that interesting. Yep, the man is bland all the way down.

We're in the mid-Florida hinterland, away from the retirement and tourism strip, in the industrial middle of the sunshine state, a vast stretch of mid-tech industries indistinguishable from any other state, save for the avocets (sort of a cross between gulls and flamingos) rooting about by the roadside.

Insofar as Romney has Florida territory, this is it – prosperous workers in high-end manufacture, pulling in good wages, many scientifically trained. They've got retirement plans, college funds and share portfolios, and they respond to the talk of 'management' and the President as a CEO of USA Corp.

Or Romney hopes they do. The trouble with offering yourself as the eminently reasonable candidate, up against the war hero, the preacher or the New York wise guy, is that you measure your success by systematically lowering the temperature of the room. McCain can get whoops and air-punches (from those of his supporters with the strength to lift their fists) when he says he'll be a 'leader, not a manager' because 'Americans don't surrender'. When Romney starts talking about his Massachusetts assisted private health-care program, the only possible response is a studious nodding of the head, one of the few signs that people here are breathing.

'We know we can do it cos we've done it,' Romney says, giving his stump mantra that leads directly into his CV – turned the Winter Olympics around, turned the state of Massachusetts around. It's like he's sitting across a boardroom table at an executive head-hunter interview, rather than trying to connect with a crowd. Why is he so studiously avoiding any last trace of the prophetic, the visionary, the uplift needed to float a campaign? Is it because he believes he just can't swing it, given his opponents' credentials? Or is he desperate not to remind people of his missionary (i.e. Mormon) heritage, cleaving desperately to the secular, the professional, the unobjectionable?

Romney appeals to the Chamber of Commerce conservatives

across the nation. He's Mr Rotary, straight down the line on all the issues: business, immigrants, abortion, the war, etcetera. McCain is prepared to talk about the complexities of things like illegal immigration, climate change and so on. Not Romney.

'My opponent wants to put a green tax to pay for global warming. Hey, it's not *America* warming, it's *global* warming. Why should we pay for it?'

That goes down well with a loyal crowd, and Florida is a closed primary, GOPers-only, so every candidate is playing to the base. Romney's strategy makes sense, but would that hard line, and the CEO style, work for the electorate as a whole? Given the current polling, the only chance the GOP has of winning is to keep hold of the Nixon/Reagan/Dubya Democrats – and that means a completely different strategy. Hitherto, these voters could be tempted over with social and cultural themes – the war, gay marriage, etcetera etcetera. That strategy appears to be well and truly busted. A lot of those things (gay marriage is a good example) just don't seem to matter much anymore beyond the 35 per cent hardcore. Quite possibly, such things might become live again if the Democratic candidate could be trapped in a pincer movement, but the trouble for any Republican venturing to raise them is that things have become a bit more, well, *real* for a lot of Americans, as the economy starts to tank and the war drags on seemingly interminably. Start all that stuff about 'Adam and Eve, not Adam and Steve', and it would simply confirm the deeply held suspicion that the GOP just doesn't get the degree to which people are feeling the squeeze. For the Republicans to have a chance, any candidate they put up would have to be able to project some sense of being capable of channelling the desire for change as energy.

That's especially so as the results of South Carolina's primary made it all the more likely that whoever gets the brass ring will be facing Barack Obama come November. Mr Audacity of Hope scored a massive 55.4 per cent in the South Carolina primary, pushing Hills down to 26.5 per cent and John Edwards to 17.6 per cent. That is a huge result and a crushing – though by no means terminal – blow for Clinton, with Obama taking a larger majority than even the polls were forecasting (they had him on a 10 per cent lead). The reason it is not being regarded as a slam dunk, lay down misère, comes down to questions of race, which, like it or not, have become a key question in voting patterns. Fifty per cent of South Carolina-registered Democrats are black, which almost exactly matches Obama's vote. That doesn't mean it was a one-to-one correspondence – Clinton appears to have got about 17 per cent of black voters (mainly older ones) and the remainder of Obama's vote was from white youth. Critically for the Democrats, there was almost no crossover between black and white older voters for Edwards and Obama. Neither got much of any of the other's racial group. Edwards would be lucky to have got ten black votes.

This means that the result is not unequivocally good news for Obama, as outlined by professional political slimeball Dick Morris last week. Morris argued that a crushing Obama victory in SC would make him so absolutely the black candidate (only Georgia and Alabama come close in proportional black population) that it would position Clinton as the one candidate capable of getting the vote of both groups – and Hispanics as well. You would have to be wilfully naive not to see the likely truth of that, and a brokered Democratic Convention would. However, Obama's SC victory means it may not come to that. The sheer appeal of his message of hope, change, etcetera etcetera – the spiritual, even transcendental, dimension he is giving politics – may sweep all before him. The Democratic rank and file may live up to the spirit of the primary system and deliver a result the party machine doesn't want.

But whether it is Clinton or Obama, it strikes me that the only chance the GOP has against either of them is McCain. Whatever the black–white split, I can't see Romney tempting anyone over to vote against their immediate interests, or for a continuation of the war. Nixon got a big slice of Democrats because of the '60s, Reagan because he gave the appearance of being one of the boys. Romney looks like everyone's boss, the prick in the tie from head office who's come down to the warehouse to talk about productivity benchmarks and layoffs. When he tries to dress down, it's embarrassing. Last time he was wearing an open-collar shirt, you could still see the square folds on it – the clown had just taken it out of the box, which made him look like the square of cardboard it comes with. It appeared less like casual sportswear than those weird see-through shirts Ferdinand Marcos used to wear at karaoke nights.

McCain, by contrast, has positioned himself as someone

who recognises that people are doing it tough and that there are no easy answers. His sheer battered physicality would show up Obama's youth, hi sleekness, the absence of content in much of what he says. He'd grab white Democrats from Obama and male Democrats from Clinton. The question is, how many? And there's an earlier question: will the Republican machine let him? And to make things even more complex – how many of these Romney supporters, gathered in this factory canteen modelled like a New York boho deli, people for whom Vietnam is from the history books and Reagan a childhood half-memory, would actually cross back to the Democrats, based on the question of age?

MIAMI BEACH: TUESDAY, 29 JANUARY

'Excuse me, sir, where are we going?'

Marta, the rep for Madrid's *El Mundo*, was freaking out in the back of the cab as the driver veered off the dark street and into the cavernous, even darker car park of the mall.

'We're just looking for an—' ATM, I was going to say, but there was a ker-thump and it was too late. As we'd slowed to go over a kerb, she'd jumped out and was clip-clopping over the asphalt to the bright lights of the mall.

It wasn't flattering, but I couldn't blame her. Miami is one uniquely sinister city, the tropical palms and soft breezes sheltering a vast army of the homeless, even in the art-deco reservation of South Beach. They're everywhere, they're mostly black, and more than a few are stark-staring mad, a ghost army of the unmedicated, with tinfoil in their hats, shouting about Mars.

Marta and I were both waiting for the same bus at the downtown bus terminal – what I'd assumed would be a brightly lit terminal crowded with unhealthy fast-food outlets, but which turned out to be a few lean-tos under the overpass, just waiting for yellow crime scene tape. I found a cab and swung back for her and we were halfway down the freeway before I realised that it was a gypsy cab, faked up to look real (yellow paint job, stencilled logo). I could see Marta's brain going like a dynamo. Was this some weird scam? Were the driver and I working in tandem? Had she seen this on a *Law and Order* episode?

It was a hell of an ordeal just to go and check in on the Rudy Giuliani death watch, at a university in the wetlands – a city of light, all glass bricks and po-mo concrete, like a beacon in the wilderness. Strange gig for the last night before the primary. All captive students, most of them simply curious, bored or there to take the piss, the whole thing organised by the bewildering 'Students for Rudy' group, dressed in the sort of outfit Mussolini would have put together if he'd worked in a Collingwood silk-screen collective in the '70s.

But then, maybe 'America's mayor' had simply run out of places to speak. He's been working his way up and down the peninsula for six weeks, talking to every deli, social club and stop sign on the highway that will have him. The strategy had some sense, since Florida has extensive early voting provisions, and Rudy was hoping that he could enthuse enough of them to such a degree that they couldn't bear to not vote for him right away. That relentless campaign, the strong New York links of the 'snowbirds' (retirees moved here for good to ripen like oranges until they fall off the twig), the whole 9/11 glow . . . all of it was giving him ratings in the 30s. Then the others arrived from South Carolina and he fell to 16s in a week. The man must have known it was all over, but at Florida International University he wasn't showing it. After an interminable wait in the library Starbucks, the press was herded into the student-crowded ballroom and did what's been done at every Republican meeting in the race – made a beeline for the three of four black attendees. The good news was there were a few more here. The bad news was that none of them was even remotely thinking of voting GOP. They just came along to see the funny old guy.

Or guys, cos we were warmed up by a bunch of men who looked like they'd just come from a Norman Mailer look-alike competition – New York politicians, Texas Governor Rick Perry and the actor Jon Voight. Squat wise guys, they should have been propping up a tavern bar somewhere, going over old cases. In this frangipani-shirted Latino ville lumiere, whipping it up for a walking corpse, they were a testament to the vast sense of futility that attends a great deal of the primary process.

Voight was on his third anecdote – something about how he got cast for *Midnight Cowboy* – with the Rudy aides flicking 'Has he lost it?' glances at each other, when the crowd noise started to ramp up. The Rudester had arrived!

'Hey! We're going to go out tomorrow and we're going to

win it!' he throws out, almost before he's got the microphone. Get the vote? From where? From who?

Giuliani was hoping that he could sell himself as Mr Experience – ran New York, de facto national leader for a coupla days during 9/11, yada yada. But Romney took that angle and established himself campaigning in Iowa and New Hampshire. That left Rudy with bupkis, and he's been reduced to going around with his 'tax return on a single page' prop, which he whips out at the first opportunity, making him look vaguely crankish. For an audience of students, it's bizarre, like whipping out the shroud of Turin at the Bialystok social club blintz night. Tax? What's that, dude? That thing Dad does, dude.

The results just starting to come in as I write are confirming those dour polls almost exactly. With a third in, Giuliani's on 17 per cent, Huckabee on 15s, and Romney and McCain are neck and neck, flickering back and forth between 34 and 33. The stoush between McCain and Romney got very vicious, with vast amounts of push polling by phone from both sides, focusing largely on conservative credentials – McCain's occasional liberal moment on immigrants and climate change, etcetera, and Romney's earlier pro-choice position. Giuliani never had a prayer on that front – he's undeniably pro-choice, especially in the matter of wives and girlfriends.

Speaking of beauty contests, the Democrats were also running a primary here, but because it had been moved up before Super Tuesday, all the state's delegates have been barred from voting at the Convention (as have half of Florida's Republican ones). The candidates agreed not to campaign here. And then Hills suddenly said last week that gosh it would be a shame if Floridians couldn't be represented – especially the clear majority supporting her (52, to Obama's 28 and Edwards 18). My God, the woman is Nixon in a dress.

'We've proved the polls wrong before, we can do it again!' yelled the Rudester to the Florida University crowd, getting a final whoop before departing and, no doubt, getting slaughtered. This morning he gave all his staff signed baseballs, about as clear a farewell as you get.

The students hung round, loyalists keen on a big shouting match with Ron Paul supporters protesting outside. Across the room I saw Marta, a bit shaken up. She looked over then quickly away. Fair enough. What, after all, is the etiquette when you've jumped out of a shared taxi? Besides, she was busy interviewing black students.

2

HILLARY AGONISTES

From California to California (later)

LOS ANGELES: SATURDAY, 2 FEBRUARY

'No pushing in. Quit pushing!' yelled the queue marshal at the line snaking round the California State University gym. 'Some of these people have been here all night.'

All night? To see Hillary Clinton? God almighty, people are really sucking the methadone rag of politics now. As Super Tuesday looms close, and with the Democratic race down to two, emotions are beginning to boil over.

Today's Hillarally at California State has as many people outside as there are in the huge auditorium, necessitating a sort of conveyer-belt system whereby the speakers at the rally proper – a half-dozen actors kicking us off, from Christine Lahti to Sally Field – are then shuffled outside to keep the crowd warmed up so they won't go away pissed off. With people sprawled over the landscaped hills and rocks of the campus on this glassy California morning, it was difficult not to think of the Sermon on the Mount.

The Democratic campaign kicked up a notch last week, when John Edwards announced his withdrawal from the race, two days before CNN's Democratic candidate's debate. Speculation is still rife as to Edwards' motives – was he protecting his rep from a dumper on Super Tuesday, or from the humiliation of being most likely virtually ignored in the debate? Did he want to tip things Obama's way, because he loathes the Clintons, or – a minority opinion – tip it Clinton's way because her program is leftish of Obama?

There is even the faint possibility that he did it for the good of his party and his country. That, at any rate, has been the effect of it, because by some strange alchemy, the Democrat race suddenly became intensely exciting, even for one as jaded with these two centre-right corporate moneyed-up fuckers as me. The sudden exit of the white male made it all real – that the Democrats would be sending either a woman or a black man to most likely become the next American president.

With Edwards still in the race, deep in the back of everyone's mind was the haunting idea that after six months of three-way struggle, some bunch of faceless men would just come in and say, 'Yeah, okay, a lotta fun, but a woman? A black? Sorry'. Edwards' withdrawal concretised the difference between what the Democrats were offering and what the Republicans are offering. There are major enough policy differences – on Iraq, health care, etcetera – but the new line-up of the teams suddenly makes crystal the utterly disjunctive nature of the Democrat–Republican split.

The Republican debate at the Reagan Library last week was like a drinks party at the 19th hole bar of the Crestwood Country Club golf course – four old codgers sitting around solving the problems of America over a coupla Scotches, and affirming that it's steady as she goes. Ron Paul could have been expected to give a bit of life, but he's a diffident man without a great deal of personal impact. Huckabee had more energy, but he is, of course, engagingly nuts. It was really down to Dad McCain and Mr Rotary, slugging it out to see who will go up against the black kid and the chick in November.

In the Democratic debate, with Edwards out of the way, the energy flowed differently, certainly more cordially. Was this strategic? In don't think so. I think the dynamic had simply changed and a new sense of focus had appeared. After all, it's in the interests of both to really tear the other down before Super Tuesday, and Clinton wasn't holding back any at her rally: 'I think the Democratic Party should refuse to nominate any-one who doesn't believe in universal health care', a clear dig at Obama's plan for an extension of private health insurance that would still leave 18 million people uncovered. Fair, but seeing it as a crucial distinction means believing that Hillary will deliver on universal cover, and that is a very big if.

The crucial question in the Democratic debate came near the end. Would either candidate accept a Clinton–Obama or an Obama–Clinton ticket? 'Well,' said Obama, with his dry wit, 'there's a bit of difference between the two'. Both used circum-locution to get around a yes or no ('I think Hillary would be on anyone's vice-presidential list'), and it's unlikely that either would offer the other the spot. Or was unlikely. Clinton would never accept it, but would she offer it to Obama? The idea of a Clinton–Obama ticket is so salivatingly exciting to so many that it might just be irresistible. Would Obama accept it? At the age of forty-six, it would make sense, setting up a potential sixteen years of Democratic leadership.

But, of course, there's no guarantee that such a ticket would be a slam dunk. It seems so, but not to the vast swathes of people across the country who re-elected Dubya, including the millions who were voting against their own interests. The failure of foreign and domestic policy is so clear now that many of these people will switch back, but the haunting question for the Democrats is how many white men and women out there simply would not come at a woman or a black man as president? It's not 1984, when Fritz Mondale's selection of Geraldine Ferraro sent people into conniptions, but nor is it Scandinavia, where chicks basically run the joint. Would either candidate hedge their bets and select some white Southern governor, to round up the strays?

No one really knows how these different factors will come into play, but the Republicans are caught in a fine dilemma, since the only candidate that could grab these people back would be John McCain, the Petro Georgiou of the GOP. If, as they would wish to do, they select Mitt Romney and he went up against Clinton–Obama, then I suspect the Republicans would be up for their greatest two-party competition defeat since Barry Goldwater got 34 per cent of the vote in 1964.

The Republicans in Congress seem to believe that too. In a system where – if you can believe it – incumbents pretty much get the opportunity to draw their own electoral boundaries, election to the House is pretty much a life term. Twenty Republicans have announced that they will not stand, and that figure will cascade over the next, oh God, ten months. The rats are getting out of Dodge, and Dubya's last ten months is going to be the lamest of lame-duck administrations in history. Unless he bombs Iran.

So okay, I'm excited. And I have to say that a Clinton–Obama ticket seems to be the go. Gritting one's teeth at the emerging dynastic nature of American politics – a feeling exacerbated by the excitement around the endorsements by Ted and Caroline Kennedy, and the son of legendary Latino labour organiser Cesar Chavez – it has to be said that Clinton strikes one as the more assertive, the more commanding, the less tentative of the two leaders. I can't help but feel that Obama wouldn't be able to stand up to the entrenched interests as well as Clinton. The only caveat with Clinton is the terrible fear that she may be Tony-Blair-in-skirts (she can't be Bill-in-skirts – Bill is Bill-in-skirts), and that whatever gains she makes in domestic politics will be offset by bombing Iran, invading Sudan, etcetera. I don't think that's the case – in fact, I think the election of a Democrat in November will put the cap on the whole neo-con adventure that began in the Anglosphere with the '96 election of the Rodent – but I am haunted by it nonetheless.

That's not a visible concern at Cal State where the passion is ramped up to a height more characteristic of a Miley Cyrus concert (ask your kids). But God, I get sick of being lectured by film stars and singers about structural social reform. But then there are United Farm Workers organisers, veteran black Congressman Ron Dellums ('My mother told me – you are black but you are also a multi-dimensional total person . . . and I have brought that total person to this moment to endorse Senator Clinton'), and Tom Petty's 'American Girl'. And the same thing, but more, going on at the Obama gig across town. It would be impossible not to conclude that something, something is happening.

WASHINGTON, DC: SUNDAY, 10 FEBRUARY

'Okay, here's a joke,' said the kid walking behind me in the seventy-nine dollar suit, to his two companions. 'Bill and Hillary get married and Bill says, "Hillary I want you to promise me one thing – never look under the bed". On their twenty-fifth wedding anniversary Hillary's tempted and looks under the bed. There's three beer bottles and $2500 in cash. Hillary goes to Bill and says, "Sorry, Bill, I just had to look – but what's the deal?" And Bill says, "Well, every time I cheated on you I drank a beer and put the bottle under the bed".' The kid can barely maintain his mirth by now.

'And Hillary says, "Well, three in twenty-five years, that's not so bad, but what's the cash for?" And Bill says, "That's what I got on the returns".'

In that terrible, terrible joke – almost an anti-joke, the sort of thing that sucks mirth out of the world – is the American conservative crisis in embryo. The teller was one of the several thousand attendees at CPAC (Conservative Political Action Committee Conference), the gathering of all the great and good from the right, or one part of it. Dubya had addressed the true believers yesterday (a 7 a.m. thing for which people had camped out all night in a queue down the corridor of the Regency Ballroom of the grand old Omni Shoreham Hotel) and McCain had also made his pitch to tepid applause and actual booing when he started talking about illegal immigration. CPAC is the looked-forward-to event of the year for the hard right, but the thing had had the stuffing knocked out of it on day one when Mitt Romney (the 'polystyrene shell in a human-shaped space', according to Jon Stewart, and the 'man who looks like he just dropped a tooth-whitening strip,' according to Dave Letterman) announced that he was dropping out of the race. Not because it was an embarrassing and squalid farce, but because to continue would 'help our enemies'.

You could pretty much feel the deflation after the Mitt hit the fan. He was a pretty piss-poor conservative record-wise anyway, but he was all they had, the only guy willing to kiss the helmet however many times it took ('We should double the size of Guantanamo Bay!' and 'Europe has a declining birth rate because they have lost faith in the Creator'). The only one who reassured them that nothing, really, had changed.

There's nothing remotely like CPAC on the Australian scene. It's a creature of the Political Action Committees formed decades ago to bypass campaign funding laws and which are responsible for the most vicious of the attack ads. They've largely been bypassed now, due to a campaign finance law they truly loathe and whose name – McCain–Feingold – suggests in two words the problems the Republicans are heading towards. But they continue to fulfil their role as a focus for highly specific political formations in a manner that's a huge headache for the National Committee of the party – a three-day political bacchanal that reinforces the sense of political separation and balkanisation. You can get the tenor of the thing from the session titles ('What Do Liberals Have Planned For Your Money?', 'Is the GOP Still Lost?', 'Hugo Chavez Democrats – How They Silence The Right'), but the point of CPAC is not that it's merely a gabfest, but that it's a gathering of the tribes, not a million miles different from a *Star Trek* convention. So there's a uniform, especially among the kids who make up about 40 per cent of it. Boys wear dark blue or grey suits and ties patterned like an Axminster carpet, and hang in packs either alpha (Romney clones and the occasional Marine buzz cuts) or, erm, omega (tending to pale weediness, acned obesity and an armful of Ann Coulter books). The girls are all in pearls, Oaks Day dresses and levels of make-up that would have a Russian cosmonaut's wife suggesting they go easy on the blue eye shadow. The outfit's a costume, of course – back at Penobscot University they'll all be in standard-issue mall-wear – but for now they're making a point.

They're also scarfing around for the internships and research positions with representatives, senators and think tanks, etcetera, that will come up in their thousands – or hundreds, if the polls are any guide. With the right poised to most likely lose their control of Congress and the White House in a massive repudiation of their whole programs, you would think there'd be a degree of soul-searching, or at least tactical discussions of the upcoming struggle. But you gotta look and listen long and hard to find any of that. When not cracking their funny, funny jokes, the deep Red-staters (confusing, isn't it) talk in the private language of their sect.

Ask a question about welfare in the bar, where you think people might unwind a little, and you get, 'Hey, newsflash to the ghetto: the government is not your baby-father!', as Chad told me (not his real name, but he looked like a Chad). 'All universal health care is a single-payer system: the taxpayer.' 'Liberals don't doubt God – they think they are God.' And on it goes. Older delegates will give you a more rational conspectus, but the kids are hopped up on the sort of Mark Steyn/Ann Coulter rhetoric that seems to act as a prophylactic against thinking. Indeed, both of them were here too, feeding the furnace. Coulter was in the exhibition hall – a one-stop mega-mall of sub-causes, from the demographic death of Europe to Mormon home-schooling – signing copies of her new book *If Democrats Had Any Brains, They'd Be Republicans*, her queue only diminished by that for Newt Gingrich on his comeback tour.

Nevertheless it was the Newt who put a crimp in the love-fest, by giving a fire-breathing speech pointing out what was obvious to all those abstaining from the Kool-Aid: that the Republicans were in deep trouble, as judged by the roll-out for Super Tuesday votes (15 million Democrats versus 8 million Republicans), the thirty or so GOP Congressional reps quitting this time round, the zero for six result in the 2006 Senate race, etcetera.

'There is something happening in this country and we don't understand it,' Gingrich intoned. 'And we are not even close to ready to fight the 2008 race.'

The pain on the crowd's faces was visible, but it was more bewildered than anything, like Ralph McTell had just told the pub he wouldn't be playing 'Streets of London' that night. What? Us? Out of step with the nation? We *are* the nation. Does not compute. For the press, it was like the thing had suddenly got interesting for the first time since Huckabee's entourage had followed their candidate in, all denim and gingham and the smell of banjos, to the naked horror of the assembled. Debate? Discussion? The conference was actually . . . conferring.

Fortunately for the crowd, Newt's solution to the problem was a program he had written based on 'electronic town hall consultations with 45 000 respondents', and thus 'the program of the American people'.

'Eighty-five per cent of Americans want us to defeat our enemies,' Gingrich said. 'We just have to explain to them that if we don't fight them over there, we'll be fighting them over here.'

So the wormhole to reality closed and we were in the bubble again. The trouble wasn't a decisive shift in the attitudes of the American public – it was just bad PR.

If that reassured the crowd for a while, they were in for a

rude shock that evening as the results of the primaries came in. As was their nemesis, Hillary. Obama stormed home in Washington and Nebraska, polling in the high 60s in states where a black person is either lost or the Black Eyed Peas touring. In Washington there's even a high Hispanic population presumed to be going for Hillary. Obama got 57 per cent to 36 per cent in Louisiana, further evidence that he can take enough of the white South to get over the line. And then Hillary's last line of defence fell, with today's Maine caucus returning an Obama vote by about 58 per cent to 40 per cent.

The stunning set of results confirm that Obama could win anywhere, which will tend to snowball his results in future primaries. And he has now pulled ahead of Hillary by about a dozen delegates, crossing the thousand mark for the first time.

This was bad news for the GOP (they reckon they'll do better against Hillary), but the real kicker was the turn-out for their primaries. Part of this is due to the fact that McCain is now the presumed frontrunner, but even so, the figures are dismal. Barely 15 000 people in the entire state of Kansas turned out, thus giving Huckabee a huge victory, 60 to 24 per cent. Washington was a Tasmanian beauty contest – no one won, with the 'other' vote (votes going to withdrawn candidates) pipping McCain for top spot on about 26 per cent. Short of a Chinese burn on his old war wound, its hard to think of a bigger vote of no-con from the cons. The result – two states lost to Huckabee (though no one gets the Louisiana delegates) and one pyrrhic victory – should have Red-staters pissing razor blades.

You wouldn't know it in the exhibition hall as CPAC closed. One of the last stalls to pack up was the 'stophernow.com' group, which does a profitable sideline in Hillary-hate novelties. Their most popular item? An inflatable Hillary punching figure. 'A fun way to beat Hillary!' says the ad. The only thing funny about it is that no one seems to have noticed that, when knocked down, the thing just bobs back up again.

ALEXANDRIA, VIRGINIA: TUESDAY, 12 FEBRUARY 2008

Through the dark streets of Fairfax goes the cab, the driver, a Romanian, an electrical engineer, and blatantly, cheerfully illegal and I are looking for the university. Andrei is refusing to play the grateful immigrant, tears of joy, etcetera.

'It's a place,' he says, shining the flashlight on street signs. 'The pay's good. There's a lot of bullshit.'

Northern Virginia is really part of the far-flung dormer suburbs of Washington, but most of the towns here predate the inauguration of that revolutionary imperial capital. Roanoke is down the road, the first stab at a permanent colony in 1585, and Alexandria and the Georgetown centre of Washington predate the city itself by a century or so.

The streets are gorgeous Georgian arcades snapped up en masse by the Washington political class, and they're the sort of places where you can get six kinds of antique chafing iron or a Vietnamese fusion takeaway, but not milk. No capital, not even Canberra, is so differentiated from the daily life of the mass of people it represents. Even the gas station is done in red brick with a white hexagonal spire.

The university has disappeared into the darkness and we are both grousing about the occasional outbreaks of public dysfunctionality in the States – small things like the lack of signage and integrated public transport, etcetera, the little indications that public space is slowly evaporating – when we turn the corner and there it is, a towering, elephantine fauxlonial structure, brightly blazing into the night. Talk about your city on the hill. Perhaps the whole beacon-giganticism-facade effect is appropriate. We're here to see Bill Clinton.

George Mason University looks like it was put up three weeks ago, but by, well, masons. The man's statue is in the forecourt and a random sample of half-a-dozen students has no idea who he is. Yet of all the second-tier founding fathers he probably has the greatest claim to shaping the modern form of the US, refusing to sign the Constitution until a bill of fundamental rights was attached to it – the eventual form of which was based on his draft of the Virginia Constitution. Without the bill, America after Reagan and Dubya would be a puritan state with criminalised abortion, mass censorship and Guantanamos for American citizens from sea to shining sea.

So it's kinda appropriate that Mr Clinton is here, cause not much ever stopped that Bill from doing what he wanted to do. In the three-storey atrium of what can only be described as a colonial-era shopping mall, the student body has gathered en masse, jammed in wall-to-wall, with faculty and trustees watching from the balconies. The secret service presumably believe that Bill isn't going to get a head-shot from university staff, having not considered the possibility that a women's studies lecturer might have a gun license.

Half an hour before the start and the crowd is already surging and churning. People arrive early because they know they need to get through the metal detectors – this week there were three shootings on campuses, and the final one has barely been discussed. It's a pretty white university, but even then it's a pretty white assembly – hard not to conclude it's the safe crowd, kids who bought the official college sweatshirt and know they shouldn't but kinda like Nickelback.

'Five years ago this man came to my campus.'

On stage, there's a heavyset, close-cropped kid in a bottle-green suit, the universal uniform of the political chancer, somehow having levered himself up to be introducing the former President of the United States and giving us his autobiography. He's already halfway to an internship, working the VIP lounge set up behind a curtain. He gets off before the booing really gathers force but even he can't put a kink in the gathering excitement.

It's not just the fact that it's an actual (ex-)President; it's the fact that it's Bill. There's an acoustic duo on, grinding through a series of tribal anthems like 'Baby One More Time' before ending with 'Living On a Prayer', which gets the crowd into a call and return to rival the Obama rallies. Most of these kids heard Bon Jovi cos their parents had it – it's about as close as you get to white ritual, the sound of suburbia. Hard to deny the power of it. It's a quasi-spiritual moment, but so is just about everything in America.

Then as the heat continues rising and a couple of people have fainted, the curtain parts and there he is, Slick Willie himself, his 'Hi, how y'all doing' started before the band is off the stage. The hair is white, the face is flushed, possibly he's just been fluffed before he came on, but he's up and raring to go. Heckling from a small claque starts immediately from a small and, it must be said, gutsy group, waving hand-written posters with 'Hillary + 4 years =' and then a hammer and sickle. If only. 'I'm glad you're here,' he says, 'but they came to hear me not you'. The roar of the crowd wipes them out. It's the pure juice.

But boy, can this bloke go on. Every other candidate is exhausted by now. Hillary's husky, Obama seems to lose himself in the middle stretches of his stump and McCain is starting to make a few too many slips for people not to get a little worried about it. Calling a friendly endorser 'the Governor of Vietnam' was my favourite. Maybe he knows Holt.

But not Bill. He's working as hard as any of them and he's still up and enjoying it as much as on day one. Day one 1991, for that matter. This is the mark of the true politician, the man who can think of nothing better than to be in a student union forecourt on a bold cold Monday night, talking to gormless sophomores about the reform of health-care records keeping.

He needs to be. As results are coming in now from Virginia – the only state so far reporting – Obama is predictably killing Hillary 62 per cent to 37 per cent. This was expected, at least in the last week or so – so much so that Team Hillary is in Texas already, campaigning for 4 March, an admission of defeat. DC has no exit polls and Maryland is keeping its polls open till 9.30 because of weather-caused chaos. But there's no reason to believe that it will be any different to Virginia – and DC may be a real crusher for Hillary, trending up to 70 per cent for Obama.

Make the vote large enough and Obama will have an absolute majority thus far – i.e. Obama will be leading even when the superdelegates are factored in. At which point, the 250 or so superdelegates that Hillary is counting on will be in play. How willing is she to take this to the wire and beyond? A slip-up in an interview reveals all. 'There's still big primaries to come,' she said. 'Ohio, Michigan . . . I mean, Ohio and Texas.' No, she meant Michigan – which she won because it was uncontested, after being stripped of its delegates. She's clearly contemplating an attempt to get those delegates seated, relying on the idea that the party would swallow their bitterness and get behind her. Her former press advisor Lisa Caputo signalled that this was on the cards in a slot on TV where she argued, against ridicule, that Hillary won Michigan and Florida.

Bill makes a good case for her – it needed to be good, because the man was on for two hours, piling anecdote on anecdote in the classic Clinton style. Jesus, I knew how Gennifer Flowers felt. You've been on your feet for sixteen hours straight and Bill's just getting his second wind. He wound up on an anecdote that went for fifteen minutes, starting as something about Iraq, detouring through a golf game, almost losing us, and then revealing that the caddie was a 9/11 fireman, a former Republican. 'Hillary was the only one who was talking about the problems we'd have from the smoke and fought for us,' this guy allegedly said. 'She was the only one who knew what it was like to be me.' God, it was good, slick as a coin trick, hooking and reeling us in.

They're going to need every one of those to be in with a prayer. More Clinton staffers have just quit, a governor ally is throwing out the idea that America isn't willing to elect a black governor, and it is getting very, very ugly.

No less so for John McCain. The Huckabee is holding him down Virginia, at 47 to 45 per cent, which was expected but nevertheless a continuing embarrassment. Bad for McCain – who now thinks he may actually have to turn his guns right-wards and engage Huckabee – but great for Hillary, because the general view is that Obama would be a better bet to beat a strong McCain ticket. The lead is turning as I write and would give McCain sixty delegates – but it ain't over yet.

But I think Hillary's toast. It seemed clear last Saturday, and it seemed clear as the crowd drifted out of the university hall – named, improbably but truly for a Bill Clinton appearance, the Johnson Center. Vox pops turned up 'Obama voter', 'Oh, I'm just curious', 'I came to get a taco and he was speaking so I hung out', and 'I dunno – I'm half-and-half for Hillary' (the latter not an unusual comment, except for the fact that they were carrying one end of a Hillary banner).

When it all wrapped up, Andrei was waiting for me on the rank. Did the spectacle of open democracy enthral him?

'I was thinking how the buildings look the same everywhere,' he said, bathed in the light of the monumental hall. 'Still, here, they stay up.'

Whether Hillary will remains to be seen. In Texas she'll either strike oil or the Alamo.

SUNDAY, 24 FEBRUARY

Raymond Chandler once said that the best way to get a stalled plot moving was to have a guy come through the door with a gun. As the primaries move towards week eight, the possibility of a reasonable performance by Hillary would kick them into another month (to Pennsylvania, the last big state, in April, and then to a state-by-state competition for every last delegate), at which point both candidates and observers will pass out from a mixture of boredom, exhaustion and enervation. Though the powers-that-be are hitting the campaign with everything they have to keep it rolling – an artfully constructed near non-story on a possible McCain sex scandal, a meeting Obama once attended at which former members of the '60s urban guerrilla group 'the Weathermen' were present – nothing's really been firing.

Comes the hour, comes the man, with Ralph Nader announcing his candidacy on Sunday's *Meet The Press*, one of the few programs that doesn't make you feel like you're being shouted at in a lift by a 55-year-old divorced man with a urinary tract infection on his way to a tax audit. Nader is running as an independent for the second time – in 2000 he ran on the Green ticket, in 2004 as an independent with endorsement of the Reform Party (whose previous candidate was the hard-right Pat Buchanan). Now he seems to have Green backing without official endorsement.

The Republicans have greeted the candidacy with glee, Democrats with dismay. The latter still believe that Nader's 2000 candidacy cost Al Gore the election, with the close Florida result. Nader's point has always been that Gore's campaign was so centrist, lacklustre and presumptuous that he couldn't take a brace of states which Clinton had held in '96. And also that without an organised candidate to the left of them, the Democrats would take that vote utterly for granted. If, as Nader has remarked this time round, the Democrats can't win against a perpetual war candidate who promises more of the same, then they should 'wrap it up and re-emerge in a different form'.

Whether the GOP are on the money seems highly dubious. Nader's 2000 candidacy took 3 per cent of the vote – the standard percentage that left-wing third parties take whenever they emerge. From 1900 to the 1920s, the Socialist Party took 3 per cent of the presidential vote – sometimes with their candidate campaigning from prison – and though the class composition of that vote was very different from the kaleidoscopic coalition Nader grooves on, the political intent is the same. It's the vote of those who simply won't accept that the Democrats as the lesser of two evils, when so many of their policies are tilted directly against the interests of the people they purport to represent. A century ago in Australia and the UK those people jumped ship from liberalism and formed Labour parties. The fact that this never took off in the US is the reason why, in America, you can hold down a full-time job and still be perpetually homeless, without health insurance or pension plans.

Nader's endless campaigns are, in that sense, atavistic, an endless restaging of the failure of American radicalism to establish its own political agency. By now, the working class that would form the base of such a party is so fractured – a car worker (those that remain) can pull in $US100 000+, the waitress who serves him coffee lives on a base three to four dollars per hour plus tips (and the tips are taxed) – and so overridden with ideology about self-reliance, etcetera etcetera, that forming and holding even the most moderate alliance is close to impossible.

Whether this has a wider political purpose is debatable. What can be said is that it is utterly pointless electorally. In 2004, faced with a lacklustre establishment candidate like John Kerry, candidates from the left, including Nader, could only muster less than 1 per cent of the vote. Nader argues that there is a new desire for truly independent candidates, saying things hitherto unsaid, hence his 2008 run. Yet he has to deal with the fact that, for many people, Obama is that independent candidate, someone outside the system, speaking a different language. Nader is right to point out that it is bollocks, of course – policy-wise, Obama is a centrist candidate with the image and rhetoric of a revolutionary. But my suspicion is that most of those smart enough to see through his act are also smart enough to see the continuing futility of splitting the progressive vote. Nader will do better than '04, but he won't break 1 per cent.

Nevertheless that may still be enough to sink Obama if the race comes close. Polls at the moment indicate that he's running around 50–44 against McCain, but that will come way in. Many Democrat supporters are getting more terrified everyday, as Obama's apparent lack of argumentative and debating skills becomes apparent. Everything this man says off the cuff, in response, in debate (everything that is not, as Nader has noted, in the 'liberal evangelist' mode), is so lacklustre, piss-weak, unfocused and, above all, diffident, that at times it amounts to car-crash television, the sort of thing you watch through parted fingers. In last week's Texas CNN debate, Hillary once again had him on the ropes in terms of argument, command of detail and sheer mental toughness – but all to no avail. She is being slated by the commentariat for sticking with the plagiarism non-issue – her gag about Obama offering 'change you can Xerox' falling achingly flat – but what else could she do? She's campaigning like Howard at this stage, aware that a tsunami is running against her, looking for any possible way to stem the tide. But if Obama's poor debate and soundbite performance can't do it, then nothing can. She's just vamping, hoping desperately he shot two crack dealers in the head, circa 1996, and that this will hit the wires 3 March.

Thing is, even in the general election, it may not matter much if Obama gets pasted again and again by McCain. His very diffidence may be taken as a mark that he's outside the system, as tentative and unburdened with assumptions as the atomised and disconnected masses he's drawing back into politics. Quite possibly his very inarticulateness is a sort of political judo, to make everyone else look slick. He needs no favours from Nader or anyone else.

Mind you, if Nader has bestowed any gifts on anyone, it's McCain, who is now no longer the oldest dog in the race. President Nader would be seventy-four a few weeks after taking office in '09.

So why does he sound younger than anyone else in the game? And is he the hero or the villain?

DALLAS: WEDNESDAY, 27 FEBRUARY

When it goes, it goes, it goes, it really goes . . . Last night's debate had been spoken of as Hillary Clinton's last chance. It wasn't, of course, in itself. She had to win it hands-down, launch a whole new policy initiative and drop a safe on Obama's head, to really have a chance. But in the end, it turned out to be she who did the cartoon thing, running furiously in mid-air, long after she'd gone off the cliff.

It opened with another interminable debate about their strikingly similar health-care plans – both favour a process of subsidising private health insurance, rather than any sort of extension of direct provision. Clinton's criticism of Obama's proposal is that it would leave up to 15 million uninsured.

That's a worst-case scenario, but fair criticism. Yet Clinton's guarantees on her own scheme seem to demand a fair whack of faith that the process of 'mandating' (making it compulsory to have health insurance) will work better than, say, compulsory car insurance. There is also the problem that mandating is not only, in effect, a huge cash transfer to private health insurance – an invitation to an increasingly punitive system that criminalises poverty and/or bad money management – but it also ultimately simply shifts poverty around. People simply go without food or heat to pay for the insurance they will be prosecuted for not having. Neither party is going to stick their neck out for efficient direct provision, which might get the average American health care standard up to somewhere in the realm of, say, Latvia.

With the policy so minimally variant, the thing pretty quickly collapsed into pettiness, and much of it was Clinton's fault. Her initial complaint that she always got the first, narkiest questions, may not have been untrue, but what of it? If 'never complain about the media' is the first rule, then 'never complain about getting the first question' is, like, the zero-ist. Clinton later referred to the fact that she barely had time to sleep, but that she didn't need to – a remark that said it all. It was followed by an excruciating reference to a *Saturday Night Live* sketch from last week, in which their Hillary had done a big riff about the easy ride Obama was getting: 'Ohhhh, someone get Senator Obama a pillow.'

It was . . . well, I don't know what it was. There isn't language for someone quoting a parody version of themselves as an ironic mode of referencing what the parody was ripping the piss out of in the first place. The metamorphosis to Tracy Flick was complete, capped off by her desire to not only speak in the debate but to moderate it as well, cutting off the hosts repeatedly.

It was scrappy and painful to watch and partway through I switched over to the dubbed version on the Spanish channel. Here was the real Hillary, with a stronger, darker, and dare I say sultrier, voice. Hillarita sounded like someone who had suffered much – perhaps in the Mexican slums – and risen from poverty to the commanding heights of a global perfume empire and the love of a Swiss count, only to have a stranger appear from her past and seek to undo it all. You could almost hear the castanets.

If only at this point Hillary could run dubbed, she'd romp it in. Spanish Obama, meanwhile, sounded like a Barcelona tram conductor. I suspect foul play in the dubbing choices.

DEEP IN THE HEART OF TEXAS: TUESDAY, 4 MARCH

When the United States begins to break up – in about 2050 or so – Vermont will be one of the first to go. This state of dairy farmers, antique sellers, Ben & Jerry's and draft dodgers, within reach of the Canadian border, not only rebelled against the British, it rebelled against the Americans, splitting off from New York State in 1777 and maintaining itself as an independent republic until 1791. It sends to Congress the only representative – the tireless Bernie Sanders – who describes himself as a socialist, while it also elected a Republican governor, albeit one to the left of most Democrats. It was never going to go Clinton's way once the Obama-slide started, and with about 7 per cent of the primary vote counted as I write, it's looking like the margin will be between 55–60 to about 24–40 for Clinton, the three stray percentage points going to Edwards, Kucinich and other waifs and strays on the ballot, or – who knows, it being Vermont – Jerry Garcia and Harvey the Rabbit.

Rhode Island, the other east-coast state in the race, doesn't close its polls till later, but all the pundits are saying it may be a more difficult one for Obama because it has the highest proportion of Catholics in the country, around 60 per cent of the population. Why do they think this would be a factor? Because there is simply nothing else to say. Every other demographic variant is nailed down and bleeding from a dozen orifices. We've looked at half-white Hispanic blue-collar female registered Democrats as compared to half-white Asian pink-collar male independents yada yada, and every variant in between. Rock choppers are just about all that's left, and it is only a matter of time before Mac–PC, HD–Blu-Ray and bitch–dom variants are factored in.

With no less desperation, the networks are simultaneously parsing the sliver of votes out of Texas and Ohio (less than 1 per cent) for something to say, which usually commences with 'Well, it's too early to say . . .' Currently, Hillary is taking Ohio 60 to 40, and Obama leads Texas by the same margin. The Obama margin in Texas looks ridiculous, given the high support Hillary commands from the Hispanic community. If it holds then something has gone seriously wrong (again) with her campaign, and ditto with Obama's in Ohio. Either result seems unlikely and both together would simply be too much of a headroot to cope with. One can only presume that both votes will come into about 53–47, or even within that, by vote's end. It doesn't help that something has gone weird at CNN, where they're reporting results from less than 1 per cent of Texas precincts, but listing the total votes from those precincts as around 700 000. This would mean a total vote of 70 million, which, I suggest, is an excess. It seems the wrong set of numbers has been loaded in at either end.

Whatever the case, there ain't going to be a Texas result any-time soon. I'm downtown in the vast concrete hell of Houston, a once grand city that appears to have woken up one morning in the '70s and thought, 'Know what would look really good here? Eighty blocks of multistorey car parks'. Folksy, it ain't. If you're reading this you can presume that I haven't been mugged for my laptop. Anyway, a few blocks down from the maximum security Greyhound station, in a hotel ballroom, they're assembling for one of the precinct caucuses that will award the final third of the primary votes. This is a small one, but there are reports of queues of up to two hundred wanting to get in, insufficient space, the possibility of multiple sittings, etcetera etcetera. Hitherto this was hardcore political junkie territory, since the deal was done long before the Texas primary occurred, and the only people turning up were those who wanted to select their local school board, and so on.

This is overwhelmingly a black crowd and overwhelmingly

unwilling to talk to a gawky white guy from 'Austria'. It can nevertheless be said, duhhh, that they are overwhelmingly pr-Obama. In terms of public education, health care, etcetera, Texas is pretty much down there on the bottom, and Austin aside (a sort of grand corral for all the state's freaks), the big cities have an edgy air to them. There's no pretence here that patronage, or at the very least ethnicity, doesn't figure in the calculus – that Obama is for the blacks and Hillary is 'for the maids', as someone pretty crudely put it. It's largely the same thing as in South Carolina – a lot of people unwilling to talk about politics, beyond polite answers to one or two questions.

On the Republican side, McCain is hoping that tonight's results will be enough to take him over the edge, with the 1191 delegates he needs to claim pre-Convention victory. If this occurs, there's a rumour that Bush will endorse him tomorrow, which is like hearing that Jeffrey Dahmer's coming to lunch. He is running about 56 to 32 per cent in Texas currently, with about 300 000 votes counted (a figure the frikkin' machine is telling me is 2 per cent of the precincts, which must be bullshit). Huckabee might have been hoping for a better result, but 32 per cent is a good result given that it is effectively a protest vote against the presumed incumbent. And it's a pretty worrying one for McCain, suggesting the big splits he will have to do to keep both the middle ground and the whacko right (to use the psephological term). Already he's pulling back from his 'in Iraq for a hundred years' pledge, coming back to 'as long as we need to be after the fighting stops', etcetera etcetera.

Ah! CNN says the votes are reports of early voting, hence the screwy numbers. It also officially projects that McCain has won the GOP nomination on these numbers.

So, from the deathful Lynchesque lobby of a chain hotel in this deathful town, that's the interim report.

And there is eerie silence still on the Vermont border . . .

SANTA FE: SUNDAY, 9 MARCH

There are two theories about Barack Obama, who won Wyoming's primary 60–40 on Saturday, netting himself an extra (woo-hoo) seven delegates, to Hillary's four.

The first is that he is a babe in the woods: a bright, distinctive person who has fashioned himself through successive identities (Hawaii stoner, undergrad lefty, thinker, community organiser and then legislator) into exactly the type who could win the 2008 election. America, in this take, is so bewildered, with so many people outside of the political system, so distanced from a basic sense of power, that a different type of political discourse – essentially a pre-political discourse – is necessary to win them.

Thus, there is no point talking about what sort of health system should be achieved before you remind people that it is something that can be done, and that they can play a part in doing it. No point talking about class in a world where so many float in a hazy social flux, with very little sense of identity coming from work. No point talking more than vestigially about race, at a time when race consciousness has diverted into the fantasy world of wealth and power portrayed by rap, movies and P. Diddy merchandising. And so on.

Obama, it is said, has understood this, but never understood that it would hit a brick wall at some point in the process, as it went up against the no-holds-barred politics and personae of Clinton and McCain. Hence, Obama will either lose the nomination or the presidential campaign, and will go down in history as one of the great quirky moments in American politics, before normal service resumed.

The second version has Obama developing, same as the first, with the addition that he knows exactly what he's doing, and come the campaign proper, on the base of a changed political discourse, he will add a bit of old-style politics. He'll throw a whole display village worth of kitchen sinks at McCain, nailing him to war and recession as the candidate of the old world, with an unstable temper to match.

Obama's history would suggest the latter is true. He moved into politics via the south side of Chicago, and you don't get a bigger or older machine than that. Prior to that his community organising had taught him that you had to apply radically different methods to different constituencies. Among the disenfranchised poor, some people have to be put together from the broken pieces of them lying on the ground, while a more organised opposition has to be shirt-fronted right back down to the other end of the street. Obama, by this assessment, is smarter than a bag of geeks.

However, his current performance has many people leaning

to the former. Outflanked by Hills in the firewall/Super Tuesday II primaries (i.e. Ohio and Texas), with a lack of drive, poor tactics and a fuzzy message, this loss has been 'Bama's 'tell', according to some. No Lenin of the stockyards, he – Mr Yes We Can – is more Hamlet, with a program conceived in a bounded nutshell, eaten up by a movement facing nothing better than the anti-inspiration of a Hillary coronation. Facing the resistance of the real, he collapses into diffidence, the very opposite of the audacity he's trying to summon up in others. More of a sniff of that, and party heavies and superdelegates will chance just about any grassroots revolt to seat Hillary as the nominee, convinced that only she has what it takes to destroy McCain.

Many of those wavering will be making their decision over the next few weeks. The Pennsylvania primary on 22 April will be a test not only as the last big delegate haul, but as to whether Obama can give the sort of campaign that would indicate he has the guts to go all the way.

There is now no possibility that either candidate can get over the line on pledged delegates alone, and precious little chance of Hillary overtaking 'Bama, given the proportional nature of the voting. However, if it were possible to somehow include Michigan and Florida in the race, that could change. Time ran out today to call an actual primary proper, but some sort of mail-in primary – with its exciting possibilities of fraud on an elephantine scale – is being mooted by guess who.

Camp Clinton is also keen on the idea of a dream joint ticket (Hillary's almost exact quote being 'I think it's a good idea as long as I'm president'), the sort of dream, for Obama, from which you wake up screaming.

The point is that there has never been any doubt about Hillary's ability to tear the joint up, but Obama is being tested at every moment, as to how he stands up to a whirlwind of aggression, i.e. McCain.

And here is where my theory of Obama's psychic judo comes in, because I think he would play McCain like a cheap fiddle. It's been five days since McCain got the nomination, and he's already had one classic snap moment when a reporter asked him a complicated question about his 2004 discussions with John Kerry, about becoming the latter's vice-presidential candidate. His answer to the suggestion was basically 'No', but having knocked it on the head, he had to bludgeon it around a bit, laying into the reporter in a way that looked to a lot of people like an uncontrollable outburst. All Obama would need to do is to tickle that reflex – which, you have to say, may not be unrelated to six years in a jungle prison – and present himself as Mr Cool versus the man who wants to blow up the world.

Or be ridden over. For which, it must be said, he is getting a lot of practice. The Mississippi primary is on Tuesday, which he can't lose. In theory.

THURSDAY, 27 MARCH

Torture and assault charges have been filed by US prosecutors against two men suspected of beating an Australian tourist and throwing

him into a burning fire pit on a Californian beach. Robert Schneider
was found in the surfside pit in Ocean Beach with third-degree burns
on February 27 . . . San Diego locals Carl Gregory and Roseann
Iovine announced plans to host an 'Australian barbeque' on April
13 to support Mr Schneider's recovery.

– San Diego Union Tribune, today

It was never a real entity, simply a coalition of separate fief-
doms jammed together out of common interest. Unwieldy,
host to demagogues and local machines, fond of useless wars,
by 2004 it looked like it would split apart altogether before
a recent surge gave some people cause for hope. Now that is
disappearing too. What does the future hold for these people,
that some call the Democrats?

Far more is at stake in November than the mere matter
of who runs the biggest armed forces in the world. Loss by
the Democrats – which, if current numbers stayed as they are,
would be a slam-dunk – would have to be a decisive crisis for
the party.

By common consent Dubya is in the running for one of the
coveted bottom three slots in the 'worst presidents ever' stakes.
The wooden spoon usually goes to Warren G Harding, eased
into the nomination by party machines during a deadlocked
convention. Of his scandal-plagued administration, someone
remarked 'he was unfit for the office and he never should have
been there' – that someone being Warren G Harding.

Union general Ulysses S Grant is the Carlton of the list,

always bobbing somewhere round the bottom three for basically being a burnt-out alky through a crucial era of reconstruction. Nixon is usually in the bottom five of meta-lists, an average of getting in the top ten on right-wing lists and below bottom on liberal ones. Carter used to limbo pretty low, but has been rising like a navy diver, as those whacky ideas like energy self-sufficiency and not backing every murderous brigand who calls themselves a freedom fighter, start to be re-examined.

Frustration and political enmity usually get the incumbent called the 'worst ever' by someone. But this time it looks like the real deal. The neat way in which the W Bush era's incompetence comes together as a neat package is pretty extraordinary. Cutting taxes while embarking on a war that you then utterly mismanage, cocking a snoot at the rest of the world while it buys up your finance capital, demonstrating dysfunctional cronyism in a straightforward national emergency and then deregulating your way to a full-force money-market melt-down . . . If Dubya isn't a North Korean agent, he should retroactively invoice.

Harding gets the wooden spoon not only for the 'teapot dome' scandal, which exposed his cabinet as a group of corrupt profiteers, but for a rep as a 'do-nothing' president. In fact, his administration reorganised government accounting into its modern form, established the Veterans Affairs Department, released WWI protestors from jail, and sent food aid to the USSR during the post-civil war famine of 1921. Match Teapot Dome with Halliburton, and Harding still has a clear lead. During his short reign, the US consolidated its post-war prosperity and the jazz age boom took off.

Other presidents have authored disastrous wars (LBJ), been mired in scandal (Nixon), dropped the ball during an emergency (Hoover), let the country drift towards destruction (Pierce), given evidence of physical damage to the language areas of the brain (Reagan) or hugged a giant rabbit (Harvey), but they all had something – something – on the assets side of the ledger. Bush has nada, nil, zip. In terms of achievements, he's running neck-and-neck with Harrison, whose claim to fame was catching pneumonia at his inauguration and dying a month later.

Yet with all that, with all that, the Republican contender for the nomination, a man who, whatever his personal virtues, promises a substantial continuity with what has gone before, is now the heir presumptive to the presidency. Leading both Democrat contenders as preferred president – and now leading Obama, by some measures, by up to 10 per cent – McCain is also benefiting from the worst possible finding for the Democrats – that up to 20 per cent of Obama supporters and 30 per cent of Hillary supporters would consider switching their vote if their candidate doesn't get the nod.

How to make sense of that figure? Well, first off, a degree of domestic fury has to be factored in. Running away with the Republicans is a bit like threatening to run off with the waitress/ shoe-store salesman who's writing a novel, and start over with a Subway franchise in rural Ohio, like they do in the sitcoms. The figure is at least partly buoyed by people letting their fantasy of revenge off the leash – it's pretty rare that the commemorative Franklin Mint John Wayne collection gets put down the garbage crusher, still less that the cat is left by the highway exit, but if no one talked the possibility out, the 'couple attack each other with K-Tel knives-like-the-chefs-use set' stories would crowd out the garage sale announcements in the local rag.

But exactly how much of this is sheer rage and how much would come to pass is a trickier question. The three candidates are less a left–right split than a set of overlapping circles. One tranche of Hillary's support, sorry to say, simply won't back the black guy. A smaller group of Obama male supporters won't back the chick. Beyond that, another section of Hillaryites won't back anyone white, black or – as it happens – beige, who sits in a church being lectured to by a priest who sounds like a one-man convention of Black Panthers and 9/11 Truthers. And a final section of Obama supporters see both Obama and McCain as representatives of a new politics with more in common than divides them – and an alternative to the duplicity of war-hero Hillary, dodging sniper bullets from the air.

This deep enmity between the camps of two figures WITH IDENTICAL PROGRAMS is a direct result of the primary system, a marvellously inclusive process capable of delivering direct democracy, so long as people can maintain a modicum of common sense and perspective.

Now read the quote at the top of the story again.

Should, as the odds now suggest, the Democrats go down in November, a degree of thorough modernisation of the party will be inevitable. Indeed, much of this will be restoration of 19th century features – a greater centralisation of power for the party to project a unity of purpose, a less open candidate selection process such as obtained before the primary system took off. Surely they must. Surely they can't drift on with entrenched interests and archaic procedures damning them for another two or three elections – can they? Any moment of smug superiority in that sense is tempered by imagining a Labor supporter saying it in 1961. (Hillary Rodham, you are magnificent!)

And by the memory that, the first thing the good people of Charters, Queensland did in the wake of the hideous backpacker fire there, was hold a sausage sizzle for the survivors.

Or as the *Desiderata* (bootleg) put it, the one thing you can't see is your own arsehole and God surely meant it that way.

3

TO UNITY, NEW HAMPSHIRE (HA HA HA)

Obama's Hard-won Victory

WEDNESDAY, 7 MAY

By the time Hillary Clinton appeared on stage in Indiana to claim that her 3 per cent margin was a victory in the tiebreaker primary, and to declare that it was 'on to the White House', Barack Obama was already swinging the guns around to former Navy flier John McCain. No one on Hillary's podium could possibly have thought it was a good result – neither the candidate herself, nor her pinkish white-haired lurch of a husband behind her, nor Chelsea, less a daughter than a child kidnapped by a weird cult of two. Though the possibility of Hillary actually overtaking Obama on delegates had disappeared months ago, she nevertheless required a big win in Indiana to continue with the story she has been telling to stay in the race – that only she can win in the heartlands of America, the socially conservative working-class voters purportedly turned off by Obama's liberalism. You couldn't get a better test case than the 'Hoosier' state, the self-proclaimed crossroads of America. Yet despite weeks spent consuming gallons of shots in trucker bars, and a variety of traditional smoking meat products across the state, she could barely hold Obama to a tie. Her victory speech lacked the fire of Pennsylvania, a victory Indiana has gone a long way to cancelling out.

In the gruelling, dying fight she has conducted in the last six weeks – since Obama won Super Tuesday and then some – Hillary Clinton has given the Republicans more ammunition to throw at the Democrats during the campaign proper than that old deluded alcoholic Charlie Wilson shipped to the Mujahadeen (Al-Qaeda, beta-testing version) through the whole of the '80s. She has brought back in Obama's connections with Tony Rezko, the Chicago slumlord who once did a few very small favours for a younger Barack. She has brought in the Reverend Jeremiah Wright, Obama's pastor at the Trinity United Church who runs a good line in radical black African theology, from a judicious slating of the USKKKA for its crimes to the loopier shores of blaming the CIA for AIDS. She has run her notorious and much-parodied 'it's 3 a.m.' TV advertisement, with small children sleeping through a global crisis while Hillary, in pantsuits, works through the night (which seems to suggest that if you can't vote for Hills, Johnny McCain might be your next best bet). And she has sailed very close to the wind of outright racism in order to scarf up a few Southern and Appalachian votes.

Save for the last, all of these are fair game, but the judgement a candidate in a primary contest always needs to make is, is it worth it, in the long run? Hillary's long run is looking like a long shot and at this point some sort of party loyalty should take over. She's running like it was anyone's game when everyone's calling it as a over, especially after the Indiana result.

Obama, meanwhile, was on fire, having taken North Carolina by an impressive 14 per cent, an unquestionable victory in practically every demographic. The energy flowed back into him and his speech essentially combined the theme he has been running on – the potential for hope and change within American life – with his more recent appeal to his own patriotic credentials, in the story of his father choosing the country as a beacon of hope.

'To those that hath shall be given' is the rule in politics, and the same press that had been talking up Clinton for weeks was now eager to hurry past her to the main game, the campaign itself, which by rights should have been underway for two months now. Though many people – many women especially – are going to be understandably disappointed that the first viable female candidate for president is going to fall at the last hurdle, and though Hillary and Obama's policy programs are virtually identical, the contest between Hillary and McCain would have been between two variations on the same style of politics, two of the same sort of people. Though McCain is portrayed as ancient compared to the other candidates, Hillary is only a decade younger than he is – both are children of the period prior to the '60s social revolutions, both in their own ways formed by it. Obama, born in the '60s, is the first Gen X contender, and a head to head between he and McCain is not merely a contest of values, but of two different ways of seeing the world, two different ways of being.

Born in the Panama Canal Zone – a fact that almost denied him eligibility for the presidency – the son and grandson of admirals, it was inevitable that John McCain (John Sidney McCain III) would join the Navy. And had all things been equal, he would have lived out his working life inside of it, finishing with the admiral's stars and bars on his shoulder. But then came Vietnam and six years as a high-profile POW. The experience not only made him a hero, and a symbol of America's confused relationship to the war, it also took him into civilian life as his career stalled for reasons of both physical health and temperament – his famous red-hot anger, which may or may not have been a product of his POW experiences. Like most leaders of that champion of traditional values, the Republican Party, his first marriage ended in multiple infidelities, including that with his current wife, Cindy, princess of an Arizona brewing fortune, whose family connections gave McCain his leg up to the Senate.

Cindy, by the way, is something else She's been at her husband's side throughout the campaign and if there's a vote they're trying to get from her appearances, it appears to be located entirely in the S&M subculture. Favouring scarlet leather jackets over black turtlenecks, with her bottle-blonde hair scraped back so hard you fear her head may slingshot off at any moment, it always looks like McCain has borrowed one of Qaddafi's female bodyguards for the duration. 'I'm very grateful for the continued support of my ruthless henchwoman, who knows thirty ways to kill . . .'

In the senate, McCain was a mostly loyal Reagan Republican for twenty years, and only recently branched out into a variety of more creative bipartisan legislation, on issues such as illegal immigration and campaign finance reform. That it is a certain type of life, and he a certain type of person, is evidenced by the fact that his boilerplate memoir *Faith of Our Fathers* was made into a TV movie for the Hallmark channel.

Faith of Our Fathers was filled with racy military anecdote, massaged by its ghost writer. Barack Obama's *Dreams from My Father* is devoid of these, but it is by far the more interesting book, the story as much about Obama himself as it is about his Kenyan father who came to the US as a graduate student. Obama's mother was a kinda proto-hippie who became an anthropologist and married first a Kenyan, and then an Indonesian. Obama grew up in Indonesia and Hawaii, and attended college in California and New York before becoming a community organiser in Chicago. Schooled in the orthodoxies of postmodern leftism and identity politics, he transcended them in his encounters with the more complex issues of organising a mixed community of Chicagoans left high and dry by factory closures, a role that seeded much of the approach he would adopt in his presidential campaign.

Obama is, in short, a hybrid person, a product of the tremendous mobility and transformation that began in the post-war years and burst into full flower in the '60s. His mother went looking for something other than the life assigned, pretty much at the same time as Betty Friedan's *The Feminine Mystique* was being published, and she found it, briefly, in a man whose passion was finding an African path to socialism. In Hawaii, where 'Barry' Obama stayed as his mother returned to the East, he was a dope-smoking slacker; in California, a black leftist talking of racist discourses; in Chicago, a Christian, organising among those who had lost everything in their lives. If the meaning of John McCain's life is encapsulated in the idea of duty, the meaning of Obama's is that you have to make not only your own life but your own self – have to put your self together from the available parts on offer – and that that is the dominant truth of the contemporary era.

Obama's challenge – of making your self and making your life – feeds into his politics, his understanding that what so many people want is a basic, entry-level sense that they are part of their society, that they can make an impact on the world. As does McCain's notion that, with a few modifications, the current set-up is working fine. It is the belief that people can find the meaning of their life in inherited institutions and attitudes, that they can slot into preordained roles.

I suspect that only the absurd extension of the Democratic primary has delayed this competition between two fundamental views of the world – and one that flows into their respective policies. For whatever his occasional liberalism on the occasional social issue, McCain is a straight-down-the-line kind of guy, living on the usual hypocrisies – the bloke who married well, preaching the virtues of free enterprise. Obama's philosophy is one that nudges Americans back in the direction that maybe, just maybe, the different parts of society – community, state, market – working together, might be able to deliver a better outcome than the obvious basket case of current American society. In a rich country, where tens of millions of working people live in terror of any disease that their insurance company might refuse to pay for, neither party will offer what most Americans now seem to want – universal health care. But McCain's answer to this is pure rhetoric, nostalgia and the abandonment not only of the poor, but of working people en masse.

Six months ago, the electorate preferred Obama to McCain by about 13 per cent. Now, after the Reverend Wright issue, and Obama's San Francisco 'elitism' speech, they are running evens. Yet in all the issues that face Americans today – health care, Iraq, climate change – opinion runs 70 to 30 per cent in the direction of the position Obama holds. If America goes against him and for McCain in November, it will not be out of belief in what McCain is professing, but of fear – fear of the unknown, fear of abandoning easy symbols, fear of . . . just fear.

McCain is pointed towards the past, Obama towards the future. If Obama's campaign has a meaning, it is not only, as his stump speech refrain goes, that 'we are the people we have been waiting for', it is also that we are the dreams our parents had, that any next generation is a synthesis of the disparate energies and half-completed projects of the last. As Hillary Clinton has reached ever more desperately for an angle, talking of 'obliterating

Iran' and of representing 'hard-working white people', Obama's candidacy has come to seem its antithesis, something calling out the best in people, the angels of their nature. Whether he can successfully make the case against McCain's pugnacity and his projection of endless American power – his assertion (as a Vietnam vet, of all people) that Americans never surrender, versus Obama's notion that America has an urgent need to both face its own failings and repair its relations with a multipolar world – will determine not only how Americans live but how we all face the century to come.

TUESDAY, 13 MAY

'Every economist has said the gas tax holiday is a bad idea.'

So said former Clinton White House staffer-turned-pundit George Stephanopoulos, to Hillary Clinton, during a high-profile interview on ABC's *This Week*.

'Oh well, elite economists can say what they like,' Hillary shot back.

The interview, conducted in the days before the North Carolina and Indiana primaries, had a ritual, kabuki air about it, a public encounter between two people who had had hundreds of private political arguments in the '90s. The game, as before, was: 'How far can you go?' How willing would Hillary be to track deep into Republican territory in an effort to outflank Barack Obama in the last big primary showdown? The answer, as if one needed to ask, was, 'All the way, baby'.

Hillary, the anti-elitist from the political elite.

Ever since the withdrawal of John Edwards, who had made poverty and the union movement his focus, Hillary had moved her rhetoric, if not her program, to the left. But she hadn't abandoned her essentially technocratic pitch of 'solutions' for America – the idea that what is required is not the airy inspirational rhetoric of Obama, but the application of the best people and ideas after eight years of wilful stupidity from the Bush administration.

With the 'elite economists' remark, that all changed. Last night, she was celebrating a 40 per cent victory margin in the West Virginia primary, to which that attack on the pointyheads had undoubtedly contributed. Though this sort of campaigning is unlikely to win the presidency for her, it is not impossible that it will lose it for Obama.

Weeks earlier, the leaking of the Obama 'San Francisco' tape – in which he spoke of poor Pennsylvanians as victims, rather than subjects, and their enthusiasm for guns and fear of immigrants as a set of symptoms rather than values in themselves – established a distinction between Obama and Clinton's attitude to the people they were campaigning among. John McCain's suggestion of a 'gas tax holiday' in summer gave her the opportunity to set the division in concrete, running the elite/populist divide right through the middle of the Democratic Party. If, ultimately, it didn't do much for Hillary, as the Indiana polls would suggest, it demonstrated how limited the application of the left/right spectrum is to American politics now.

Whatever one's feelings about consumer taxes, the gas tax holiday was a stunningly bad idea. The proposal was to suspend the eighteen-and-a-half cents in the gallon tax on petrol during the high summer period. The move would do little to alleviate the real problems working Americans now face from rising gas prices – in particular, the increasing cost of the morning commute, or of basic shopping in suburban areas. As Obama noted, the total average saving over the summer would be thirty dollars. Nor does the holiday act as a spur to business by lowering costs over any significant amount of time. Instead, it would increase cost uncertainty and undermine the ability to plan ahead – would it be extended, would it be increased?

Initially proposed by McCain, he gave it a symbolic swoosh by declaring that he wanted it to run from 'Memorial Day to Labour Day', the two holidays that bookend summer. McCain knew that there was no chance the proposal would make it through the Senate, but the gas tax holiday was meticulously designed to appeal to the rather forlorn hope that the escalation of gas prices was not the mark of new conditions in which increasing global demand had made cheap gas a thing of the past. It was also intended to contrast with the Democrat's call to seriousness and acknowledgement of the need to address deep structural problems. Forget the mopers, McCain's proposal seemed to say, it's still morning in America. Sure, there are issues to address, but let's enjoy the summer. On the other hand, it stopped short of saying that everything was fine. It was diluted Reaganism, combining reflexive optimism with popular tax-cutting.

Somewhat amazingly, McCain had this initiative taken away from him when Hillary not only endorsed it, but also added an anti-corporate spin by suggesting that it was about time the oil companies started paying. There was no accompanying suggestion about how they would be prevented from passing that new cost on to the consumer without more stringent price controls, but since she had no suggestion about how the actual proposal could be brought to fruition, that didn't seem to matter. Effectively, McCain and Clinton had carved up the populist territory between them, offering to let their policy be guided by general acclaim, rather than its role in a more comprehensive program, each giving a right or left spin to add political branding.

Obama had come out swinging against the gas tax holiday, less out of political courage than a lack of options. The proposal not only ran against the grain of his appeal to Americans to face the challenges of a changing world, he was also never going to win a populist petrol pissing contest against a crusty old vet.

By the time the proposal hit, Obama's San Francisco speech had thoroughly positioned him as an elitist member of the executive class, an image reinforced by his gawky performance on the campaign trail. While Hillary downed shots in bars, Obama came across as the nerd at the beach party, emerging blinking from the library into the sunlight. It was not that Obama spurned the ritual of modern campaigning, he just did it appallingly badly. Faced with the famed 'Philly cheesesteak' – a roll oozing chopped meat and melted cheese – after a day sampling various wursts, he couldn't handle it, but promised to 'come back for it later'.

Hitherto, Obama had avoided the familiar Republican charge of 'elitism', largely due to the originality of his political rhetoric – his near-total avoidance of any of the standby themes of American liberalism, state programs and issues of race and gender. This was partly because the wilder fringes of the right were going after his unusual background – Kenyan father, schooling in Indonesia, middle name Hussein – but also because he simply didn't fit any handy class mould. Obama knew both poverty and privilege, post-'60s hippiedom and old-fashioned Protestant application.

What was new about his pitch, for someone from the Democratic left, was its universalism, his argument that practically everyone, aside from the wealthy, has been marginalised by the system regardless of their identity. The right could do little but attack its airiness, its lack of content – a difficult move, since the Bush administration has been the epitome of lackadaisical ennui for the past two years.

Obama's canny strategy hid an obvious fact – he was both a member of the elite and an elitist, by virtue of his political practice. His political path seems to have been set by a period in New York in his early twenties when he read a variety of deeper sources – religious texts, the classic existentialists, Nietzsche. With the exception of the last of these, such writings had fallen out of favour among the young American left of the 1980s, and particularly the subject of the will, of making meaning. Even Nietzsche's texts were regarded purely as proto-deconstruction, discourses on the meaninglessness of systems, rather than an assertion of the will to live and act in the world.

Obama's move into the world of community organising was the proverbial 'leap of faith', in this case, into a context he was not part of, but that he wanted to transform. Joining the organisation created by the founder of community organising, Saul Alinksy, Obama effectively took on a form of activism whose principle is the transformation of the people being organised. Community organising, as practised in areas of the US devastated by factory closures and neighbourhood decline, combined a series of techniques drawn from psychology and sociology to address the loss of given frameworks and sense of identity provided by working life.

For Alinsky, change came when people had reached a point of despair, when the loss of an old world had become undeniable. At this point, community organising was as much a process of reconstructing will and individuals' self-belief. Every activist or organisational process reflects on its own processes and techniques, but community organising in particular abstractly reflects on the manner in which it rebuilds, or applies, a sense of meaning and process. It is no exaggeration to say that Obama's primary campaign has been an application at the national level of the techniques applied in the south side of Chicago.

But there is no way of having such a relationship to people without being willing to frame their values and attitudes as 'symptoms' in a false consciousness model. Thus, to the wider public, Obama's public positions – 'hope, change, we are the people we have been waiting for', etcetera – sit ill with the fairly old school new leftism of his San Francisco speech:

You go into some of these small towns in Pennsylvania and, like a lot of small towns in the Midwest, the jobs have been gone now for twenty-five years and nothing's replaced them. And they fell through the Clinton administration and the Bush administration, and each successive administration has said that somehow these communities are gonna regenerate, and they have not. And it's not surprising then they get bitter, they cling to guns or religion or antipathy to people who aren't like them, or anti-immigrant sentiment or anti-trade sentiment, as a way to explain their frustrations.

Liberal commentators have criticised the mainstream media's focus on this speech, as if it were on a par with the disinformation campaign around Obama's alleged Muslim childhood, madrassa and all. Yet they are obviously entirely different matters. Voters, whatever their material circumstances, are hardly deluded if they choose their leaders based on a candidate's attitude to the values that give their lives meaning and express their cultural identity.

Hillary's decision to go full bore with the notion of 'elitism' was thus doubly opportunistic – exploiting not only the gulf that had opened up between Obama and his desired projection of himself, but also willing to employ the full irrationalism that Republicans have marshalled in other areas such as the early stages of Iraq (Rumsfeld's shrugged 'Stuff happens' comments, for example, as the place began to fall apart), intelligent design in the classroom, abstinence-based sex education, and a host of other areas.

Hillary, who had marshalled a huge brief of economic reasoning against the Bush tax cuts, was willing to construct the argument over a gas tax holiday as a battle of the pointyheads against the NASCAR set. Given the extreme likelihood that Obama will be the Democratic nominee, such a deep division not only drives the populist division down the middle of the Democrats, it is effectively an argument to a section of Hillary supporters that they might be better represented by McCain.

Populism was hitherto a style that appeared on both sides of the left–right divide. Once those formations start to lose their sway, the axis of division swings around – to experts versus the people, abstract versus concrete, theory versus experience. Older-style political movements based on an idea about the world, an account of how values relate to facts, are capable of maintaining a relationship between experts and rank and file within a movement, based on the trust arising from a shared project. In that sense, Hillary's desperate attempt to throw the switch on what remains of Democrat unity is a measure not merely of her desperation, but of the attenuated nature of the party itself, at least among its elite.

Indeed, she took it further in the wake of the Indiana result, with a remark about being the only one who can appeal to 'hard-working white people', an adjectival combination with a very nasty edge. Though much of the criticism of her has centred on the very fact of her continuation of the contest, a healthy party with clear boundaries around its beliefs should be able to bear a vigorous contest for the leadership, even such a public one as the US primary process. Forget God and guns – it's Hillary who is less the cause than the symptom of a politics that has lost much of its meaning.

MONDAY, 19 MAY

God, oh God, please let it be over soon, now, anytime, soon. Somebody do something. Somebody do nothing. Anybody do anything. It's like waiting for the electrician. Nothing interesting is going to happen, but nothing else can be done until the bell rings.

Latest: Obama leading in Oregon by between eight to fifteen points, depending. Hillary leading in Kentucky by about twenty to thirty. No surprises, absolutely no surprises, in either forecast. Hillary has to win Kentucky big to not lose; Obama can weather a disappointing Oregon result.

Obama – now not even bothering to campaign against Hillary but focusing directly on McCain – spending time in swing states, estimating himself to be seventy-five short of the 2026 delegates needed, calling on Clinton to concede.

Clinton warning against any premature victory celebrations, which is a bit of a desperate situation to find oneself in. She is now an acute source of psychophysical pain to me and many others, like a trace memory of childhood scalding whenever she comes on the teev.

Yes, she has a right to keep campaigning. No one denies she's got a right. And if she had a different program – continuing the war and socialising health care, for example – then she would be offering something different. But it's the sodding same, with bells and whistles.

Make it stop.

Warren Buffett has endorsed Obama. No big surprise. He's always had a social liberalish streak.

More significantly, 'Bama also got the endorsement of Robert Byrd, the 90-year-old veteran Senator from West Virginia, days after Hillary took the state. To say Byrd is a conservative Democrat is something of an understatement: the guy was a member of the Ku Klux Klan. Mind you, that was in 1942 – he was a Grand Cyclops, apparently – and he has subsequently apologised profusely. Now he's just your average bloke who stays at home on a weekend to do some chores and singe the lawn.

Hillary will probably counter by getting the backing of the KKK. 'Racist? Oh, that's just elite sociologists talking.'

God knows, if the whole campaign is like methadone now, then next week (Montana and South Dakota) will be like sucking the cotton wool in a Panadol bottle. A perfectly tepid half-life of politics.

Everything is stuck. No matter how much Obama tries to turn the guns onto McCain, it just can't be done in any serious way until round one is out of the way.

And of course, Hillary could still win. She could still win.

Possibilities:

1. Assassination of Obama. Highly unlikely, though the most plausible culprit at this stage would be an enraged white Hillary supporter, or possibly Gloria Steinem.

2. Big scandal as yet unexplored, though God knows what it would be that FOX News hasn't thrown at Obama yet. There's lots of stuff from his Illinois voting record that will be thrown during the general election, but nothing of the 'video of farm animals' level they would need. Jump the shark. Fuck the quokka. Sniff the chair.

3. Mixture of intimidation, influence, etcetera, by Clintons in post-primary hiatus to get enough superdelegates back for a narrow victory.

4. Food poisoning at Convention.

None even remotely likely, but NUTC.

So, as the Democrack-up continues, McCain is getting a free ride on a bunch of stuff, most specifically the fact that his campaign against Washington lobbyists has had to be close fought lately – he's had to sack three of his staff for being, um, lobbyists. Two of them worked for the Myanmar junta, a moderate faction thereof. Which is McCain all over, really. We will work with a *moderate* faction of the junta.

There's also the endorsement by Pastor Jim Hagee that McCain sought and then had to qualify, due to Hagee's anti-Catholicism. Hagee's an ultra-Protestant who basically sees the Pope as the Antichrist. Even worse/better are his views on Jews.

Like most evangelical fervid supporters of Israel, it's conditional on the idea that on Judgement Day, half the Jews will be saved and half condemned – and that such fates are predestined, i.e. half the Jewish population are satanic creatures with no souls. Jewish suffering – including the Holocaust – is held to be God's punishment for Jews deserting their role as chosen people, i.e. becoming secular and assimilated in 20th century Europe.

There appears to be no footage of Hagee saying this bilge, which must be the only reason FOX News isn't running with it full-bore. I mean, what other reason could there be?

But as Obama will need to hang on to the Democrat Jewish bloc, given his qualms about incinerating Iran, I will be very surprised if the issue doesn't come up in the general campaign.

If there is one. If there ever is one.

Stop press: Phil Beavis, vice chair of the Waxachie (MO) county Democratic Party has endorsed Obama. What does this mean for the campaign? CNN will be debating the issue for the next eight hours.

Make it all stop.

MONDAY, 26 MAY

It's Memorial Day here, a holiday that began as a commemoration of the Civil War Union dead (and thus of the subjugation of one part of the country by another) and became a memory of American dead in foreign wars. In Texas, there are military parades. In Nebraska, relatives visit and clean the graves of the fallen. And in Portland, folks have a late mushroom and asiago omelette brunch in the Pearl District, browse Powell's for new anime and then take in a movie at the Living Room, preferably black and white, preferably Brazilian. Semper Fi, o cap'n, my cap'n.

Six more weeks here and I will no longer be able to understand myself.

God knows what the country will look like next year, when once again one part of it has subjugated the other, but even with a Democratic grand slam the place will still be embroiled in foreign wars. The question is whether the US will be led by someone who's trying to back out of them – someone who defines them as exactly the wrong relationship the country should have to the world – or by a man who, despite subsequent back-pedalling, is easy with the idea of being in ever more exotic locales for a hundred years.

Currently, the polls would suggest the latter scenario, with McSame leading Obama by around four points across the board – more than enough to grab a few more states than Bush took from Kerry or Gore. But we're a long way out and a lot can and will happen. However, one thing is certain – if Obama is to win this, the election will have to be rendered qualitatively different by his candidacy and campaign than any before.

If Indecision '08 merely runs in the grooves of red state–blue state culture wars that have gone before, then Obama may as well give up now. Of all the possible scenarios for an Obama victory, the least likely is the one that Democrats have been working on for the past three years, when Hillary was seen as a shoo-in.

Consider, from worst to best for Obama:

SCENARIO ONE: The current state of play is that the Democrats hold New England, the north bit of the industrial Northeast, and the Pacific coast. The GOP holds the South, the Southwest, the Midwest, the Great Plains, and the Northeast remnant – Indiana and Ohio. Bush got 286 electoral college votes, Kerry 251.

The assumption has always been that the Democrats must win either Ohio (20 votes) or Florida (27) in order to regain the White House.

Given the current polling of Obama among certain sectors, that is looking unlikely. Indeed, one possible result is that Obama not only fails to gain either state, but loses New Hampshire (4), the most ornery of the New England states, and maybe even Michigan (10), for a true debacle and an entrenchment of 'McCain Democrats'.

SCENARIO TWO: This would have Obama losing these states, but gaining GOP states that the silvertailed Kerry couldn't get – New Mexico (5), Iowa (7), maybe even Colorado (9), to do slightly better than Kerry, without actually winning.

SCENARIO THREE: This has Obama holding all the states Kerry took, taking neither Florida nor Ohio, but taking some of New Mexico, Iowa, Colorado, Nevada (5), and maybe even South Carolina (8), in such a way as to give him the eighteen votes he needs for a narrow victory.

SCENARIO FOUR: This assumes that much of the 'won't vote Obama' thing is pique that can be magicked away, both by Obama going head to head with McCain and by a remorseless worsening of everything the latter is in favour of. In this scenario, Obama gains one or both of Florida, and a couple from the New Mexico etcetera list, to take the Democrat vote above 300 and lay the basis for a reconstruction of the electoral map.

SCENARIO FIVE: Now the grand slam. Obama takes everything below the GOP waterline, leaving the Republicans with redoubt states like Texas and Idaho. With the Democrats also gaining a 50–60 seat majority in Congress, the conditions are set for a decade or more of Democrat power, and the chance to appoint several Supreme Court justices, effectively setting the terms of American political culture for the next three or four decades.

So you can see why things are a little fraught on the Democrat side, but also why Obama supporters are more confident than the terrifying stories of white working-class desertion would have one believe.

Two factors are key here – one is the winner-take-all nature of a state-based selection process. Take the state by one or one million votes, it don't matter (except for Nebraska and Maine, shittily enough) – the electoral college votes are yours. New Mexico went to Bush by 6000 votes last time, and a few other states are so close to the waterline that it is generally assumed that sheer Bushhatred will carry them for the Dems.

Second is the small-state weighting. Electoral college votes are arrived at by adding congressional districts to Senate seats. Since every state has two senators, that means small states punch above their weight. Ohio has eighteen districts and New Mexico has three. The latter is one-sixth the size but gets one quarter of the electoral college votes (20 against 5). To get twenty electoral college votes from three close smaller states – New Mexico, Nevada, Colorado, say – means convincing fewer people than one close big state.

Usually, that's a goose–gander sauce thang. This year it may be different, because so many of these states may be composed of the sort of people – Hispanic Americans, mixed culture, outlaws in general – most likely to have some sort of general identification with Obama. Effectively, his status as the first postmodern candidate may be enough to outflank the rustbelt/sunbelt states that it has hitherto been assumed the Democrats have to win.

Risky strategy? You bet. But the Democrats ain't got much else. Which means that . . . Hillary's still in the race. Why? Because if she were the candidate, most likely none of this outflanking nonsense would be needed. After all, she's not the one getting endorsed by frikkin' Castro (de facto). The Dems would take not only Ohio, but quite possibly regain a chunk of the South – Kentucky, Mississippi, etcetera – plus the Southwest, to put together an electoral college vote not seen since, well, since the last time a Clinton ran.

Who's to say that won't become so obvious, so compelling in the lead-up to the Convention, that there won't be a sudden superdelegate crossback? Who's to say it's not possible that they won't feel it not merely their prerogative, but their duty, to history?

For the party, for the country, for the Union dead?

FRIDAY, 30 MAY

From *West Wing Side Story* (grovelling apologies to the usual . . .):

Rosahillaria:

> *Puerto Rico*
> *You lovely island*
> *Island of votes in the sixties*
> *Always the primary's going*
> *Even though no one will be voting[i]*

Anitobama:

> *Puerto Rico*
> *You ugly island*
> *Like a pile of big donkey faeces*
> *Still, this primary's blowing[ii]*
> *Difficulties keep growing*
> *Lead over McCain's slowing*
> *And the press is lying*
> *And my buzz is dying*
> *I like the fact that I've ALREADY WON![iii]*
> *Which I may or may not have mentioned*

Both:

> I want to govern America
> I want to govern America
> Although it's proving very hard
> I want to frikkin' govern America!

Rosahillaria:

> I like Florida, Michigan

Anitobama:

> Then you can have half of them[iv]

Rosahillaria:

> Let a hundred flowers of thought bloom

Anitobama:

> Then decide it all in smoke-filled rooms[v]

Both: Chorus

Rosahillaria:

> I've got the popular vote in America!
> From getting the bloat in diners there![vi]

Anitobama:

> You're going to split middle America!
> And fiddle, while burns America![vii]

Rosahillaria:

> I've torn you a new one in San Juan

Anitobama:

> *A pity you've no pot to shit on*

Rosahillaria:

> *You've still got an insane pastor*

Anitobama:

> *Well . . . everyone thinks you're a bastard*[viii]

Both: *Chorus*

Rosahillaria:

> *We'll go all the way up to Denver*
> *Though Democrat hopes may all end there*

Anitobama:

> *Just goes to show in America*
> *Many jobs (snows) in America!*[ix]

Endnotes

i. Hillary Clinton won the Puerto Rico primary with a vote in the high 60 per centers. However, none of the people voting will be able to cast an actual vote in the election – the Democratic primary was invented years ago as a sop to the wider Hispanic vote. The two dominant parties in Puerto Rico cut across the Republican–Democrat divide.

ii. Though Obama will win the Montana and South Dakota primaries, the Puerto Rico victory gives Hillary yet another meaningless symbolic occasion to disrupt the process of choosing a candidate.

iii. Despite Puerto Rico, Hillary now has no chance of getting an actual majority, without tempting back some superdelegates who have already pledged to Obama.

iv. The Democratic Rules Committee met on the weekend to sort out the problem of the Michigan and Florida delegations. The eventually agreed-upon compromise was that all the delegates would be seated but would only get half a vote each. Delegates would be awarded to Obama in Michigan (he wasn't on the ballot) based on a complex proportional formula.

v. Hillary's rep Harold Ickes argued that the deal was a blow against democracy and diversity in the past – and then said the whole deal would be referred to the Credentials Committee, the ultimate backroom fix.

vi. Hillary reiterated the claim that Obama's inability to connect with common people – i.e. through eating hideous foods at photo opps – indicates that he will lose the country.

vii. Hillary's supporters practically disrupted the DRC meeting with loud chanting and walkouts.

viii. After the Trinity Church featured another pastor doing a big piss-take of Hillary as an angry white witch, Obama quit his church.

ix. The origin of 'snow job' is apparently either as an excuse for absenteeism at work (snowed in at home), or a military term for embedded positions faked by piling up snow drifts. Interesting, huh?

TUESDAY, 3 JUNE

By the time Hillary came out on stage in New York – about 9.30 p.m. eastern seaboard time – the tension was close to frikkin' unbearable across the nation. With only two half-deserted, misbegotten states— I'm sorry, proud frontier, great plains, best of America thangs to report, and with CNN now forecasting on the basis of exit polls that Obama now had the delegates necessary for the 2118 majority (the revised number following the reseating of 50 per cent of Michigan and Florida), she would concede. Wouldn't she?

For the first ten minutes of her speech it seemed like, hell no, she wouldn't. Congratulating Obama early on the whole campaign and noting that she is 'proud to call him my friend' (presumably because it indicates an admirable ability to speak through gritted teeth), she quickly got out of that ditch and talked about 'standing up for the best values of my party, making sure that every voice is heard and that every vote counts'.

Uh oh.

'I think of each of your votes as a prayer . . .'

Gaaaaaaak.

'I am so proud we stayed the course together . . .'

Okay, maybe she is conceding. Maybe the first bit was just a last canter around the track. Now she's talking in the past tense.

Huge noise, stomping at intervals.

'Everyone came together – red state, blue state, purple people of every age, colour . . .'

Purple people?

'I am committed to uniting the party . . .'

Fantastic. She is conceding.

'None of you is invisible to me . . . I see you wherever you are . . .'

She is now claiming superpowers, X-ray vision.

'I have been fighting for you my whole adult life . . . Like the soldier who gave his spending money to the campaign, the 11-year-old boy in Kentucky who sold his bike . . .'

That poor kid again. He must be getting such shit down on the blue grassy knoll.

Chants of 'DENVER DENVER', i.e. go all the way to the Convention.

'Where do we go from here?'

That's it – you don't ask that question unless you're looking for a future direction.

'I will be making no decisions tonight . . .'

WHAT? WHAT? Obama's got 2127 delegates according to CNN. He'll get another 30 superd's after tonight. It's over.

'I want to hear from you. Write to me on the website and tell me what you think we should do.'

My God, it's Nancy Drew. The first choose-your-own-adventure campaign in history.

'We'll think about what is best for the party in the days to come.'

She goes off to the tune of 'Simply the Best' by Tina Turner, à la what? She took a few hard knocks too? Obama as Ike? We all suffer at the hands of skinny abusive black men?

In St Paul, Minnesota, minutes later, Obama (there, where the Republicans will meet, in order to stick it to them):

'Thank you to my grandmother . . .'

The cool Hawaiian one, not the racist . . . or was she the racist one?

'She put everything she had into me . . . this is the end of one historic journey.'

Bye bye, Hillary.

'I will be the Democratic nominee for the president of the United States.'

Would you get that through your thick goddam sorority preppie skull?

'Senator Hillary Clinton has made history in this campaign . . .'

Big ups for not slipping up on 'has made' and making it 'is'.

'I congratulate her.'

Booing mixed amidst the cheers – none of that in Hillary's speech. Obama giving a summary of Hillary's life – eulogy for the living, a gold-watch speech.

'I am a better candidate for having had to compete against Hillary Rodham Clinton.'

I couldn't think of a better strop for my gleaming razor . . .

'We aren't the reason you came out . . . We owe our children a better future . . . Let us unite . . .'

Going the big picture. Then he wheeled round and stuck it to McCain, Hillary vanishing into the dust.

'I honour, we all honour, John McCain . . . But nothing he will say here is about change.'

Change. There's a theme we haven't heard much of.

'Tough direct diplomacy, which means we don't cower from every petty dictator . . . Change is about renewing our schools and returning to science and innovation . . .'

Much more content in this speech, basically turning the Democrat agenda on John McCain rather than fighting it out with Hillary, the lineaments of his presidential campaign being set.

'. . . college be a birthright for every American . . . that's why I'm running for president of the United States . . . I look forward to the debate with the other side . . .'

That is, a real debate, not a trench war with the Clintons.

Then we go into boilerplate about the politics of fear, from 1776 through the Civil War to WWII, civil rights, glass ceilings, etcetera etcetera.

But still, it soars. Hillary can never top this. It must really hurt to know that.

'This is our moment, this is our time . . . We will be able to look back and say that this was the moment . . .we ended a war, we slowed the rise of the oceans . . .'

Slowed the rise of the oceans? Oh, global warming.

'. . . restored our place as the "last best hope of man".'

Goes out on Springsteen's 9/11 song 'The Rising', so at least that wimpy noncommittal number has at last found a meaning . . .

A damn powerful speech (another one). Even the CNN gang slightly moved by it – imagine what it would have been like if Hillary had conceded and endorsed him. The pure surge of power.

So we go on. Yet there is no relief. The days, weeks roll on, waiting for Hillary either to concede in some afterthought, or to fight on in a mad destructive frenzy.

We go on. We go on.

MONDAY, 30 JUNE

I know what we start here on this field will end on the steps of Capitol Hill next January, as Barack Obama takes the oath of office as our next president.

– Hillary Clinton

I know that, because of our campaign, because of the campaign that Hillary Clinton waged, my daughters and all of your daughters will forever know that there is no barrier to who they are and what they can be in the United States of America . . . They can take for granted that women can do anything that the boys can do, and do it better. And do it in heels.

– Barack Obama

They met in Unity, New Hampshire, a place chosen because no one has yet named an American town 'Bitter Alliance, Nebraska' or 'Not-Gagging-On-What-I'm-Saying, Wyoming'*. Though both would deny they'd colour-coordinated, Obama's blue tie was of a shade identical to Hillary's pantsuit, giving the appearance that he'd torn a strip of it off her and wrapped it round his neck in triumph.

The rally – in which Hillary urged her supporters to put the past behind them and back Obama, and Obama sang the praises of his erstwhile opponent – was, as Pat Buchanan noted on MSNBC, 'an arranged marriage with a pre-nup'. Obama needs Hillary to corral her supporters and lead them back into the Democratic mainstream, and Hillary needs Obama to help pay off some of her mammoth debts.

Though Obama can't directly pay a portion of his massive fundraising haul to Camp Clinton, he can try and direct donations coming into his website to pay directly to the Clinton campaign. Whether they will do that depends on how much they know about where the money's going – Clinton's campaign owes at least $5 million to Mark Penn, her chief strategist, and another $5 million to herself.

---

*There's a Truth Or Consequences in New Mexico, named after a radio quiz show. Also Intercourse, Pennsylvania, named by literal-minded Amish farmers, and Boring, Oregon, named after a local, but which (in typical blue-state Oregon fashion), has become an ironic rallying point. Others include Muck City (Alabama), Steam Corner (Indiana) and, of course, Frankenstein (Missouri).

With the Clinton's wealth estimated at $110 million, and Penn's payment going to his powerful consulting organisation, it's not exactly a draw for the sort of donors Obama has been relying on, the fifty or a hundred dollars here and there.

Most likely the debt will be repaid by Obama's 'bundlers', the fundraisers who specialise in finding ten, twenty, a hundred people to donate the maximum $2600 an individual can give to a candidate. Those who've donated the maximum amount to Obama now have their slate cleared to donate to Hillary. Two thousand such donors – not such a huge number – would knock a hole in the debt, at least part of which is money owed on hall rentals, etcetera, rapid payment of which is politically imperative.

The corollary is, if course, that Obama now has access to Hillary's donors and bundlers and, though that is a smaller resource than Obama's Iowa-esque floodplain of money, it will help enormously now that Obama has knocked back public funding for his campaign.

The announcement last week by the Obama team that they would go private was greeted with astonishment, dismay and a quasar's-worth of spin by the punditocracy. Obama had previously asserted that he would take public funding for the campaign, but that was before it became clear just how willing people were to contribute to his run. Public funding limits a candidate's general election budget to $84 million (in 2008) once s/he's been nominated by the party convention.

For John McCain, who has accepted public funding, that's

a good bet. He raised a total of about $115 million to the end of May, compared to Obama's $287 million. More significant, however, is the amount that has come from small donors – $200 or less – compared to those who've given close to the maximum $2600. Almost half of Obama's money to date has come from those small donors, almost 150 000 of them, which means they can be returned to. They would only need to part with another $600 each, on average, to exceed the total public funds available to McCain. And that is before we have even counted new donors who have held back so as to be able to give a maximum amount to whoever the Democrats pick – Hillary contributors, John Edwards' contributors, independents drawn to the Obama movement over the coming months. There is also the small but increasing number of Obamicans – Republicans who believe that McCain is simply too compromised, too bellicose, too nothing-much-at-all, and Obama at least offers a chance for fresh thinking.

Thus Obama has rich fields yet to tap. There is potentially another $200–300 million out there for him to throw at McCain during the three months between the Convention and the election.

McCain, by contrast, knows that his funding sources are fast drying up. His main primary rival, Mitt Romney, worked off a base substantially composed of maximum contribution supporters, and Mike Huckabee was working off a base in the hundreds. There is much less of a guarantee that supporters of either candidate would be willing to donate to McCain, in the manner Obama can rely on. Despite the rhetoric, you could barely run a sheet of paper between Hillary and Obama's plans on Iraq, health care and the economy. By contrast, Huckabee's supporters want the Constitution rewritten to include the Ten Commandments. McCain will be fighting to get them to the polling booth at all, let alone part with money for the kids' home-schooling.

Thus, things are looking grim for McCain. When *Newsweek* came out with a poll putting Obama 15 per cent ahead, it was dismissed as an outlier. When the *Los Angeles Times* followed up with a poll having him 12 per cent ahead, it was clear that something was going on. *RealClearPolitics'* poll of polls now has Obama running 7 per cent ahead.

So, it's still a long way to November, but there is more than a hint of desperation around the Republican camp, and its minions in FOX News and elsewhere. Obama's private-funding decision – he had hitherto strongly supported public funding – and his support for the recent 5–4 Supreme Court decision striking down a handgun ban, has made it clear that he's no hapless liberal in the Kerry/Dukakis manner. He really wants to win, and he's not going to be outflanked on issues that are not at the economic/foreign policy core.

Nor does there seem to be much joy from the '527' groups, the 'independent' attack dogs who ran ads such as the Swift Boat Veterans attack on Kerry in 2004. New regulations have made direct attacks on a candidate's character impermissible for such groups. Faced with this appalling demand that they focus on the issues, many right organisations have said they'll sit this election out.

Meanwhile Obama has launched a twenty-state ad campaign, including such Republican strongholds as Alaska, in what is the start of a fifty-state strategy.

Oh yes, there will be blood.

TUESDAY, 8 JULY

'She sent one email to [my assistant] Reggie [Love], who forwarded it to me. I [wrote] saying, "Thank you, Scarlett, for doing what you do". And suddenly we have this email relationship.'

It was May and Barack Obama was clarifying his relationship with pulchritudinous actress Scarlett Johannson, who was claiming to be 'in dialogue' with him. Johansson had recorded an automatic phone message (a 'robocall') for the Minnesota primary and had appeared in the slick/creepy *Yes We Can* video by the Black Eyed Peas' will.i.am, in which leading celebs sang along to Obama's speeches.

'Dialogue' was something else, however, and leaving the assertion unchallenged would open the campaign to charges of flakiness. After a bit of shillyshallying, it was obvious that the candidate himself would have to make clear that the girl with the pearl earring would not be part of the new administration. Thus did Barack Obama, who has already broken a few records, excel himself – becoming perhaps the first man to say 'no' to Scarlett Johannson.

These days, most candidates would kill to be associated with just about any actress, with the rule-proving exception of Lindsay Lohan. But one look at the roster of A-listers who've lined up with Obama's campaign and it's clear that Scarlett's barely in the top twenty. The stars have come out for candidates before, but the mobilisation for the candidate of 'change we can believe in' is like nothing hitherto seen.

Oprah Winfrey has organised Hollywood fundraisers for him, raising millions. Robert de Niro has opened for him at events in New Jersey. Ben Affleck has helped Moveon.org make an Obama video. Samuel L Jackson skipped the Oscars to man the phones for him during the Texas primary. And then there was that shattering syzygy of supercharged charisma, when, in April, Obama and George Clooney shared the stage to talk about genocide. Obama's Hollywood base is so chock-full that stars who would get red carpet treatment in any other campaign are tacked on almost as an afterthought. Forest Whitaker was barely noticed stumping out in Colorado, while Kerry Washington never made it out of the South.

Barack Obama's thunderous campaign is not the first – and certainly not the first Democratic – presidential tilt to have attracted the interest and support of celebrities, but it is quite possibly the first in which the candidate has more of what film stars and musicians provide – a magical glow of charisma and specialness – than the celebs themselves. Politics, as the old adage goes, is showbiz for ugly people, and when, in the 1970s, Hollywood people once again became seriously interested in politics, political professionals saw a way of giving old white male political hack candidates a connection to the millions of younger potential voters who increasingly looked to the mass media for sources of identity and values.

But it's worth remembering how separate these two worlds were until pretty recently. Bill Clinton may have acquired the title of 'first rock star president' in retrospect, but in 1992 he was still a slightly goofy looking governor from Arkansas, and campaigns were sufficiently hidebound that the Clintons' choice of Fleetwood Mac's 'Don't Stop' as a theme song was sufficiently exciting to become a talking point.

It was only during Clinton's two-term presidency that the world of celebrity and politics started to really come together – as smart, well-connected film stars and musicians, once employed as marginal extras, came to the centre of political causes. Today, it seems unremarkable that George Clooney should be not just the hood ornament of a campaign around Darfur, but the engine of it, and that Angelina Jolie should be some sort of spare UN Secretary General floating around the world. In a world where Bono had been seriously spoken of as a possible head of the World Bank, anything was possible.

But, by the 2000s, as celebs started to move en masse into left-liberal politics, their support had become very much a mixed blessing. The wave of anti-'elitism' deployed by right-wing parties managed to shift the idea of the elite from economic to cultural differences – thus the socially conservative corporate rich who ran the Republican party could present themselves as more representative of the average voter than celebrities living in a very different world. Nor did many celebrities do themselves, or their preferred candidates, any favours with some of their whackier and less self-aware comments. From John Travolta lecturing the world on global warming from the proverbial stairway of one of his many jets, to Sean Penn running a full-page *New York Times* ad attacking George W Bush for 'deconstructing civil liberties', to Jolie and Brad Pitt using the African nation of Namibia as their personal maternity ward, by the time of John Kerry's 2004 presidential run, A-list involvement in politics was beginning to look less like citizen involvement and more like the self-indulgence of a new aristocracy – especially given Kerry's New England patrician demeanour and his billionaire heiress wife.

The Republicans' 'elite' angle would seem to have worked – Dubya was returned by a 3 million-vote margin in 2004, recording increases in support in dozens of rural and industrial counties decimated by his earlier cuts in social services. The loss marked a break in Democratic politics – having had the advantage of youthful glow from Hollywood interest in the '90s, celebrity endorsements were now crowding out any notion of the Democrats as a popular party.

It's clear that, from the start, it was an issue the Obama campaign were going to consciously address. Though actors and rap stars have been used to open events, the whole shtick of Obama standing on a podium with an endless string of action heroes has been avoided. Indeed, there's been an emphasis on shots of the great and good sitting on a phone bank in some regional office, patiently calling the backblocks of the Midwest to grab that extra caucus vote. Come the Party Convention at the end of August, they'll be a secondary presence at best, with Obama accepting the nomination in the 73 000-seat Mile High Stadium in Denver, the true star of the show.

It's a measure of the dilemma faced by the Republicans that they will have to follow that extravaganza with their own Convention, a mere few days later, and that their nominee is a man whose oratory is far better suited to the small meeting and the informal press briefing than the roar of the stadium. To put it bluntly, nothing is going right for John McCain. Any hope that the war of attrition between Hillary and Obama in the primaries would give McCain an advantage has faded away, and public perceptions – that McCain represents a past, inadequate to the challenges of the present – have set hard. Polling averages suggest Obama has a solid 6 per cent lead, and nothing in McCain's message or style suggests he has the capacity to overtake him, unless extraordinary events occur.

Indeed there is something a little depressing about the McCain campaign, which may be why he can claim so few celebrities of his own. Even Mike Huckabee had Chuck Norris, former kickboxing superhero, now home-gym plugger, who would rassle up the crowd before the Huckabee himself emerged to give a truly insane speech and then knock out a few old rock'n'roll songs on bass with his band. McCain, by contrast, has been scratching for some time to find anyone to give him a bit of glamour, and for a while was in the unenviable position of being endorsed by Wilfred Brimley, the old character actor (you may remember him as the tubby, shifty bloke in *The China Syndrome*, or indeed half-a-dozen other films) whose previous political activism has included a campaign to decriminalise cockfighting in New Mexico. He is currently most visible to the American public as a spokesman for a major blood glucose monitor manufacturer. He hasn't, it will surprise you to hear, been exactly front and centre of McCain's Straight Talk Express, and it was with considerable relief that the McCain team finally managed to secure Sylvester Stallone – and a measure of their desperation that Rocky's their main man. Celebrity star power is all about either freshness (as in Johannson) or authority (as in Jack Nicholson's last-ditch ad for Hillary, late in the primaries). If Stallone didn't exist, cultural studies departments would have invented him as a teaching aid.

Though McCain has always been a reasonably solid conservative, and has now abandoned any earlier positions that might have even the slightest whiff of liberalism (to the extent of refusing to vote for the campaign finance reform bill that he himself introduced to the Senate), there will never be any real love for John McCain from the conservative heartland. Despite his war service, he doesn't fire up the imagination the way the immensely less impressive George W Bush ever did, simply because his conduct suggests that political solutions are sometimes an eclectic mix, and demand working with the other side. Hardcore Republican celebs like the estimable Mr Norris want a good and evil scenario, while hitherto Republican moderates like Clint Eastwood are repelled by what the party has become.

Yet even if John McCain could field the whole *Vanity Fair* Hollywood-issue cover, it would do him little good, for the simple reason that celebrity is all about irresistible fascination, and Barack Obama is the most fascinating man in America, perhaps the world, at the moment.

'Who the devil is Obama?' remarked Pat Buchanan, the conservative but not unsympathetic commentator, as the candidate tracked to the centre-right on a whole range of issues (federal wiretapping, gun ownership, Iran), confounding conservative expectations that he would run as a hapless liberal. Everything about Obama – from his eclectic world-music style origins as a half-Kenyan raised in Hawaii and Indonesia, to his future as a president of historic import from the very moment he's elected – draws people in further.

For the professional political class, it is an obsession with one of the sharpest politicians of the era, who combines quasi-spiritualistic oratory with meticulous grassroots organisation and deft policy manoeuvre. For the general public, it is a fascination with someone like them – black, white, brown – post–WWII, post-'60s, a man who gives the impression that he was once at sea in his own life, found a way through and understands that old stories of American triumphalism or secular-liberal smugness don't work any more.

The most extraordinary expression of this was last week's interview with the Obama family, including his two daughters under ten, in which the mysterious Chicago leftist/secret Muslim/whatever was revealed as a goofy suburban dad, being assailed by his family for leaving his briefcase in the hall. 'We didn't plan it this way,' the interviewer said later, as sections of the interview played across the media, 'the daughters just wandered into the shot'. The next day, Obama told breakfast TV: 'It was a one-off, we won't be doing it again, wouldn't let the kids be interviewed if we could do it over.'

Haphazard? Plotted? Either way, he gets the benefit of the best presidential family portrait since JFK, and also to deny that it was planned. And the channel the interview was for? Access Hollywood.

Scarlett who?

4

MILE HIGH IN THE MILE HIGH CITY

The Democrat Convention, Denver

SAVANNAH, GEORGIA: WEDNESDAY, 20 AUGUST

A black car pulls into a driveway, surrounded by flashes and crouching paparazzi – has Britney shaved the rest of it off? Is Paris in there? Lindsay? No, it's some boring white-bread senator, suddenly being tagged 24/7 because he's a possible vice-presidential candidate for Barack Obama.

The Obama campaign, in what is becoming its increasingly irritating manner, has done a slow striptease with the VP announcement, first announcing that it would be distributed by email and txtmsg, then that Obama had made his decision, then that it would be any day now, then in the next twenty-four hours, and so on, and so on . . .

The candidates the media's settled on as favourites are Indiana Senator Evan Bayh (of an old Democratic family), Governor Tim Kaine of Virginia, and Senator Joe Biden; the first two offering an advantage in key swing states, the third a senior Democrat providing gravitas and connection to unions and white working-class voters.

The wider field includes Kansas Governor Kathleen Sebelius (women, Finnish–Americans), Georgia Senator Sam Nunn (armed forces creds) and Wesley Clark (the retired general).

And, of course, there's Hillary, sui generis.

The whole process has been as arbitrary as, well, most of the post-primary Obama campaign, with Nunn a strong favourite for a while before dropping back mysteriously, and Wesley Clark a strong candidate to neutralise McCain to whom no one's paid much attention.

'Any clues on the nomination, Rick?' one CNN anchor asked a roving reporter.

'Well, we saw Evan Bayh and Tim Kaine today and neither looked like their lives were about to change for the next seventy days,' said Rick. 'Judging by the look on their faces.'

God, oh God. Everything about this is the Obama campaign at its worst – meaningless tech wonkery (the txtmsg thing), making it all about the process rather than the content, and ultimately giving John McCain another few policy-free days with which to keep hammering home his message.

When this slomo campaign began at the conclusion of the primaries, the thought was that it was a deliberate strategy – Obama would run as the de facto incumbent, releasing one policy after another, while letting McCain continue to beat himself up. Then, post-Convention, with their huge pile of funds, the Obama campaign would attack McCain from all sides, leaving the old codger neither time nor funds to reply, thus making it a double whammy.

That's how it went, except for the details – Obama didn't occupy the airwaves with any policies and McCain didn't beat himself up. Instead, the Republican landed some rather telling blows to bring the race to near equal.

A month ago, Team Obama looked like it was sailing to victory, in a smooth and self-assured manner. Their candidate's world tour had coincided with the Iraqi Government's announcement that its view on the future of the US occupation pretty much concurred with the Democrats' policy of a sixteen-month withdrawal. The trip culminated in Obama's triumphal appearance in Berlin. McCain's staff had responded to this high-profile stuff with a mix of cute stunts that were too clever by half. Though they'd abandoned the practice of having McCain shoot the shit with a half-dozen journos on the circular couches at the back of the Small Talk—sorry, *Straight Talk* Express, they were still putting McCain in situations where any hope of dignity was forfeited: campaigning in supermarkets and knocking over jars of applesauce, holding hands with the Dalai Lama and, while Obama was speaking to 200000 enraptured Germans, appearing in some Bavarian wurst restaurant somewhere in Ohio.

The point was well taken – that McCain was willing to sit down with average people where they lived – but the faux German setting, the wood panelling and lederhosen on the wall just looked weird, like a lost scene from *The Cremaster Cycle*. While McCain bumped into supermarket shelves, Obama scored a three-point basket, first throw, in front of cheering US troops and addressed the world about peace from a mountain in Jerusalem. McCain's campaign, in the throes of reorganisation, was trying a bunch of gimmicks that only served to portray their candidate as a sitcom-ish grandpa figure.

Even so, the measure of a failing campaign is not that it makes terrible mistakes – everyone does that – but that it cuts its losses and changes direction quickly. McCain's team didn't let go of the cheap shots – indeed, they would go lower and cheaper than anyone had expected – but they extracted their man from them. They got him back in his boring, dutiful small-town meetings, circling chain hotel ballrooms and town halls, mic in hand, taking questions from, well, codgers. In parallel, his team used the internet and small-release ad schedules to get scurrilous gossip bouncing around the news programs. The 'Paris Hilton ad', painting Obama as a Paris/Britney-esque celebrity, and the one ludicrously associating Obama with high petrol prices, served to take the fight to the Democrat. They were widely assessed as damaging McCain's image of integrity and credibility, but it was clear his team was of the belief that they had no choice but to gamble.

And it worked. In the space of a week or two, the running was entirely reversed. The Obama campaign, having established their candidate as ready to serve, simply went off the boil altogether. They rolled out no new policies, they launched no new attacks and Obama's televised appearances were the candidate at his worst – the vague, laidback, slightly superior seminar leader, rather than the presidential candidate who wants to lead, who wants the job yesterday.

So it went from that point on. The Obama campaign was utterly reactive, humming and hawing on offshore drilling, waffling on Russia's invasion of Georgia, and so on. When they finally started throwing back at McCain, they did so days late, dollars short. Their response to McCain's 'Paris Hilton' ad was an ad showing a series of clips from McCain's impressive list of TV and movie cameos – the equivalent of yelling 'So are you!'. (True nuff. The old guy is actually a really good comic actor, judging by his numerous *Saturday Night Live* appearances.) When, in an interview with New Age evangelist pastor Rick Warren, McCain defined 'rich' as anyone earning more than $5 million, the Obama campaign took days to do what they should have been doing all along – accurately portraying McCain as a very rich establishment figure, with policies that would continue the squeeze on anyone earning a bit less than $100 000 a year.

With this, and other missed opportunities, you couldn't help but wonder what Hillary – though not short of a dime herself – might have made of all this great material.

Slowly it began to dawn on horrified onlookers, this author included, that this was not a new low-key campaign of rolling to victory by energising a base (the much-vaunted new politics), it was the worst sort of old Democrat campaign – diffident, half-hearted, frequently and easily ambushed. Despite many losses in exactly the same manner – Kerry '04, Gore '00, Dukakis '88 – the party was repeating the same smug, elitist, unassertive strategy of old, assuming that the Republican vision was simply too stupid for people to adopt, so long as the Democrats didn't scare them into the arms of the right with talk of real change. Nothing symbolised this better than Obama's casual comment that inflating one's tyres can save up to 5 per cent on gas costs – and his mocking of the Republicans' 'pride in their own ignorance' when McCain made fun of the suggestion as hot-air energy policy. Had Obama not noticed how McCain had parlayed offshore drilling (an utterly ineffectual response to the US's energy problem) into a symbol of American Promethean determination to make the earth yield bounty? (Nonetheless McCain still opposed drilling in the Alaskan wilderness reserve, the only worthwhile oil field left.) Had Obama not forethought how wimpy and lame the tyre inflation thing would sound? After a decade as a professional candidate in a polity now utterly dominated by questions of symbolism and identity, why was Obama now running so dead?

It should have been obvious that running as the de facto incumbent was only one part of a strategy, the second half of which was to break the public identification with McCain as the embodied essence of the American people. McCain's war record made this tricky but necessary – he had to be challenged as a fraud on foreign policy, a man who couldn't tell Shi'ite from Sunni, trading on his POW chops to present himself as an expert, a multimillionaire declaring the economy to be 'fundamentally sound', a serial adulterer running as a values candidate. That would have caused collateral damage on the Democrat side, especially for the Clintons, but since they weren't helping anyway, what the hell.

Instead, it's all been an utter mess, the signs of a campaign suffering internal conflict, like the flight path of a plane in which people are fighting for control of the cockpit. The erratic course is most probably coming from vicious infighting between the Obama core staff and the Democratic Party hacks who got hired as soon as the primaries were over. Unsurprisingly, Obama's lead has shrunk to about 1 or 2 per cent averaged over all polls (though to a degree that's been caused by one or two polls having McCain in front by as much as 5 per cent – Obama's still leading most polls).

The trouble is not merely with strategy. Most telling is the change in Obama himself. Gone is the soaring rhetoric; the energising, if light on content, speeches; the canny, prophetic speaking to the sense of spiritual mission which lies at the heart of American political self-conception. The candidate who has reappeared is the community-activist-turned-lawyer, speaking of sensible solutions and policy wonkery, and displaying a worrying diffidence when he's dealing with a situation that isn't a stadium speech. McCain addresses every question fired at him like he's asking it to step outside and the energy makes for good TV. Obama just sounds like the law professor he was, considering the pros and cons of tortious claim of estoppel. Or something.

Sixty per cent of the country want to vote for a Democrat according to the polls. Forty-five per cent say they'll vote for Obama. Do the math(s).

When a breakthrough finally came, it was nothing that the Obama team did. It was McCain, delivering a spectacular own goal by responding to the question 'How many houses do you own?' with the answer 'I'll have to get back to you on that'. Any response ('Ten, I've been very lucky but I know many people haven't been', or 'My wife owns them, I'm a kept man, I'd advise you all to marry a beer heiress') would have been better than portraying the thing that millions of Americans are lying awake at night worrying about as an accounting detail.

The fact this magnificent blunder was the only thing that gave the Democrats a lift on the way to their Convention is a measure of how poor their campaign has been.

Whatever the choice of VP adds, if Obama can't find a centre, can't want it, chew it up, spit it out, etcetera, then even digging up Reagan and running with what's left wouldn't help the man. My money is on Wesley Clark. It's the longest of long shots – Kaine seems the safer choice – but my thinking is based on the idea of neutralising McCain's military experience. I also figure that if my tip comes true, my powers of prescience and acute political analysis will become renowned, but if it doesn't no one will notice.

It didn't come true.

The msg techno Democrats received today was that the choice is Joe Biden, but the Obama team's clever-clever process of building suspense – which was also, of course, a way of netting yet more contact numbers for email alerts and calls – was somewhat undercut by the press staking out every candidate's home and watching the comings and goings.

Joe Biden is a stunning choice – stunning in that it's so ordinary. A lifelong senator of more than thirty years, he is a party grandee and has been a primary candidate twice (notably in 1988, of which more later). He's a supporter of the war in Iraq and has close relationships with the credit card industry, helping to ram through a law making it more difficult for people to declare bankruptcy and cancel their card debts.

But he also has solid credentials in terms of foreign policy, with decades of experience in meeting world leaders and framing policy approaches. He is a strong, old-style Democrat, with a long history of connections with trade unions and middle-class suburban people. For the Obama team, the choice is one from strength – they believe they're winning and they want to consolidate their support among the base. But also, importantly, Obama wants a genuine partner in power, a wise counsel who will make up for his lack of years in the job with memories and experience of earlier crises.

Biden doesn't come without baggage. His candidacy of 1988 was derailed when he had been caught plagiarising a speech from UK Labour leader Neil Kinnock (of all people), and he has a famous habit of being gaffe-prone and prolix. Joe Biden's never had a thought he didn't want to express, and he's never seen a relative clause he didn't want to insert. Soon after his VP candidacy was announced I saw him on TV accepting an award from the National Organization of Women – Biden had been instrumental in getting federal funding for women's shelters at a time when such things were exotic, crazy feminist ideas – and he said this:

'My father once told me that only a small man hits a child, and no sort of man . . .'

The obvious stinger line is 'no sort of man hits a woman'. Did Biden go there? Nooooooo. What he said was:

'. . . and no sort of man, unless he's acting in self-defence, or unless he's had some sort of total psychotic breakdown, for which he's not personally responsible, but I mean, I'm not trying to excuse anything . . . no sort of man hits a woman.'

You can see the problem.

Denver awaits the Convention. The Democrats will be working hard to make sure it's a triumph, because this may be their last chance to get a badly failing campaign back on track.

DENVER: SUNDAY, 24 AUGUST

'I'm feeling really terrible,' the bloke at the Union Station bar said. His suit was crumpled, his rosette slightly askew. He couldn't have looked more like a Convention delegate if he was wearing a panama hat and carrying a placard saying 'Ma, Ma, where's my Pa? Gone to the White House, Ha! Ha! Ha!' (the famous cry in the 1890s from opponents of Grover Cleveland, who'd fathered an illegitimate child, as, of course, you knew).

'It's altitude sickness,' said this wearied traveller, remembering two days and nights spent in a Santa Fe motel watching the funny lights move across the ceiling. 'You need to drink four litres of water a day and take eight deep breaths every ten minutes.'

'Does that mean I'll stop feeling like this?' the bloke asked.

'In about a week.'

'But we're only here a week.'

Indeed. It takes the particular genius of the Democrats to hold a week-long convention in a place that takes at least a week to get used to. After two weeks at a mile-high altitude, you actually feel great – you're running with 20 per cent more red blood cells, your lungs have been doing push-ups for a fortnight, and you go striding across the Rockies. First week? Fuhgeddaboudit.

Here we all are in the Mile-High City – half modern wreck, half restored chi chi warehouses turned into reiki massage juice bar condominiums. Denver had been waiting for the Convention for a month before it got here – gussying itself up, turning itself out for the tens of thousands of delegates and others ready to attend. As soon as you arrived it became clear that the town had become the Convention, and vice versa.

A mile-wide security cordon has been thrown around the Pepsi Center (another Democrat special – choose the cola with 15 per cent market share) and fleets of media crews are buzzing around interviewing each other. The Convention starts at the Center tomorrow with a keynote address by Michelle Obama, an event that already has me clenching my glutes in tension.

Quite aside from her 'for the first time I am proud of my country' remark, the only bum note in the Obama family inter-view granted to *Access Hollywood* was when she was asked to describe the most romantic thing she did for her husband. 'Well, I look after his kids,' she replied, opening the must-never-be-spoken-of crevasse in the elite professional marriage.

Never really a professional politician's wife, she must have got with the program to be giving the Convention speech, but the gaffe potential is awesome. Also speaking will be Jimmy Carter, a sepia-tinted historic figure for anyone under forty, but owed what is due to presidents past. There'll also be a tribute film for Ted Kennedy, who is slowly croaking in Massachusetts, and in honour of his life's work, an intern will be groped live on stage.

Tuesday will be a potential biggie, with Hillary giving her right of repl— sorry, speech, and a bunch of supporters (unkindly labelled the 'Hillarytards' by political blog *Wonkette*) ready with signs and shouts to express their dissent from an Obama ticket. The Convention floor manager said with thin-lipped quietness that an orderly Convention would be 'managed', and one suspects any protestors might find themselves waking up four days later in a Tijuana prison with a half pound of brown heroin in their back pocket. At least that would show some decisiveness.

If by any wild, weird chance Hillary is planning an upset and has organised numbers for a coup on the floor – and I don't think for a second this is likely but bring it up as a sort of presci-ent political insurance – we'll get some hint of it then, more by what she doesn't say than by what she does.

Of course on Wednesday, as well as famously prolix speaker

VP candidate Joe Biden, we will also hear from Bill Clinton, which in terms of hubris, delusion, false piety, wit and sheer danger is going to be like watching a gay man doing a solo performance of *What Ever Happened To Baby Jane?* at the Melbourne Fringe. Wednesday is the day Hillary has to release her delegates to Obama (confusingly, prior to her roll-call vote) to allow for him to be voted in with full Convention support.

Thursday it all moves to the Invesco Field stadium for the roll call, and if the upset happens then all of a sudden it will be Hillary addressing the assembled masses.

No, of course it won't happen. Obama will give the speech and it'd better be a farkin' good one if he's to get this half-arsed campaign refocused and back on the road.

Around all this there's a range of caucuses and fringe meetings in various hotel ballrooms – the women's caucus, the af–am caucus (African–American), the vets, etcetera. There's been no mention of a middle-class caucus and still less one for the working class (that dread phrase which must never be mentioned).

And around all of that there are the protests. Chinese-style, the city authorities have awarded a 'protest park', although perhaps they won't use them Chinese-style as a way of rounding up dissidents for re-education (or, as it's called in the US, 'education').

There was a protest march through the streets of downtown today, a couple of thousand people from what appeared to be dizzyingly divergent groups, all looking pretty much like a letter/number protest from the turn of the century (you know, J18, S11 . . .). That one of the groups is called 'Recreate 68' would appear to indicate the bind that the movement appears to find itself in, its innovations ossified into custom, its insurgent radicalism become a conservative repetition.

But aside from about 2000 parties, there ain't much happening tonight. FOX News, in that standard way, has been reduced to running a half-hour special about its own broadcasting HQ ('This is called the Green Room . . .') and unless Hillary can save us all this is pretty much how it will run all week.

DENVER: MONDAY, 25 AUGUST

Down Stout Street among the restored brick warehouses and the bland Midwestern office buildings, comes today's protest march – the theme different but the personnel the same (anarchists in tie-dye and black face masks, nu-skool communists with tight-cropped hair and a predilection for denim, '60s veterans with Santa Claus beards or feminist battleaxe earrings). Today it's prisoners' rights, with a dozen people in Guantanamo-style orange jumpsuits and the Hannibal Lecter masks the authorities are wont to use.

In tow, a phalanx of police in black from head to foot, machineguns strapped down the middle of their body armour, thick barrels hanging pendulously between their legs. The march turned into the grounds of the massive Stalinist-lite Denver courthouse building, one of the designated protest parks, à la Chine.

I hadn't meant to follow the march. I was looking for dried apricots (low GI) and the thing happened to be going towards the Walgreens pharmacy. By the time it swept past there, the police had locked in around it, along with about forty hors d'oeuvres (pigs on horseback) and other officers using such a dizzying array of transport that they seemed to be trying to win a bet – the Segway squad lurking round one corner, the BMX flying division on the right flank, and an expanded golf cart peopled with the top brass bringing up the rear.

We were all poured into one corner of the courthouse gardens. Batons were drawn. Various megaphones were starting up: 'Obama isn't the change we need, revolution is the change we need! Only Communism can—'. The cordon moved a couple of steps in. I realised that I hadn't yet picked up my press pass. Curse you, Zone Diet. I heard the sound that's a familiar prelude to a police barney: the low hum of a large van pulling up. 'Stand back from there!' a cop barked. Here it comes . . . 'You're on the road – you might get run over.'

So not exactly 'Recreate '68', though that time may yet come. But there's no doubt that the city's in carnival mode, the whole of its expansive downtown dominated by the Convention. T-shirt sellers, face-painters (recreate '86) and a select bunch of Christian lunatics with enormous signs that seem to hold about two-thirds of the Bible. 'Hey, are you a fag? Well, what about my civil rights to hate you?!' yelled one at a thin man in a bicycle helmet – probably an accurate target for the barb, but nasty nonetheless. By employing such tactics, each fundamentalist has earned a police detail of about twenty-five, thus swelling every appearance into a traffic-stopping mini-demo.

In Starbucks, CNN is playing the Convention prelims – people who know someone who knows one of the stage crew, standing at the podium for a souvenir photo. There's a long queue of them, and FOX News is videoing them from the other end, so they're all looking back to that camera. Having both CNN and FOX on the screen would show a perfect loop.

Back on the street, we run into a fast-moving mini-demo of Hillarytar— of Hillary stalwarts, about twenty of them, with three media crews in tow. For the most part white woman d'un certain age, they have cardboard Hillary masks tied to the back of their heads, which is deeply, deeply disconcerting.

Serial interviews are being conducted. 'Hillary got the most votes, the rules were stacked against her', etcetera etcetera. Not untrue, save for the fact that Hillary agreed to the rules and thought they would shift things her way. US crews throw in questions about Hillary having asked her supporters to pull it in, and they respond that they want to stand for her. 'Given that Hillary and Obama have identical policies, what difference does it make?' I ask, in a Westminsterish mood, and the question seems to throw everyone. 'I don't think that's relevant,' says one.

Further down the road they pose with an eight-foot inflatable man, advertising a nearby grill house – an homage, I guess, to Bill. 'HRT has a lot to answer for,' says a man beside me, who I just made up so as not to have that joke hung round my neck.

At the Big Tent – set up on a vacant lot downtown by an alliance of powerful blogs and progressive organisations – bloggers in rows are tick-tacking away, like they were in a sort of online-content Nike factory. The space was designed for minimum connection between actual human beings and maximum connection between disembodied websites. None of the TVs are turned to Convention coverage – they're covering a debate about progressivism, which is being conducted on the second floor of the tent – and the bar is a single table shoved into the corner (the juice stall and massage centre, by contrast, is expansive). 'We open at 7 a.m.,' says the nice young woman filling in my registration, 'for yoga.'

By contrast, the Wazee Street Bar, where I hastily reassembled my news desk ten minutes later, has all three news channels on and a reliably destroyed bunch of bar flies whose only experience of blogging is the occasional alcohol-induced trousers emergency.

'Howdchew like Denver?' says one, ordering a vanilla vodka and Grand Marnier shooter. 'Svery dry,' he says, answering his own question.

By now, the actual convention part of the Convention is under way, the stuff that every political party has to undergo (minutes of the Credentials Committee, report of the Rules Committee), though generally not attracting coverage by nine television networks. The ratings will be low, of course. At least, the Democrats should hope they are, because these appearances show the internal apparatus of the party as it is and as its critics have charged – a party which has come to be dominated by the '60s social movements, as mainstream working-class membership and involvement evaporated from it. So in the rapid three-minute appearances that fill the rest of the afternoon we get too many people with chunky wooden jewellery and slim-hipped timeserving congressmen to give any sense that this is a mass party, rather than a coalition of all who have been hitherto marginalised.

'You excited by the Convention?' I ask.

'Sdry, Denver.'

Most of these speakers – a large bald female pastor is up now, a sort of cross between Skunk Anansie and Sue-Ann Post – have worked hard for the party and given decades of their life to the fractious task of running a sprawling and only semi-real organisation. The charge of takeover is only half-true – the Democrats lost a lot of their base because reactionary union leaders led the rank and file away in the '60s, out of sheer pique at the party's push for civil rights and its anti-Vietnam war message. The social movements were filling a vacuum created by the corruption and reaction that paralysed the American labour movement for twenty-five years.

Nevertheless, considering NAFTA and the failure of a health care push in the Clinton government, you can't say that the Democrats worked too hard to get them back, and the rollcall of speakers this first afternoon says it all. The only union leader to speak is the head of the teachers' union. Could the organisers not find an Ohio engine parts shop steward, a middle-aged working mother doing split shifts between the Pancake House and cleaning rooms at the Days Inn? Could we not hear about the wreck of New Orleans from an average Joe or Joan, rather than a musician who 'had to take flight with my tribe of friends when the levees broke' and who has made a documentary film of her experiences?

It's not that I think these people have any less right to be up there. And if the Democrats can elect a half-Kenyan, ex-leftist senator of two years standing to the White House, then they will have pulled off a game-changing coup with little parallel in the country's history. It's simply that there's a missing middle in the way the party is presenting itself to the wider public.

By the time I wander down to the Pepsi Center and pass through the quietly, professionally paranoid security, the afternoon segues into a musical interlude. Man, they've got a huge, hot and tight band rocking it out. The GOP will never top these guys belting out 'Respect' and 'Are You Gonna Go My Way' – it'll be Wilfred Brimley doing 'Tea for Two' on the paper comb. The floor of the Convention is full with people bopping to their various level of ability – that is, there are black people dancing and white people shifting their bodies around like they're balancing a load of bricks on a trolley.

The moment that pierces the heart is a young girl, about twelve or thirteen, singing a wobbly but never off-tune version of Alicia Keys' 'No One' ('No one, no one/can get in the way of what I'm feeling'), which seems to take all the aspiration in the auditorium, all the hope, and lift it simply to the ceiling. Three minutes like this is often all you need to remind you where you stand and why. Then there are some more party goons. (Stop press: before the end, some workers and unionists come on, but even then they're giving testimonials to Barack Obama's magical powers, rather than talking about their own day-to-day struggles.)

The Convention is, as the network talking heads have said, the chance the party gets to present itself to the nation, less mediated by the spin, counter-spin and news cycle agendas. Even though fewer and fewer people have been watching it over the decades, it still commands far greater attention than would, say, the standard ALP Hobart/Terrigal-based smorgasbord of shit sandwiches that pass for party democracy.

(Caroline Kennedy on now, talking about Jello Biafra's soon-to-be-latest recruit.) The last six weeks have been opportunities lost, coming off the solid lead from the primaries and Obama's Europe trip. Everything has to go right from here on.

Trapped in the Pepsi Center and with no chance of getting into the media room, your correspondent realised, not for the first time, that watching it on TV would be far more real. Back to the bloggers' Big Tent.

We're all hanging on tenterhooks to see what Michelle Obama will do to open the Democratic Convention. Terrorist fist bump with her tiny terrorist daughters? Shout 'Off the pigs, man!' and 'Fight the power!'? Introduce, by video link, 'My very good friend Fidel Castro?' Here we go . . .

It begins with her brother giving what amounted to a best-man-at-the-wedding speech about his sis as a little girl, preceded by a film of his mum talking about the struggles of South Side, Chicago, etcetera etcetera.

Then the girl herself.

I come here tonight as a sister . . . as a wife . . . as a mom . . . as a daughter . . .

She opens by working through her identity and then on to talking about her dad, who died of multiple sclerosis and 'got up an hour early to dress himself', etcetera.

Her voice is thin, not projective, not coming from the belly – nervous as hell. Last time this happened it was Teresa Heinz Kerry in 2004 addressing the Convention in four languages – like watching a verbal luge.

Isn't that the great American story? It's the story of men and women gathered in churches and union halls, in town squares and high school gyms – people who stood up and marched and risked everything they had – refusing to settle, determined to mould our future into the shape of our ideals . . . People who work the day shift, kiss their kids goodnight, and head out for the night shift – without disappointment, without regret . . .

Only in the United States of America is working yourself to death a cause of pride.

The military families who say grace each night with an empty seat at the table. The servicemen and women who love this country so much, they leave those they love most to defend it.

Great line.

People like Hillary Clinton, who put those 18 million cracks in the glass ceiling, so that our daughters – and sons – can dream a little bigger and aim a little higher.

rubitinrubitin

See, it's . . . See, it's . . .

Too much of that Chicago-speak.

Millions of Americans who know that Barack understands their dreams; that Barack will fight for people like them; and that Barack will finally bring the change we need.

Not enough about the exceptional nature of Barack. She's laying it on with a trowel, but is a shovel required?

And in the end, after all that's happened these past nineteen months, the Barack Obama I know today is the same man I fell in love with nineteen years ago.

Tears! Tears! Yay!

He's the same man who drove me and our new baby daughter home from the hospital ten years ago this summer . . . Feeling the whole weight of her future in his hands . . .

Gaaaak . . . but it seems to be working.

They'll tell them how this time, we listened to our hopes, instead of our fears. How this time, we decided to stop doubting and to start dreaming.

Good penultimate lines.

Let us stand together to elect Barack Obama President of the United States of America!

Great final line!

Stevie Wonder's 'Isn't She Lovely' plays while their two kids join Michelle on stage. It looks a little strange without Dad – a black single mother. Strikes an odd note. *AND SUDDENLY THERE HE IS ON THE ENORMOUS SCREEN.*

'Hi, Daddy!' calls one of his daughters.

That's a hell of a moment, but what a risk. A live cross to Obama speaking from Kansas City – a producer's nightmare.

'How about Michelle Obama?' Barack jokes. 'Now you know why I asked her out so many times – you want a persistent president.'

He speaks a bit about the people he's staying with, but his youngest daughter keeps talking too – never work with children, animals or a live video cross . . . It winds it up pretty well, but a bit flat.

'I love you, Daddy!' the daughter yells again.

Perhaps it was all too clever by half.

Half an hour after the speech has wrapped up, C-SPAN is droning on at the Big Tent as everyone is trying to work out ways to crash the *Slate* party a couple of doors down. Callers being fielded on Mrs Obama – everyone thinks she did well, even the confessed McCain supporters, and she may have turned it round, at least for a while.

She did well, but it was hard to top Ted Kennedy earlier – the dying liberal animal, roaring out that this time we can dream, we can hope, change is possible.

We can hope.

Tharin Gartrell was got first, high on meth – Nazi-crank white-trash drug of choice – driving erratically in a van, containing rifles, ammo, wigs and more Nazi crank. Gartrell resisted bravely for minutes while in a cell but then coughed up the whole 'plot' to assassinate Barack Obama. It involved two of his white supremacist friends, who were arrested at 4.30 a.m. on the Monday morning, one of them – a Mr Adolph – trying to evade escape by jumping from a sixth-floor hotel window.

Police have since been trying to play down the idea that it was a plot, suggesting instead that it was a lunatic neo-Nazi cranked up fantasy, even though the rifles in the van had threaded barrels, allowing for the use of silencers.

The whole thing was fully laid out in a press conference late Monday during and after Michelle Obama's speech. Your correspondent missed it because he was too busy trying to chat up Daryl Hannah.

For some reason she was at some 10 p.m. thing about urban farms, a sort of late-night green discussion which sorts out the truly hardcore wonk from the priss. Why she is interested in urban farms God only knows, but there she was with twelve greenish dweebs and a few tired journos and bloggers, down-gearing on the free beer. Dressed simply in a black sort of shift, accessorised only by her husband, a man a full two feet shorter than her who appeared to have sewn his hand to the small of her back, she glowed like a quasar, moving through the crowd to the bar where I was slumped.

There has only ever been one use for the line I used then –

and that was at a party with an undersea theme at an advertising agency some years ago, which featured, among other things, several starving actresses dressed as mermaids, seated in giant papier-mâche clams.

For every male who hit puberty around the time of *Splash*, I said, 'Didn't you play that mermaid in that movie – I remember you seated in a giant shell or something. I suppose a shuck's out of the question?'

In my defence, I don't think she heard me above the TV noise – some assassination plot thing, I wasn't paying attention – and if she did I don't think it registered, because as the Q&A had established, she was out to a vegan lunch, dude.

'Aren't urban farms a bit bourgeois?' she was asked.

'I think we really have to re-appropriate terms like that,' she twinkled.

Ah, sweet early '80s. Bring me my skateboard and my *Juke* magazine. I fade into a *Smash Hits* fold-out reverie.

DENVER: TUESDAY, 26 AUGUST

Since the Convention opened, as dozens of speakers have lined up to give their five-minute spiel, effectively the same speech has been repeated endlessly. It begins with a reference to the speaker's parents' – or grandparents' – struggle in low-paid manual labour, segues into an assertion that the current speaker's presence here today is a validation of the American dream, goes into a story about a constituent's ghastly experience of health care/job loss/sub-prime failure, and ends with an endorsement of Obama as an answer to all this. So we heard from and about the victims, and from the leaders and officers – but nothing from the missing middle, people fighting day-by-day union struggles, community struggles, and the like. But nor have we heard from the leaders an account of what has happened, and a clear alternative program. Interestingly, one of the few who did was Ted Kennedy, dying from cancer, who managed to roar out a bracing assertion of what the party should stand for, with references to a more inclusive citizenship and to the sort of determination that got the country to the moon. *To the Finland Station* it wasn't, but it was exceptional in this context for setting out a broader idea of what the party should be for, unmitigated by personal anecdote or childlike concrete illustrations. Left presidential candidate Dennis Kucinich was another speaker who bucked the trend. Viewed by many as a nuisance – given his insistence on running an impeachment campaign against George W. Bush in the most recent congressional session – he nevertheless got the Convention crowd to their feet with a 'wake up, America' refrain. You didn't need to agree with some of the assertions ('Wake up, America – we went into Iraq for oil', 'Wake up, America – the pharmaceutical companies took over drug pricing') to feel that at least an argument was being made, an argument about what had happened to the country. And when his three minutes were up, we lapsed again into the parade of anecdote and identity.

But is the Kucinich approach politics waiting to be reborn – or the dying shout of an older politics which cannot flourish in the postmodern hall of mirrors?

Looking around the wider spectacle of Convention Denver, it was difficult not to feel that the political carnivale was becoming a bit of a freakshow pantomime. The protest of the day was a 9/11 Truthers rally, God help us, with half the anarchists who'd been in yesterday's perfectly proper Guantanamo protest joining in, suggesting that one section of the US far left is effectively mirroring the same mythical religious politics of the dominant right culture here. In a world of bewildering meaningless complexity, it's the seduction that one single idea could explain it all.

The coalition of protest groups – or coalitions, following several splits – had promised up to 25 000 people at their protest and Denver had budgeted $50 million for policing. In the end there have been barely a thousand, and while some of the protests – on Guantanamo, wiretapping and the American prison system – have been focused, others have been dominated by political fantasy, such as a march by the manically energetic ultra-Maoist parties calling for 'communism immediately', or, passing by the window of my Starbucks base an hour ago, the several hundred strong procession of 9/11 Truthers.

Faced with the need to justify their huge expenditure, the Denver police have started assigning phalanxes of dozens of cops – many on Segways – to follow marches of two dozen. 'This is what a police state looks like' the anarchists chant. Really? On Segways? This is what a Jacques Tati film looks like. Much of the protest is really the dying embers of the late '90s

anti-globalisation movement, hamstrung by its internal contradic-
tions. The 'Behavior Guide' for the protest convergence centre
detailed a bewildering list of self-administered regulations from the
sensible ('No videoing in the center') to the self-managing Stalinoid
('No rumours – if you have news report it through appropriate
channels – no group-based arguments'), and so on. Bizarrely,
the anarchists had succeeded in creating a space that felt terribly
un-free. Where, on the street, one wondered, were the unions and
the workers? Where were the Hispanics? Where were the blacks?
Why were these groups so willing to invest all their political will
in a party that was displaying very little of such? How have they
been persuaded to subordinate themselves to a process trying to
draw a politics out of such thin air?

Meanwhile in the auditorium the rollcall of sob stories continued after midget firebrand Kucinich had brought the crowd
roaring to their feet. Towards the end of the evening Mark
Warner, the immediate former Virginia Governor, gave a pretty
good long-range account of rebuilding America after the Bush
wrecking crew has been turfed out.

But really we're all waiting for the night's main act, Hillary.
She was generating the sort of nervous excitement Sam New-
man's handlers must feel after the first sedative dart has hit his
calf and it's ten seconds to show time. Would she do us proud?
Or would she take the whole thing down in a flaming zeppelin
of suicidal vengeance? The Convention hall was full to bursting, the Big Tent was crowded to the gills, and after the usual
sickmaking intro film, away we went:

I speak to you as a proud mother . . . a proud American . . . AND A PROUD SUPPORTER OF BARACK OBAMA!

Missing was 'proud wife'. Big surprise.

The time is now to unite as a single party with a single purpose.

[Loud applause in the Big Tent] The time to unite would have been four months ago, but we'll let that pass.

It's a fight we must win. I haven't spent the past thirty-five years in the trenches advocating for children, campaigning for universal healthcare, helping parents balance work and family, and fighting for women's rights at home and around the world . . . to see another Republican in da house . . .

Leaving out the more direct remark: '. . . to see another Republican win because you lunatic bozos are pursuing some mad God-knows-what vengeance thing in my name . . .'

So I say to you – No way, no how, no McCain! Barack Obama is my candidate and he must be our president!

In short, I repeat, cudditout sisters! Would you lunatics stop using my name to rip the party apart?

Your stories reminded me every day . . .

Oh God, stories . . .

The single mom who adopted two kids with autism . . . discovered she had cancer . . . her bald head painted with my name on it . . . The young man in a Marine Corps T-shirt . . .

Sooner or later, we'll hear about the young boy who sold his bicycle and computer games, and has now learned a valuable lesson about politics.

To my supporters, my champions – my sisterhood of the travelling pantsuits . . .

Knock it off. Just knock it off.

We have a lot of work ahead.

Keeping Bill shut up, for one.

Jobs lost, houses gone, falling wages, rising prices. Clean energy . . . health care system . . . workplace . . . blah blah blah . . .

It's all pretty boilerplate, but it's great stuff because it's what Obama should have been saying for the last month. If Hillary was the candidate, McCain would be bleeding from all orifices by now.

Iran for president . . .

Iran for president? Oh – I *ran* for president . . .

I want you to ask yourselves: Were you in this campaign just for me?

There are a few shouts of yes from the auditorium.

Or were you in it for that boy born without a body, the woman with nine pod children . . .

She's bringing it round to try and emotionally blackmail the Hillarytards back into the camp.

We need a president who understands pod babies and people born without bodies . . . Democrats know how to do this. As I recall, President Clinton and the Democrats did it before. And President Obama and the Democrats will do it again.

Loud applause from the Big Tent blogosphere – I suspect some of these people are biased.

Michelle . . . Joe Biden . . .

Namechecks.

Now, John McCain is my colleague and my friend.

Though her smile seems to say, I hope cancer eats him from the taint upwards.

It makes sense that George Bush and John McCain will be together next week in the Twin Cities. Because these days they're awfully hard to tell apart.

Big applause.

Seneca Falls . . . 1848 . . . women's rights convention . . . Eighty-eight years ago the 19th amendment guaranteeing women the right to vote forever enshrined in our Constitution.

More applause in the Big Tent, except from two kids in suits over by the corner – Mormons or Republican youth, or both, it's kinda hard to tell.

Harriett Tubman had one piece of advice. Don't ever stop. Keep going.

Harriet Tubman? That's a damn strange image – are we trying to smuggle Barack into the White House by the Underground Railroad?

We are Americans. We're not big on quitting. But remember, before we can keep going, we have to get going by electing Barack Obama president . . . That is our duty, to build that bright future . . .

Soaring rhetoric here. Very moving – she never puts a foot wrong. Man, if we'd had six weeks of this the thing would be all over.

DENVER: WEDNESDAY, 27 AUGUST

'I am honoured to be here tonight to support Barack Obama.'

Wednesday we got the other half of the twofer, as Bill Clinton strolled down off the porch to give his endorsement at the Convention. By now Team McCain had come off the road completely for the week to assess their VP picks. Speculation swirled as to whether they would try a spoiler by announcing it on the Thursday morning of Obama's speech.

'Everything I learned in my eight years as president . . . has convinced me that Barack Obama is the man for this job.'

Well, it was about time. Ten minutes into Bill's nervously awaited speech, he finally cracked it to say those little words necessary to seal up the breach below the Democratic waterline: 'Barack Obama is ready to be President of the United States.'

The hall erupted. They'd already given the guy a five-minute standing ovation, which had been beyond anyone's control, the force of pure love coming through. The moment the bloke was on the podium, trim, focused, red skin and white-haired like some old southern gentleman, everyone just lost it, and it took a while to get some semblance of control back.

He began with a few weak jokes ('I'm just here to warm up for Joe Biden') and then he got into the by now familiar rundown of how the Bush lack-of-Administration had screwed everything up, reduced us to eating twigs, no one likes us, etcetera. It was pretty low-key and there were a few mutterings in the room about whether he still had it, whether he was going to deliver – was this old tired Bill, post zipper job?

But then he threw in the stuff about the leader we need and Obama being that leader and the whole place went apeshit.

He rolled out what Obama would do, how his policies were better. But then he really started to lift it to the roof in a return to a denunciation in detail of the Bush era – indeed, of the last quarter century of Republicanism.

'Once they got control of both houses in 2001 the country really saw what they were like.'

Then suddenly the old Bill was back, the hell raiser. 'The parents of children with autism who told me on the campaign trail that they couldn't afford health care and couldn't qualify their kids for Medicaid unless they quit work or got a divorce . . . Are these the family values the Republicans talk about? What about the military families pushed to the breaking point by unprecedented multiple deployments?'

He lifted it from there, the old firebrand from the '90s, reminding us how singular he had been in his own victories, portraying the way America could be.

'People the world over have always been more impressed by the power of our example than by the example of our power.'

'. . . proof of our continuing progress toward the "more perfect union" of our founders' dreams . . . like me, you still believe America must always be a place called Hope . . .'

And the hall erupted again.

Whatever its half-truths, confusions or fudges, which are an inevitable part of any discussion of the American example, it was a powerful thing. Bill had delivered and a million or so buttocks could unclench.

So now the unity is official, first Hillary and then Bill getting the thing in line and pointed forward. Whatever Clintonite dissidents the GOP can dig up would have to be utterly marginal. But will they get out on the stump? Or is this as good as it gets? Knowing the Clintons, knowing how they embody the best and worst of mainstream left politics, they will do their bit unless it looks like the campaign is going down screaming, at which point they will disappear, already focused on '12.

But last night and tonight they gave what only they can give, and that is not nothing, that is not nothing at all.

Wow. Something of the Clinton magic must be rubbing off – even John Kerry gave a thunderingly good speech in his wake. And then, history repeating itself in the well-known manner, we had Biden.

Let me make this pledge to you right here and now . . . No longer will the eight most dreaded words in the English language be: "The vice president's office is on the phone."

There's an Irish lilt to the guy, an ease of speech, which people have talked about.

'*Should Mom move in with us now that Dad is gone? Did you hear the company may be cutting our health care?*'

He's voicing the poor, like a one-man show in Carlton.

Barack Obama is the great American story . . .

It's the first point at which you start to get that slight itch of, actually how long is this going to go on?

John McCain is my friend.

Everyone who's been up there has had to say that – the follow-up sentence is, but I'm going to ram this podium up him sideways.

Then he gets into the riff. 'John McCain wants to . . .' i.e. pull out people's eyes and frag the sockets:

That's not change – that's more of the same!

The audience pick it up but the time lag doesn't fill you full of joy.

Then he switches to Obama's policies and another riff:

That's the change we need!

It's theatre restaurant politics – get 'em singing along and they don't notice the chicken's grey. But it's going on a bit – I hope his VP thing is paying off in terms of hard-hat votes, cos he ain't no Hillary.

Should we trust John McCain's judgement?

Another repeated riff, making four so far.

John McCain was wrong and Barack Obama was right . . .

Repetition is the secret of his prolixity – the man is a walking villanelle. He got off just as the trapdoor was poised to open.

DENVER: THURSDAY, 28 AUGUST

'Thank you, thank you,' he called from the circular podium, above the roar that continued to roll back and forth like a wave. 'Thank you, thank you.'

It sounded like it would never stop, a creature awakened. Finally: 'With profound humility and gratitude, I accept the nomination.' And the roaring was off again. On the anniversary of MLK's 'I have a dream' speech, Barack Obama was speaking to his destiny.

The crowd had begun forming hours earlier on Thursday morning, snaking back from the stadium through the rail yard hinterland that separates it from the city proper. The tickets had long ago been spoken for, but with the usual chaos that is essential to online distribution, rumours abounded of open access, and then counter-rumours, and it all went round and round. There being no wifi, the press drew straws and the unlucky 10 per cent had to stay behind and watch the thing on TV.

Watching the live feed from the stadium had the usual hypnotic effect of random TV, with the spectacle of roadies setting up that can fill up the odd ten or twelve hours. Here we got our first chance to see the much talked about 'Roman' set, which *The Drudge Report* had built up as some sort of Caligulaesque extravaganza, but turned out to be a single curve with a few columns and a couple of Roman-style (Fauxman) TV banks – it looked like the carpark of an Olive Garden restaurant. Yet cable news, right on cue, built the non-story into a rolling debate point.

Me, I could have watched people plugging in speakers until Obama was ready to speak, but they put on some musicians instead. There was will.i.am, intermixed with another rollcall of Democrat hacks, including the shadowy Obama campaign manager David Plouffe and Nancy Pelosi (seemingly for the sixth time).

By now we've had the rundown eight million times: my grandfather was a slurry worker from Waxahachie, I taught myself to read from old billboards which got me to Harvard, and I know for a fact that Obama was sent here as a baby in a rocket when his own planet was dying. Could it get more low-key?

Yes, it could. Not only because Al Gore came on with six new depressing statistics but because he was followed by Michael McDonald, formerly of the Doobie Brothers, the only rock musician who can slow down 'America the Beautiful'. Then a vaguely Maoist self-criticism session of former Republicans who've lost their jobs, cars, health insurance, corneas, etcetera, and have come round to the Obama vision. We had about eight generals up on the stage as well, making you wonder who was running the military store, until you remembered that of course no one has been.

By now the place was packed to the rafters, the delegations down on the ground, spectators up in the stands, with a sea of flags and the mountain twilight setting behind the high stadium walls. Then, at around 8 p.m., with Senator Dick Durbin making the intro – chosen, I presume, because he is as effectively featureless a human being as it would be possible to invent, against which Obama's singularity shines like a blood diamond – and with another of those set-up films which always sound like the biography of John the Baptist by Jesus Christ, suddenly the man was there and we were launched into it.

'We meet at one of those defining moments . . . America, we are better than this . . . We are better . . . more honourable . . . more compassionate . . .'

He went through the usual spiel of anecdotes of work and health horror stories, before getting to: 'Enough! This moment, we must say, enough!'

He launched into the now familiar one-two attack on McCain – great guy and hero, political sack of shit – and then detailed the failures of Republican policy. He segued into the different ideas that Dems and Republicans have about what constitutes a good society, and then back into the people in his life who had inspired him to reach for – and this will be the title of the speech in retrospect – 'the American promise'.

What was the American promise? That everyone pursues their individual goals but that the nation rises and falls together. Living up to that promise took him to some concrete goals – tax cuts for the 95 per cent of working families and ending oil dependency in ten years with $150 billion in funding. The promise of universal college education, of ending insurance discrimination against the chronically ill. America's promise at home segued into America's promise in the world, and the toughest attack he's made on Republican foreign policy to date. From there he jumped into a magnificent riff about the 'last best hope of man', really jacking it up to another level.

The final part brought us back to the notion of promise.

'I stand before you tonight because something across the country is stirring . . . What the naysayers don't understand is that this election has never been about me. It's been about you . . . The change we need doesn't come from Washington, it comes to Washington . . . The change we need is coming – I've seen it, I've lived it.

'In America, our destiny is inextricably linked . . . We cannot walk alone . . . We cannot turn back. We cannot turn back . . . Let us keep that American promise and hold firmly, without wavering, to the hope that we confess . . .'

With another roar from the crowd he was off the stage, and then back again with his family and the Bidens.

There ain't a doubt in hell that we have just seen one of the great American speeches, renewing old themes while tapping into the nation's deepest roots. But will it be enough to take all the people with him – and does it mark the renewal, in fire and iron, of a flagging campaign?

Or was it one of the great speeches? In retrospect, away from the excitement, the spectacle, the feel of a whole city turned towards one event, and the desire for it to be such a moment, it seems less likely to even be in Obama's top five. Would it linger in the memory, resonate and grow by repetition over the days ahead?

We never got to find out. On Friday morning, as hurricanes queued up in the Gulf of Mexico to batter Texas and New Orleans to a bloody pulp, Team McCain pulled off a coup by announcing their VP pick – Sarah Palin, the 44-year-old Governor of Alaska, and suddenly all bets were off, and Obama's 'American Promise' speech was as distant as a sepia wax cylinder recording of Ulysses S. Grant asking for a refill.

The prospect of the Republican VP had filled almost everyone with that emotion for which there is presumably a word in German – the dread of imminent boredom. (Although since that covers most of German life, it may be too general for a specific word, like with Eskimos and 'snow'. Where was I? Snow . . . Eskimos . . . boredom . . . dread . . . Palin VP . . . ah, yes.) Would it be Mitt Romney, McCain's loathsome rival for the nomination, a Mormon whom the conservative wing of the party liked? Tim Pawlenty, the young Governor of Minnesota, also good on the values thing and able to maybe swing that state into the Republican camp? 'Bobby' Jindal, Indian–American (subcontinental, native American), about twelve years old, but staunch conservative? Or Joe Lieberman (D), the D standing for 'douche bag' since he ratted on the Democrats and threw his lot in with McCain?

It's a measure of how unprepared we all were that Lieberman – because of his former affiliations and lack of popularity, to put it mildly, with the Republican base – was the most exciting possibility, even though McCain and Lieberman together looked like a prostate medication commercial.

So when we were introduced to a young, pretty, fashionably dressed governor, who shoots wolves from a helicopter and has twenty-nine children, the whole thing got pretty quickly turned upside down.

5

MINNESOTA FISTULA

With the GOP in the Twin Cities

SAINT PAUL: SUNDAY, 31 AUGUST

'I just cannot understand how Democrats can hear Osama bin Laden and not understand. I mean, what part of "We want to kill you" do you not get?'

Trapped in the airport shuttle buses, heading into Minneapolis proper, we all shifted uneasily, as the large woman, a delegate from Montana, broke the unwritten rule of shuttle etiquette and filled the space with standard-issue FOX News news.

'Are you a liberal or a conservative?' she asked, bearing down on me.

'Well, uh, I'm from Australia, the politics don't really match up,' I lied, ready to invent impenetrable ethnic conflicts if necessary. 'I write for some left papers *and* some libertarian websites.'

She stared at me long and hard. 'How is that possible?' she asked, confused.

'How's Montana doing?' someone said from the back. 'Last time I heard, it was going over to Obama.' The rest of the journey was taken up with her hip replacement.

It was the third such conversation I'd had or heard since touching down – itchy, combative, the old big guns of the Culture War being wheeled to the front.

For those who had come straight from Denver to the eerie city of Saint Paul – a sort of lesser, evil twin to Minneapolis, stuffed with Hopperesque Victorian architecture that no one has got around to demolishing yet – it was a strange feeling, with the Democratic finale still humming in the memory. Whatever one felt of the politics of spectacle or identity on display in Denver, few could deny that it was an intoxicating performance, with Obama's 'American promise' speech mixing a series of more concrete proposals with an echo of his lofty rhetoric of the primary season.

McCain's job was to try to gazump Obama's performance. And gazump it he did, with a Friday morning announcement of his vice-presidential choice – Sarah Palin, the 44-year-old Governor of Alaska, with some twenty months experience. Formerly, Palin had been the mayor of Wasilla, which is basically an outlying suburb of Anchorage, with a population variously figured to be between 6000 and 9000 people, depending on which source you use. The announcement spread like wildfire. At Denver Airport, every departure lounge was full of journalists following the story on their Blackberries, breathlessly relaying the same Wikipedia details to editors on the coast. Restaurant and retail staff stopped to watch CNN on the airport screens. Rumours had said the job might go to local Minnesota Governor Tim Pawlenty or the awful Mitt Romney – so the sight of old buggerlugs standing beside a woman, who had achieved the improbable feat of looking younger than Barack Obama, was pretty hard to top. The universal description of the choice was 'exciting'. 'Hillary Clinton put 18 million cracks in the glass ceiling,' Governor Palin told the assembled press, 'and the women of America aren't done yet!'

According to some reports, senior Republican officials had another word for the promotion of Palin: 'terrifying'. The choice of Palin hints at the nervousness that McCain's inner circle feels about the way the polls are going – it suggests they think victory over Obama will only be achieved by making audacious moves. If the McCain camp had been convinced that it was steadily pulling ahead of Obama, it would have chosen someone to emphasise Obama's inexperience, such as Romney or Joe Lieberman. The choice of Palin is an attempt to punch through, to change the terms of the contest. It got early results, with the Obama team releasing an initial statement damning Palin as a 'cynical' choice.

In the sphere of the American commentariat, where wishful thinking has long since taken the place of analysis, left-liberals such as Maureen Dowd damned the choice as desperate. The right celebrated it as a choice the left 'feared'. A more dispassionate analysis would suggest that only Palin's subsequent performance will retroactively establish one side as bearers of deep, reflective wisdom and the other as 'out of touch with the American people'. What one can say is that it is a high-risk choice, which would not have been made in any other election year.

Palin is a practically lifelong Alaskan, who worked briefly as a regional TV sports reporter before becoming a local councillor in the early '90s, and then mayor of Wasilla. She rapidly gained a reputation for toughness against an entrenched political machine, sacking her own police chief and later resigning her subsequent appointment to the Alaska Oil and Gas Conservation Commission and filing corruption complaints against fellow Republican members of that body.

Off the back of that victory, she won the Republican primary for the governor candidacy and then the governorship itself in 2006. While she won a lot of support for highly visible stunts, such as selling the former governor's recently purchased Learjet on eBay, she also gained the undying enmity of a section of the Republican establishment, a feeling amplified when Alaska patriarch Senator Ted Stevens was indicted two months ago on charges of corruption, thanks to Palin.

The drive, the efficiency, the independent streak, make up a part of her attractiveness as VP candidate – the other attraction is her solid social conservatism. A Pentecostal Christian, she is hardline anti-abortion and anti same-sex marriage, and on creationism she supports 'teaching the controversy'. For her, the personal and political are intertwined – she became a poster mom for the anti-abortion movement when she gave birth to her fifth child despite knowing he would have Down's syndrome, a move that is now portrayed by right-wing commentators less as a personal choice than an heroic expression of cultural resistance.

In that sense, Palin's a safe choice for Republicans. Many suspect she was selected to satisfy the Christian right faction of the party, which would have departed permanently had McCain insisted on his other maverick choice, former Democrat (and Democrat VP candidate) Joe Lieberman, a social liberal.

Yet the fact cannot be ignored that compared to Sarah Palin, the 'inexperienced' Barack Obama looks like Talleyrand in his eighth decade. At least Obama has had a couple of years in the Senate. Palin, by contrast, gives no appearance of having focused on national or international issues at all. She's a familiar figure in provincial politics: someone drawn into the political sphere by an irritation with an obvious idiocy (sales tax, in her case), who then suddenly discovered that they possess the highly integrated skills which are essential to every mainstream politician. Thus, she has panache (that Learjet), but also application and energy; guts (that police chief), but also diplomacy and conciliation. In places like Alaska, where corruption has driven many capable people out of politics, or out of the state altogether, people like Palin rise quickly. Yet the other side of the coin is that her focus has practically been entirely on the parochial.

Until last year, Palin had never been out of the country, and barely out of Alaska. Unsurprisingly, she has almost no foreign policy opinions on record. A month ago, she not only pooh-poohed the suggestion that she was a VP candidate, but also questioned whether the job was worth it: 'But as for that VP talk all the time, I'll tell you, I still can't answer that question until somebody answers for me what is it exactly that the VP does every day? I'm used to being very productive and working real hard in an administration.' Her startling resemblance to Elaine Benes from *Seinfeld* doesn't help the perception of her as enthusiastic, but possibly also ditzy.

The great fear for Republican hacks is that Joe Biden, Obama's VP candidate and a walking encyclopedia of domestic and foreign policy, will take her apart in the vice-presidential debate, and it will be suddenly clear that a Republican victory will ensure that the White House is one cold-snap away from being run by someone who has spent her career thinking about snowmobiles and regional airstrips.

However, the converse may also be true – she may make Biden look like a doddering dinosaur and, with due tutelage, appear smart and fast in comparison. What is interesting is the extent to which the selection of Palin suggests that leadership and statesmanship play no real part in serious presidential politics now.

This goes for Obama, too. Part of his appeal is that he put together a new sort of political career from the standard chaos of a postmodern life – tens of millions of younger people recognise in him the same bewildering wander through college, a couple of different dead-end jobs, a bit of going-back-to-the-roots and so on. Once he somehow achieved his new status as 'probably the first black president of the United States', Obama solidified his ticket with an elder mentor: Joe Biden, less Kennedy than Obi-Wan Kenobi. Ironically, then, the Obama ticket seems almost *solid*, with two types of experience on it, in comparison to the Republicans' ticket – the offering of McCain and Palin seems more yippie-ishly improvised than the emergence of Obama over the past couple of years.

The Palin VP selection has more the mark of backroom stunt-making than an old-fashioned political decision. It looks like something decided upon by a strategy team locked in a room at the Ramada Inn for four days, coming up with a triangulated choice so brilliant that hopefully no one will notice that it holes the campaign's main selling point below the waterline.

For the Republicans, it's looking like a hell of a week. Obama got perfect weather for his extravaganza, while this week Hurricane Gustav powers towards New Orleans with the air of finishing the job Katrina started. Given the Republican Convention theme – 'Country First' – the prospect of Gustav resurrecting memories of Katrina, Bush's terrible moment of indecision, is a nightmare. In the eyes of some observers, however, it's also an enormous opportunity, where the whole Convention, apart from procedural matters such as formally nominating a candidate, could be turned into a sort of hurricane telethon.

The altered plans have at least given the Republicans the opportunity to avoid one unpleasant moment – the meeting onstage of McCain and deeply unpopular President George W. Bush. Instead, President Bush will address the Convention by video link from the White House. Vice President Dick Cheney will also be absent.

Yet even the manner in which such things are being suggested – where apparently this is a time when politics needs to be 'put aside' – is indicative of how weak the conservative brand is today, and how little confidence Republicans have in asserting a joined-up worldview. A grounded conservative party would argue that a hurricane hitting one area of a large country is not thermonuclear war, and that the choice of a candidate and expression of a program really matters. And what's more, that managing a hurricane while getting on with politics as usual is something a complex society should be able to do. Yet because the party half-suspects that such a suggestion would be greeted with horror these days, and because many of them have little confidence in such a proposition anyway, then, to paraphrase the German satirist Tucholsky, owing to bad weather the Republican revolution is occurring as muzak.

SAINT PAUL: MONDAY, 1 SEPTEMBER

Man, this is one weird party convention town, made all the more strange by the whole Twin Cities thing – Minneapolis and Saint Paul, two separate metropolises that fused together around the turn of the 20th century, a sort of urban fistula.

Halfway down Sibley Street, between the advancing lines of riot police, in the full gasmask and riot outfit – ah . . . 'pigs', now I get it – the trailing ranks of anarchist protestors and the stray wisps of gas, I paused outside a cafe with MSNBC playing on a TV with subtitles. Ah, sweet luxury of press credentials! Like the gift of the fermata, I could slip back and forth between the lines unmolested.

It was noon and the major protest rally, 10 000 strong, was just starting to move from the park spread beneath the gold-tipped Capitol dome. But the black bloc, the armed vegan bloc and the general mayhem bloc had broken off early, and were playing cat and mouse with the cops, trying to scatter and re-form close to the Xcel Energy Center arena for a front-on assault.

They never really got there – the Minnesota burglary rate will spike this week given the sheer number of out-of-town cops in situ – and the only really fun stuff was a couple of police cars set on fire and a half dozen windows of Macy's broken. But they generally outperformed the lumbering Midwestern-beefy cops, who failed repeatedly to learn that if you face an entire riot squad column in one direction, protestors will – Anyone? Anyone? Bueller? Bueller? – yes, go in the other. At Harriet Island, on the Saint Paul riverbank, Billy Bragg was opening a 'reclaim Labor Day' open-air concert and a rocked-up version of Woody Guthrie's 'This Land is Your Land' blasted through the lower blocks of the city. Oh, and according to the TV, Hurricane Gustav was a bust.

'Hurricane Gustav has not picked up the energy expected and has been downgraded to level three, and may be downgraded further to a tropical storm.' – *Weather USA*, earlier today.

Wow, these Republicans just cannot take a trick. Having

turned the whole Convention into some sort of ghastly telethon in a half-empty sports arena, in the hope it could become a moment of patriotic rallying during a national emergency, the damn emergency is petering out into a mere storm. No spectacular death tolls, houses blown to matchsticks, etcetera, just lots of sogginess. God is clearly dicking with these people. He's having a larf, playing with the weather controls to keep everyone wrong-footed.

Whatever happens with Gustav, it's too late to put the Republican Convention back on track. Today's sessions were taken up almost entirely with pious appeals to send money, blankets, tins of sardines, etcetera etcetera, and to pull together as Americans, and so on. With the Center half empty, the whole thing had the feel of one of those old 48-hour televised appeals of yore – Cure Dropsy Now – which you could tune into at 2 a.m. to see Bobby Limb weeping into his button-on collar while singing 'My Favorite Things'.

Bobby, would that you were here at this hour. A couple of stooges spoke, but I would be lying if I said I remembered their names.

It was never going to be a great day, but even before things had really got going it got much, much worse, with Sarah Palin hit by a double-whammy like, well, two tropical storms. First came the news that her 17-year-old unwed daughter Bristol was pregnant, a fact apparently released to deal with rumours that Governor Palin's most recent baby was actually Bristol's. Nothing wrong there for most of us, except for the fact that the

GOP has been hammering everyone for years on questions of values, the importance of marriage, the terrible effect of absent fathers, blah blah BLAH.

These things ain't meant to happen. Doubtless we will find that Bristol was in one of those terrible 'True Love Waits' teen virgin programs – the full title being 'True Love Waits Until Three Malibu Shooters at a Post-Prom Party Have Gone to Work on Teens Whose Sex Education Comes From *The Book of Joshua*'.

Palin was forced to make some statement about families being out of bounds for politics – which is hilarious because part of her appeal was as a fecund mother who took a Downs syndrome foetus to term. Of course, the chaotic life of the Clintons was also used as an anti-standard, though I don't remember Chelsea knitting booties.

But hey, that was just the curtain-raiser. By lunchtime we heard that Palin had retained counsel in a long-running and incredibly complex story about whether she tried to improperly interfere in an ongoing investigation into some corrupt thing or other . . . forget it Mac, it's Alaska.

It's a pretty heavy hit for a candidate who was always a risky proposition, and who even some conservative commentators are saying was a poor choice. John McCain says he knew about both issues. Cue Mandy Rice-Davies. But the example that people are beginning to mention is that of Thomas Eagleton, the hapless first VP-pick of the hapless George McGovern, who concealed his history of clinical depression and electro-shock therapy, and was subsequently replaced by the hapless Sargent Shriver. Bizarrely, Geraldine Ferraro is another example – the lustre was taken off Walter Mondale's bold 1984 pick by revelations about loose tax arrangements, unfiled returns, etcetera, although most of it was the fault of her sleazy husband.

For all the spinning, no one retains counsel in these circumstances unless actual prosecution or impeachment is on the table – and if it were to get to that stage, well, it may be all over, red rover. McCain ran on the issue of experience and the clarity of that message has been smudged somewhat by Palin's sudden proximity to the nuclear button. But he's also run on the idea of judgement, and if it turns out that he blew that too, well, what does he have? As he'd only met Palin once or twice, for less than an hour total, legal problems for her would focus attention on just how exactly he makes decisions. And whether he was being insouciant or cynical about the choice of whoever would take over as president after one double dose of Cialis too many, followed by the customary Republican keel-over at the fifteenth hole.

Barack Obama has made a short announcement to the press, saying the pregnancy is all a matter for the Palin family – Sarah, Bristol and Michael, the former Python, who in fact fathered Sarah during the filming of *Pole to Pole* – and, well, cue Mandy Rice-Davies. Someone would have to be combing through the acres of comment from Coulter, Hannity, Novak, etcetera, where they thunder about how teen pregnancy has nothing to do with society, and 'it's the family, stupid', and so on. Neither of the official Democratic candidates will stoop to it, but there has to be a few attack dogs out there somewhere.

With nothing officially announced for tomorrow, the Convention planners are presumably, even as I write, working out whether to get back to as much of the extravaganza as they can, or continue with the hurricane appeal for mittens (no, not Romney – woollen gloves). They'll have their work cut out, as significant numbers haven't bothered to show up. This evening's party for the American Conservative Union – the ol' granddaddy of conservative ginger groups – looked like a trainspotters' mixer, until bizarrely, a large Asian delegation turned up to swell the numbers. It appears to be like that all over the joint.

The anarchists meanwhile have reformed their convergence centre twice after police raids, and are promising a rematch tomorrow, their floating re-arrangement of meetings, press conferences and decision-making managed through a bewildering network of legal, medical and affinity groups. The irony is that amidst the whiff of tear gas and the charging of police phalanxes, the anarchists seem better organised, more onto it, than the Republicans.

MINNEAPOLIS: TUESDAY, 2 SEPTEMBER

'The trouble is that the Federal Reserve was established as a private bank but most people think it's a public bank.'

The voice behind me in Starbucks was piping high and reedy, hard to place as man or woman. I turned round and saw no one. Then I looked down.

'It's vital to return the currency to the gold and silver stand-ard,' an 11-year-old kid was saying. With a pudding bowl haircut and a dozen Ron Paul buttons on his neat blue blazer, he was instructing a grizzled hippie with a grey ponytail in the intrica-cies of bimetallism.

We're in Minneapolis – the cooler, bigger part, founded by Scandinavians, full of funky modern architecture and art col-lectives. It was eleven in the morning, and across the road in the Target Center, Paulapalooza, Ron Paul's alt.convention, was just getting started. The crowds were already milling: bikers, Daniel Boone look-alikes, smooth besuited delegates from the Convention proper, all eager to get in. By the end of the day the hippie–Doogie Howser conversation would struggle to make the top ten of weirdness – not that that's a bad thing.

Libertarian/Republican Texas congressman Ron Paul, whose quixotic crusade has attracted every insurgent, maverick and, most of all, fruit bat in the libertarian hinterland, has ben-efited from a phalanx of supporters who might otherwise have found themselves, with a bit more pushing, dodging the tear gas down the road. Paulapalooza is a one-day event with everyone from right-wing creep Grover Norquist to the ever-entertaining former governor/wrestler Jesse Ventura along for the ride.

Having wrapped up his long primary campaign – after hang-ing on to the bitter end – Paul has now launched a broader-based Campaign for Liberty, hoping to draw in a scattered and cul-turally antagonistic set of groups into a movement that puts individual freedom, anti-US militarism and radical institutional reduction at the heart of a new program. By his own account – in his keynote speech – he had not planned on establishing anything like this when he began his tilt at the big job in early 2007. Paul had hitherto been a presidential candidate for the Libertarian party (while also being a Republican congressman), but the combination of blundering military adventurism, constitutional degradation and financial profligacy of the Bush administration persuaded him that some sort of protest run was necessary – above and beyond his usual lonely stand within the party against things such as the *USA Patriot Act*.

What happened then was really one of the most interesting phenomena of the long campaign. From a base of right-wing libertarians, Paul's campaign – especially its sustained assault on the Iraq occupation – began to attract activists who would, in earlier decades, have found themselves firmly on the left. Many had passed out of politics through the long decline of the left in the 1990s, and the sclerosis of micropolitics and rights that attended it. For many of them Paul's simple core message – that projection of power in the world and attacks on constitutional rights at home were essentially the same process seem from either side – hit like a revelation.

'As soon as I heard Ron, I just knew that he had the answer,' said a bearded, tattooed guy, who looked more likely to be down at the anarchist protests in Saint Paul. Near him, a tattooed riot-grrrl with a Statue of Liberty headpiece was singing bent versions of the national anthem, and a buttoned down bunch of home-schoolers was leading a chant to 'abolish the IRS'. Meanwhile a bunch of more organised activists in 'Ron Paul R(love)olution' T-shirts were hauling a model blimp into place.

There were plenty of standard American libertarians around too – buttoned-down types in the standard-issue blue suit, white shirt and red tie – but it's fair to say that if Paul had to rely on that part of his base alone, he would be a footnote to the Obama–McCain race. It was the influx of young former or would-have-been leftists that sent the campaign in a different direction. A certain amount of that was visual style – the cool black T-shirts, the logo with its echoes of a more licentious '60s idea of freedom, the Ron Paul blimp that floated above events – which was all drawn straight from the Abbie Hoffman playbook. But it was also about a more confrontational style, with groups of activists throwing up rowdy events outside events by other contenders for the Republican candidacy – Mitt Romney's meetings were a particular favourite. These things involved loud music off the back of flatbed trucks, verging on the disruptive, with a definite punkish air about it – the Paulites were out to generate a bit of heat and light. (Ironically enough, the mild-mannered, white-haired Paul had appeared on the Jay Leno show with the Sex Pistols during one of their icon-killing reunion tours, which only served to make the gang of four look older still.)

Paul had no chance of gaining the nomination, of course. In January his campaign was hit by revelations in *The New Republic* that newsletters published under his name in the '70s and '80s had contained a significant amount of noxious anti-Semitism in the traditional manner – a self-contained system mixing up Jews, masons, Bilderbergers, Venetian bankers and anyone else in a grand epochal conspiracy. Paul explained that he hadn't written the newsletters himself and barely looked at them, and nothing in his speeches hints at conspiracy or anti-Semitism. But it was a measure of both carelessness and an easy tolerance for some denizens of the lower depths of American libertarianism.

However, the interesting and somewhat disconcerting thing was that this seemed to dissuade so few people from a movement and a man that exhibited, along with whatever virtues, a heavy load of crankery. Nor were any of his leftish supporters dissuaded by American libertarianism's emphasis on sovereignty, as manifested, for example, in a strict anti-immigration position, or Paul's personal opposition to abortion. But his talent for speaking clearly about the follies of militarism and the debasement of the idea of 'freedom', his call to action not wrapped up in heavy geopolitical analysis, was so singular that many appeared willing to suspend critical analysis, or even to track into vaguely delusional territory.

That was certainly the feel at the anti-Convention, storming ahead with an standing-room-only crowd in the 10 000-seat Target Center, which had the odd effect of being both inspiring and reminiscent of *The Life of Brian*. 'What we have here is a group of people who don't do the same things together, wouldn't hang out together, but who have the same shared core beliefs – which is the opposite of both of the major parties,' said Grover Norquist, one of the procession of speakers throughout the afternoon, and a pretty deeply embedded right-wing operative. And it was true enough. What was inspiring about the gathering was that it was genuinely political, not an identity/cultural affinity group masquerading as a political organisation. Nor was it unsparing of many of its own attendees, with old 'paleolibertarian', 'paleoconservative', and unclassifiable speakers like Bill Kauffman, ramming home the degree to which the movement had to turn its back on both the label and the company of 'conservatives'. The sense that this was the birth of a clear-sighted political movement being born, with a capacity to apply some critical energy on the right, and the purposeful energy in the room, was a marked contrast to what was going on downtown.

Watching most of it on live feed from across the road at the Hard Rock Café, it's hard not to like the Paultards, no matter what hideous thoughts about abortion, Jews, the Illuminati, etcetera, are lurking beneath the surface. It's the only game in town where you can find some teenager in a blue suit and party riband talking to a guy in a hemp shirt with an 'I brake for hallucinations' button. In the hall, Aimee Allen – some sort of Christian/alt/fugknows act – is rocking it out, and though it appears that at least two songs are devoted entirely to various amendments to the Constitution, there's energy, there's life.

There were two hundred arrests at the protests yesterday, eighty of them on felony charges, and most of those the catch-all 'conspiracy' charge – if there were half a dozen acts of property damage, that was it. Not a great day, as it turned out.

But as bad as it was for the armies of the night, it weren't nothing compared to the saga of Sarah Palin, which, by mid-morning, had political betting sites opening up odds for a quit/sacked result. The pregnant teenager and the trooper intimidation case (in which she appears to have misused political influence to have her brother-in-law sacked from a government job) were only the beginning of it, apparently. There was also her early membership of the Alaska Independence Party, which claims – with perfect reason – that the 1959 passage to statehood was a con job; her enthusiastic lobbying for 'earmarks' (pork attached to legitimate bills as the price of getting them through); her near-recall as mayor of Wasilla; her comments that Iraq was a 'war for oil'; her support for abstinence-only sex education; and on and on, and on, it went. Then there was Levi Johnston, daddy of Bristol Palin's baby, a dude in a football jersey with a haircut screaming 'roped in to a Year 12 production of *Footloose*', and a MySpace page that reads – I kid you not – 'in a relationship but I don't want kids'. Bad luck, dude. You *Juno*ed the daughter of the first citizen of Juneau and you've either hit the white-trash jackpot or just got yourself anchored down in Anchorage for a long, long time.

By now the whole thing has become well-meta, with the main story being the pitiful failure of the vetting process. The suggestion is that McCain dug his heels in so long – he basically wanted his man-crush, Joe Biden, and wouldn't take no for an answer until very, very late – he was left facing an invidious choice. He could either say, 'Yes, I was bamboozled, I didn't know any of this stuff', or 'No, I was aware of it all the time and I selected a 44-year-old mayor of a place with the population of forty Manhattan blocks, who publicly suggested the job is pointless, is currently under investigation for misuse of power, and all that other crap as well. Next question. Hey! Let's put sugar in the tank of the Straight Talk Express.'

Would team McCain actually ask Palin to resign? Would she resign of her own accord, given the heat now coming down on her family? The fact that this shit is even possible is a measure of just how unbelievably dumb the choice was. Hang on to her or drop her out the bomb bays – either way, it's a helluva choice. This may be the worst executive pick since Aaron Burr, who actually tried to kill his boss.

It's clear that Sarah Palin's speech is going to be the only game in town. The Palin effect has been phenomenal. Folks can't stop talking about her everywhere you go, on the street in Saint Paul, on the airwaves, in the blogosphere. Journalists hurrying back from the hurricane to their original gig at the Convention were put straight on a plane to Anchorage, to comb over Palin's life and lines for absolutely anything at all.

On the streets, events look like following a familiar pattern. The anarchists, etcetera, come out in the morning – postings on their Twitter page urged people to stay clean, sober and well-rested to get out on the field early – and march from the Capitol building or thereabouts. The police go apeshit, block off intersections and throw smoke bombs, thus tying up half the city and doing exactly what the anarchists want, which is to disrupt business as usual.

Not since the letter–number (J18, S11, etcetera) protests of the turn of the century have I had such a good time. Going into a Starbucks you never know coming out whether you'll get hit by a baton charge or an anarchist flying V formation.

Thus, amidst the pretty, pretty smoke and the cool police horses – in designer Italian eye shades – do we wait for the divine Sarah.

Meanwhile I've got a CNN live feed of the Convention on my laptop, which is showing the band warming up before the event itself starts at 6.30 p.m. central time. The Dems had a house band somewhere between Parliament-Funkadelic and Earth, Wind & Fire, but the GOP has got . . . smooth jazz. Kid you not, it's like something between the on-hold muzak in a dentist's office and the theme to a cancelled sitcom. Delegates in the crowd are waltzing to it. Christ, if only the nation at large could see this, the GOP wouldn't get nine seats. It's everything that's plastic, sexless, deracinated, lifeless, safe and deadened.

Even the dudes playing it aren't into it. Black guys in suits, they're playing with that tight-lipped contempt you see in bands at weddings held in places where the reception centre looks like the cake, all white froufrou and fake columns.

The drummer has a ponytail.

The GOP promised us a full day today, with nancy-boy fancy-pants Euro-Hurricane Gustav having turned into a bor-ing old, big rainstorm, but it hasn't eventuated. (The other three hurricanes are racked up off the coast, feeding off high-sea temperatures – BUT IT HAS NOTHING TO DO WITH GLOBAL WARMING, YOU WARMENISTS.) With half the delegates never turning up, and another bunch turning round and going back home on Sunday, the party could only put together an evening's entertainment, culminating in Dubya addressing the crowd by video. That seems to neatly defeat the one advantage of the truncated Convention – that nothing Bush-esque (except the botoxed Laura) would be here to remind the public that there's any connection between the current administration and the Republican Party.

God, oh God, the Convention has started and CNN cameras are panning the crowd as the minority leader speaks – some bloke with not so much hair as a central parted helmet. The cameras are scanning to find collections of other people with similar plastic-moulded hair. Buzz Lightyear enters the toy store.

'Please stand for the official Convention photo. Would all delegates please stand and face to the back as the panoramic camera takes the shot. This should take a minute or so . . .' Good God. These people *want* to be on *The Daily Show*.

Rage Against the Machine is playing a free concert at the Saint Paul Capitol and I'm in the Hard Rock Café watching Republicans facing backwards and smiling, rictus-style. It's like a Devo film clip.

Barry Goldwater Jr now, at the Target Center, speaking to the Paultards: 'We will take back the Republican party.' They might at that.

Then Ron Paul himself came out and the sense of exuberance spilt into the distinctly cultish.

It was nothing that Paul said, per se, that gave the impression that these massed champions of individual liberty had been waiting for nothing less than the chance to meld into one, so much as the whole iconography and staging. Beneath the giant stadium video screen relaying his face five stories high, Paul's every statement was greeted with huge applause and massive light flashes suggestive of an alien landing. The message was nothing that hadn't been heard before (though at one moment he alluded to the possibility that the 'time may come' for violent revolution, something none of the mainstream media apparently noticed). But there was a startling willingness to deliver and receive it as something iconic. On the merchandising stalls outside there were Paul pins, portraits and the man's profile cast in silver 'Liberty Dollars', an autonomous currency circulating in the South. Affection, even veneration, for someone who has shown a clear path and leadership is understandable, but this was something a little more needy.

Yet if a critical libertarian movement drawing in left and right elements is to emerge it will have to pretty quickly go beyond Paul and the particular set of obsessions that a mid-century American libertarian brings to the table. At its worst and most cartoonish, American libertarianism is ahistorical and nostalgic in its attempt to re-found the republic on the sort of simple pieties that suggest a direct continuity between the northern agrarian and puritan 18th century republic, which rebelled against the British, and the idea of freedom, liberty and sovereignty in a globalised 21st century society. For paleolibertarians – and the whole fractured collection of political subgroups is a measure of how desperate the need is for a re-grounding of American libertarian principles – floated currency and central banking is the Fall, the betrayal of good and virtuous men and women, whose bounty can be restored by a return to metallic-backed money finding its own level. Obviously, there's no chance of that, and if it were to pass, it would amount to one of the most enormous economic deflations of all time, depriving the global economy of its capacity to generate sufficient credit. The Paulites' monetary ideas would deprive them of most features of the fluid hi-tech world that make an expanded notion of liberty possible. A fair few of Paul's younger supporters – and most of the younger leftists of recent recruitment – couldn't be less interested in bimetallism, even in so far as they have a mental picture of the banking system at all. They like the no-bullshit nailing of the neo-con behemoth, exposing the way in which the protection of abstract freedom is used to cloak the removal of individual liberties. Yet the outward image of Paul's campaign is those more obsessive characters, the slightly frightening besuited 11-year-olds with their tales of currency wreckers, cabals and the illuminati. If Paul's campaign for liberty is going to march on, it's going to have to find a strict minimum program oriented to contemporary challenges, which all can agree to while maintain their differences within. More importantly, it must take it beyond the exuberance found in a leader who has spoken a few plain truths.

At the GOP, 18-year-old Ashley Gunn from Brandon, Mississippi, a teen blonde in turquoise, has come out to talk: 'A famous philosopher, Socrates, once said . . .' God help us – can the swimsuit competition be far behind?

Some blues rock at the Paultardapalooza. 'Down with big brother / I got the big brother blues . . .' Bless.

And Obama's now back with a 7 per cent lead in the poll average.

Fzzzt.

Nine p.m. Dubya addressing the Republican troops, beamed from his undersea headquarters in Crawford. Ron Paul has just addressed his adoring disciples in a damn powerful speech, which had about the only measure of plain common sense heard in this campaign.

Dubya's as wooden as hell, like someone giving a testimonial for an unpleasant-tasting cough medicine. 'John's an independent thinker, I know.' Translation: 'C_nt c_nt c_nt c_nt c_nt.'

Almost nothing to Dubya's piece – ten minutes tops? Something about a picture on the wall with sunrise on mountains: '. . . and Americans have all lived on the sunny side of the mountains.'

Laura's giving Cindy the wrap now. 'Cindy's visited refugees, war zones, Georgian crises . . .' So many disaster areas, so many painkillers.

Laura wrapping it up, and we're segueing into a film tribute

to Reagan – who HAS BEEN DEAD FOR TEN YEARS.
Or so.

It's a real contrast to Paulapalooza, where the energy was
phenomenal and the candidate gutsy in his thorough denunciation of his own party (if you don't dig too deep), not to mention
his call for civil disobedience in the face of future wars. And, of
course, his defence of hemp as an alternative fuel source.

Fred Thompson's on at the GOP and to be fair he's punching
it home, even though his voice seems strained. Still, at least he's
got an actor's delivery. Even if you find this whole worship of
military casualties in unnecessary wars a bizarre cult of death,
he's giving it a bit of life.

Strange days, strange days.

'John McCain has a face that says "Yes",' some stooge said
earlier at the GOP. Yeah, dude, but sadly, so does Bristol Palin.

SAINT PAUL: WEDNESDAY, 3 SEPTEMBER

We're all waiting for Palin. We had been established in the 5th
Avenue Starbucks, which has become the de facto blogger central
(I have stopped bothering to say 'I am not a blogger'), not least
for what has become the Jon Stewart perp walk, the diminutive
genius strolling through at about nine-ish each morning for a
big coffee and about half a dozen fan photos.

But Starbucks is not going to get us through an entire evening
of Republicans. This is going to have to be done from a bar.

Six in the evening and we have re-established the national

affairs desk in the peerless Wyld Tymes bar, across the way from the Convention compound proper.

Six cars pulled up a minute ago. Twenty riot cops piled out like clowns from a jalopy and cleared the whole mall. Then they surrounded a building while about six cops on mountain bikes rode inside. Yes, *in*. No, I don't know why either. Anarchists have occupied the indoor velodrome. (Say it in Norwegian and it makes sense.)

The Convention started again at about 6 p.m., the rest of the day having been taken up by luncheons, and bruncheons, for God's sake. No shame about lobbyists here, the buffet is rolled out wide as hell. The hot ticket was the AstraZeneca lunch, which had caviar, lobster, etcetera, piled up on groaning tables, a pure celebration of excess.

More movement in the mall outside. Cops lined up at both ends, Republicans sitting in the outdoor gardens getting nervous. Are they in the line of fire?

The McCain abortion truck crawls past. A three-ton job covered with pictures of aborted foetuses and signs saying 'McCain shame'. God knows what one stray vote McCain cast for abortion – if the mother is raped and dying, perhaps – but this bloke remembers it.

Meg Whiteman, the founder of eBay, is speaking to the Convention now, offering the standard platitudes and sales pitch – John's a different breed, tempered in the fire, etcetera etcetera, he'll achieve energy independence, this is our moonshot. This ain't interesting – it's boilerplate.

Earlier we had a woman who was some sort of Amish pretzel entrepreneur, who had started her company after her family lost their crops. Then she lost her 19-month-old daughter, and she spoke compellingly of despair and how she had then given her life to giving.

I don't mean to make fun of that, because she was one of the rare people at either convention who sounded real. But what she spoke about – of only being alive when you give to others – is, let's face it, hardly a Republican motif. Isn't it all about the individual and making your own way in the world? The giving thing is, you know . . . for *others*.

But even better, she then quoted Alexis De Tocqueville: 'America is great because it is good'. There was huge applause and cheering from people who fell asleep at page twelve of *The Da Vinci Code*. The boobies. The whole point of the quote in Tocqueville's *Democracy in America* is ironic – or let's be more precise, sardonic. De T had gone to the US to study its prison system. He observed a society building a new order and he worried about their belief that association alone, rather than deep organic roots, could sustain a society. *Democracy in America* was not a celebration, it was a warning about hubris, you tools.

But still, the woman was compelling. She knows what she knows.

Mitt Romney's up.

Romney is the awfulness test. If he just makes you want to vomit up your own spleen, you're a human being. Nevertheless, he's giving a good speech, hammering on the liberals.

Is supporting rights for Guantanamo Bay liberal or conservative? It's liberal!

Cheers.

People are stronger if raised in family homes with a mom and a dad.

You listening, Bristol?

Romney's going for the hard yards – trying to sell the mortgage crisis, etcetera, as a Democratic thing. Then energy security again.

The woman next to me at the bar is a hooker. This is too good. I'm watching Mitt Romney at the Republican Convention and the woman next to me is negotiating an hourly rate and an appointment time. For yea, I sayeth to God, send me a metaphor, and lo there is Jessica, with a white top, reading *Royal Beauty*.

God, the GOP are kicking hard tonight. And dancing to 'Life is a Highway'. Forget load shifting, these dancers are piles of marbled meat fat sliding around the back of a truck as it goes over a cliff.

Now Huckabee, telling some goddamn anecdote I can't hear cos I'm eavesdropping on the hookers. There's two of them but I think one is a sort of girl pimp. Like Romney.

Huckabee should have been the VP pick. He's got substance. He gave credit to Obama and then rounded on the Democrats. He would have got the evangelicals, no problem of cred. A foolish bypass?

Now Giuliani slamming down the attack on Obama in old NY-style. Pretty good.

He worked as a community organiser. [Scornful laughter.] *A what?*

Huge laughter. Good get.

Obama is the least experienced leader in a hundred years . . . On this we agree with Joe Biden.

Laughter. Good get.

These guys are too good. They may well upstage Palin. The amateur's mistake – don't overload the front end of the ticket.

Drill, baby, drill!

Into the John McCain spiel. Boy, this must hurt the back of Giuliani's throat.

The Democrats couldn't mention 9/11.

Obama was X . . . Obama was Y . . . Too much Obama-focused.

If I were Joe Biden I'd get the VP thing in writing.

It's a cracking speech, though. Real piledriver. This guy will be their lead attack dog.

Okay, here we go. Palin's on.

Five minutes of applause, and the bar has gone quiet – people are actually listening.

I accept the privilege of serving with a man who has come through much harder missions . . .

Cindy's holding Sarah's—no, Bristol's baby. 'It's Cindy's baby!' the bar yells.

He's a man who'd rather lose an election than lose a war . . .

Tepid applause for a line used too many times. She's got a lot on McCain – is this hitting the right note?

There's a time for politics and a time for leadership . . .

What, then, is politics?

Our nominee is a true profile in courage, etcetera etcetera, etcetera . . .

Enough about McCain, we want to hear about you. Close-up on bloke in audience – husband? Son? Who knows? Does she?

She's got a kid going to Iraq . . . and a nephew . . . Well, that's not fair.

My strong and kind-hearted daughters, Bristol, Willow and . . . something . . .

Willow – *Buffy's* got a lot to answer for. But it turns out she's named after the town up the road, a place that makes Wasilla look like Vienna at the end of the 19th century.

Everyone's got babies and they're being passed around.

Kids with special needs inspire a special love.

How many babies are there? Seems like ten.

To the kids of special needs families across America, I have a message—

'If you're poor, get fucked.' No, that wasn't it.

Todd the husband . . .

He's a proud member of the steelworkers union and a dog racer . . .

Groans from the bar. Is this a Democrat establishment, or are they just cat people? Actually, the bar's not really strong Democrat – the hookers, who've gone to a Covention party, were definitely GOP.

I was just your average hockey mom, and signed up for the PTA . . . You know the difference between a hockey mom and a pitbull? Lipstick.

Big laugh and applause.

The six-year-old's got the kid now, which brings raucous laughter from the bar. These are average or non-voters, and they're half buying it.

I guess a small-town mayor is sort of like a community organiser, except you have actual responsibilities.

Big laugh. A nasty line, but a good get.

We tend to prefer candidates who don't talk about us one way in Scranton and another way in San Francisco.

She's knocking this out of the park. But then comes back to McCain – she didn't need to.

I'm not a member of the permanent political establishment . . . And I've learned quickly . . . some in the media consider a candidate unqualified for that reason alone.

Freelance booing from crowd. A mistake of sorts, I think – it sounds whiny to all but Republicans.

To serve the common good and leave this nation better than we found it . . .

On to the generalities now . . . A bit early? A few more specifics? She is really looking good, though. It's not just the woman thing, it's the youth. She's definitely trumped Obama for the moment in novelty.

The previous governor's luxury jet was over the top. I put it on eBay . . . I took a cut in salary, which upset my husband . . .

I sacked the governor's chef, which upset my kids.

I said thanks, but no thanks for that 'bridge to nowhere' . . .

Everyone of these gets bigger ups than the last – she's really firing. Then, some dull but necessary stuff – and the audience flags. On to Obama . . .

There is much to like and admire about our opponent . . . But . . . it's easy to forget that this is a man who has authored two memoirs but not a single major law or reform . . . When the stadium lights go out, and those Styrofoam Greek columns are hauled back to a studio lot, what exactly is our opponent's plan?

HUGE LAUGH on this, but there is a danger. It's great for the home crowd but no one outside really cares.

Harry Reid [majority leader of the Senate] *said 'I can't stand John McCain' . . . What he was driving at is that he can't stand up to John McCain . . .*

This gets great ups at the Convention, but a groan of dismay in the bar. It's too nasty.

Both Senator Obama and Senator Biden have been going on lately about how they are always, quote, 'fighting for you' . . . There is only one man in this election who has ever really fought for you . . . and that man is John McCain.

It's been so full of this deeply depressing, dumb macho bullshit – all tough posturing posing as policy, which of course the party faithful loved. But how will it play for the middle ground? Nevertheless it was an effective speech. If it's not exactly true that a star is born, then at least a giant gas cloud is collecting.

From the moment it was announced, Sarah Palin's candidacy had been assessed as 'risky' by leading pundits. Palin's speech to the Convention blew most of those concerns away, yet what is most curious about her candidacy and its importance as a return to Culture War values, is how much their previously clear message – that selfish liberal values were destroying social life – has had to be contorted to fit Sarah Palin.

For right-wing culture warriors, one of the key contributions to the undermining of social life was the rise of liberal feminism, with its insistence on the right of women to work and its assumption that children are not disadvantaged by women working substantial hours. The tenor of conservative attacks was that this was the epitome of narcissistic liberalism, which didn't recognise that grounded biological differences between men and women ordained different life paths and roles, and most importantly, wouldn't acknowledge that children's development could be harmed by the absence of a full-time mother.

Bizarrely, these positions have now been reversed in the short-term political skirmishing. For the right, stray questions about whether the mother of three children under fourteen, one a baby with Down's syndrome, would have the pure focus necessary for the office of president of the United States, should John McCain slip off the perch, are 'sexist', 'outrageous', and so on. Yet if US president isn't a job that makes effective parenting impossible, then what job is?

If this is a turnaround, it's nothing compared to the sudden equanimity the right has displayed towards teen pregnancy. For twenty years the right had insisted that there was one cause for unmarried motherhood – poor parenting. Here's FOX News supremo Bill O'Reilly in 2007:

'On the pinhead front, 16-year-old Jamie Lynn Spears [Britney's younger sister] is pregnant . . . Here, the blame falls primarily on the parents of the girl, who obviously have little control over her.'

The ironies are multiple. The right has insisted that teen pregnancy has nothing to do with ignorance or lack of opportunity, and everything to do with virtue and good parenting. For this reason they, including Sarah Palin, have voted for abstinence-only education, a course of action which doesn't tend to survive six tequila shooters on prom night. Yet suddenly teen pregnancy is a morally neutral act, and everything politicised for the past twenty years is a matter of privacy. Hilariously, family values conservatives have suddenly morphed into choice freaks. It's a clear sign of the rottenness at the heart of American political conservatism – any judgement, any value, can be thrown overboard in the quest for power.

SAINT PAUL: THURSDAY, 4 SEPTEMBER

Last day of the gig and everything's leading up to McCain, who will be speaking at about 9.30 p.m., two hours past his bedtime, and may have to wander off for a leak halfway through.

Round four of the battle of Saint Paul and the protestors finally got their shit together. They managed to block off the whole northern half of the city, cannily using the overpass system the city fathers built in the '60s. The whole of Saint Paul was channelled into a single freeway entrance and four bridges, and the protestors have taken them all. Token protestors at each intersection have forced the police to close them all off, and columns run through the park to keep the cops guessing about where the main balance of forces are.

So we can't get down to our usual haunt, much less the actual Convention centre, and we're instead filing from a cavernous hotel on the hill.

Half a dozen Republicans just came in. Then they all went out, leaving one – the runt of the litter – to order for 'em. 'Six steaks,' she said, of course. One bloke came back in to make sure she got the order right, and yelled: 'And mashed potato for all!'

And mashed potato for all, my friends.

Outside, about two hundred protestors ran past the floor-to-ceiling windows, followed by two hundred cops. Very funny.

Cindy McCain's on, at about 8.30. God, she creeps me out.

Previously we had Phil Gramm, another of McCain's man-crushes. This man really has a lot of very, very close bloke friends – I bet they all rent a summer house in Crete.

The subject of the evening till now, of course, has been Barack Obama, obsessively, unstoppably, and well beyond any sort of usefulness, I think. But who knows?

Cindy speaks about how she met John – how he changed her, taught her the meaning of obligation, etcetera. How they went to Bangladesh after a cyclone and saw two beautiful children, whom they adopted, '. . . and one of them is here tonight – Bridget'.

We all know Bridget. She was the girl subject to rumours spread by Dubya's team in 2000 that she was McCain's half-black love child. Which I guess is the difference between Democrats and Republicans.

Cindy's wearing a better dress than the previous $300 000 one, which looked like it was entirely made of human skin, from someone with a large neck in order to provide the wraparound collar. Her hair looks like a bald eagle has attacked the back of her head.

The GOPers have finished their steak and gone. The table looks like a field surgical hospital.

'Cindy McCain's speech was rather subdued . . .' says the FOX News person. 'Sedated' is more the word. I am trying to be fair.

McCain film starting.

'He'd stand for hours and stare at the border of north and south Vietnam . . .the closest he could get to his son, who was a prisoner in Hanoi, a city he'd just ordered to be carpet bombed . . .'

Fred Thompson: 'When you've lived in a box, the world becomes clear . . .'

McCain on stage, out on the runway like a model.

A bizarre image behind him of a white stucco building – the White House from an uncommon angle? One of the houses he doesn't know he owns? (Turns out it was Walter Reed – but not the famous veterans' hospital. Some campaign bimbo had image Googled 'walter reed' and got a girls' high school in California.)

I'm grateful to the President of the United States [who remains unnamed] *for leading us in those dark days following the worst attack on American soil in our history . . . Grateful to the forty-first President . . .*

It's hilarious – they will not say 'Bush'.

The screen is mostly green behind him – do they *want* another round of *The Colbert Report* viewers doing PhotoShop jobs on him? Yes, of course they do.

A tribute to his mom, who is 183, and who I'd vote for.

A word to Senator Obama and his supporters . . . You have my respect and our admiration . . .

Very tepid applause initially.

Despite our differences, much more unites us than divides us. We are fellow Americans, an association that means more to me than any other.

Big applause on the Americans line.

So far it's nothing new – but it was never going to be. Palin was the star turn.

USA! USA! USA!

. . . get this country back on the road to prosperity and peace . . .

BUSH SUCKS! BUSH SUCKS!

On to Palin . . .

She has run a small business, she has worked with her hands and nose . . .

Say what? Is this an Eskimo thing? Eskimo kisses, five cents a go?

. . . with her hands, and knows what it is to worry . . .

Oh, it was just a bad line break.

I've been called a maverick . . .

And also, by most of the people assembled here, a cunt . . .

I fought for . . . more troops in Iraq . . .

The surge. Here we go.

I fight for Americans . . . I fight for you . . .

I fight for almost any reason whatsoever. What follows is a recitative of names of people who've been screwed over by the system.

Then actually hacking into Republicans.

We were elected to change Washington and we let Washington change us . . . We lost the trust of the American people . . .

This stuff is new and the audience is drawing in breath.

We're going to recover the people's trust . . .

In the bar, off-duty riot cops are piling in, taking off their helmets and rubbing the spot on their head where it chafes. What's the verdict? It's a solid speech, but apart from the GOP attack, it's not really going to convert anyone. Even given the Palin bump, will this be enough to give him the added oomph he needs, to get the extra 5 per cent and more by which he's currently trailing?

And mashed potatoes for all.

And mashed potatoes for all.

PART TWO

THE
CAMPAIGN

6

NORTH TO ALASKALA!

And Dog Days for the Democrats

'Alaska is the last frontier, the last place in this damn country where you can be free,' the ol' feller said in the Izzy Jack's bar, half the Miller Lite I'd just bought him going into his beard, presumably to be wrung out later. It's true, of course.

You can go up to the North Slope and earn six figures driving a truck, and you can get drunk, fall asleep in the street and get eaten by a polar bear. You can take advantage of the 'circle [i.e. Arctic] rule', which is pretty much what it sounds like – or you can steal another man's camp wife and end up dumped down a hole in the ice, to come bobbing up downstream six months later during the thaw. The ol' timer told me all this dead-on, even though it's entirely possible that he's a failed dotcommer paid by the tourist board to hang 'round the bars spinning tales for free drinks.

But whatever it is, it's mostly bollocks, of course. Alaska preserves the image of America as the land of free enterprise and individual effort, while quietly carrying on as a quasi-socialist fiefdom of social dividends and big-money patronage. In a few days time, every Alaskan is going to get a $3000 cheque, their share of the huge tax the state charges the oil industry. The underlying idea, unless I'm very much mistaken, is that the oil is the property of ALL ALASKANS, not merely the private enterprises that staked the claims on it. Effectively, the place runs like Norway, which has had a similar fund in place for thirty years.

Unlike Norway, Alaska hands over most of it as a cash payment, which is treated by the populace with the same prudent thriftiness as any chunk of free money is – i.e. not all of it goes on booze and crystal meth. Besides, why do boring old infrastructure and investment, like Norway does, when there's a federal government?

'We got a lot of time for Ted Stevens up here,' the cab driver told me as we drove into the main entrance of the Ted Stevens International Anchorage Airport, having passed a plaque commemorating Ted Stevens as 'Alaskan of the century'. Stevens is, of course, the still-living six-time senator who is to stand trial in Washington in September for decades of alleged rorting via undeclared gifts, the most recent being a sled dog, or 'husky money', as they call it here.

Of course they've got a lot of time for Ted – he's head of the Senate Appropriations Committee, and nothing moves in any direction without Alaska getting a little slice off the top. Consequently 25 per cent of the money in the state is big government investment, which spares Alaskans from funding their own development, which in turn frees up the money for dividends to be used as a political bribe.

The ultimate result of this is that the state is uniquely dependent, not independent – dependent on high oil prices and Washington pork. When either or both of these vanish, the underinvestment sends the state spinning into poverty, as occurred with the low oil prices of the '90s. Unlike the Norwegians, who now have around $400 billion in their investment fund, and may thus be the first entire country to take early retirement, or Venezuela, which has ploughed it back into poverty reduction, Alaskans simply let it float through the economy, inflating prices to the point where you don't get much change out of ten bucks for a sandwich in downtown Anchorage.

Of course, it's not all rents and royalties and rorts. There's the fantastically high wages the closed-shop oil industry generates – the sort of wages that, for example, allow for single-income families, which permits a woman with four children to pursue a political career as city councillor, then as mayor and then . . .

'What about Palin?' I asked the Stevens-loving cabbie (and there *is* the faintest touch of North Korea ancestor-worship about the place).

'Oh, we like her a lot too.'

'Isn't she kind of famous for starting to bring down the whole Ted Stevens regime?'

Silence for a while, then: 'Oh, fall is really here. Look at the golden trees. Well, here's your gate.'

True dat. Alaska is beautiful in every direction, the forests round Fairbanks striped gold and green with deciduous and evergreen trees planted together. Here, tonight, Sarah Palin is going to descend from the air like a returning hometown goddess and speak in an aircraft hangar. Tomorrow, she farewells her son, leaving for Iraq. On 9/11! Nice touch.

The Republicans are killing the Democrats at the moment and it's stuff like this that's doing it. The 'country first' slogan, combined with their audacious theft of the 'change' slogan and the selection of Palin, all make the GOP look like a pair of outriders. Suddenly old, tired, hackneyed, Obama and Biden look like the sort of black–white team of political pros that most big inner cities run. McCain and Palin, by contrast, look like a travelling theatre version of Hunter S. Thompson's *Fear and Loathing in Las Vegas*, two people comfortable with guns and bad craziness, and coming out of a context beyond easy summary.

We haven't been able to stop talking about Sarah Palin because her candidacy was not simply a clever tactical move – it was a genuine and multiple historic moment, arguably more significant than Barack Obama's rise to the Democratic candidacy. Why? Put simply, it's because the identity of men and women in a society – what they are allowed to do, what is seen as appropriate to them – really runs deeper than what different types of men – black, white, other – are allowed to do. We've already had one female VP candidate, of course – Geraldine Ferraro in 1984. But Palin's candidacy has an entirely different complexion, not merely because she has a good chance of winning, which Ferraro never really had, but also because she is a woman who's grown up and lived in what is effectively a post-feminist era. Amazingly, Palin's life – a professional career woman with a family, a husband both blue-collar and SNAG-ish, her set of conservative attitudes – is both the triumph of the second wave feminist revolution and the finish of it.

Even a decade ago, Palin's candidacy would have been impossible. Too many of the religious right, as well as many voters in conservative Southern and Appalachian states, and conservative blue-collar cities, would have found a career mother of four unacceptable. The fact that a number of conservative commentators who still find it unacceptable have gone silent is a measure of political cynicism – but that across the country Palin's dual role is seen as unremarkable, is a register of extraordinary social and cultural change. It is a decisive end to any hope that the whole second-wave feminist program – equality, choice, secularism, etcetera – could be held together as an assumed set of attitudes. As the former Clinton political advisor, the odious Dick Morris, noted, Sarah Palin's success represents an 'existential threat' to the Democratic Party's role as the representatives of a unitary progressivism. Palin's candidacy said to the country that you don't have to take on the whole liberal package to exercise your right to a career, full public equality and a marriage with shared duties. Palin's husband Todd is an undoubted part of this whole grand slam – a man who used the fabulous wages gained from work in the virtual closed-shop of the North Slope oil fields to be a part-time house-husband.

This tectonic shift in American culture knocked the Democrats sideways, not only because they have been running a lacklustre campaign since the end of the primaries, but because its 'theft' of a set of values and themes that the Democrats regarded as their own cut to the quick. Panic is the usual reaction to the sudden feeling of loss of self, of annihilation, and the Democrats fell for it, unable to contain comments about experience and attitude, etcetera, which, while not inaccurate, could be equally applied to Barack Obama. They simply reinforced the appearance of a born-to-rule attitude.

In doing so, the party made visible the deep cultural divide in America and the degree to which they failed to understand it. For the difference between the McCain–Palin and the Obama–Biden teams no longer turns on a distinction between the old and the new, the progressive and the hidebound, but between the heroic and non-heroic, with advantage to guess who. Suddenly with 'Walnuts' McCain and Sarah the Warrior Princess marketing themselves as a pair of mavericks, Barack Obama's extraordinary life story looks merely exotic, a Pacific souvenir. Taken together, McCain's war experience and Palin's whole life – the (very infrequent) hunting; the son going to Iraq and, godhelpus, shipping out on September eleventh; the Down syndrome child – are all visceral, physical. They're commitments to life and death, and that's the raw material of heroism. There's nothing rational about the power these factors have in selecting the leader of a hi-tech country in a globalised world – a 'hero' is as likely to lead you to national disaster – but to imagine they don't stack up well against the prosaic world of lawyers and community organisers is to revel in illusion.

The Democratic campaign has, over the past two months, become a distastefully smug assumption of right, which quickly turned whiny when thing started going wrong. It has not yet recovered and may never do so. One had inklings of that after the primary season was concluded, when it became clear that the Obama team's real passion had been for defeating Hillary Clinton, with the Republicans as an afterthought. But it was really confirmed at the Denver Convention, a gathering whose party/caucus ratio suggested more energy for play than work. Together with a British political-betting handicapper and a Bavarian bruiser from the NSW Right faction of the German greens, I toured the open-bar sessions put on by state parties, pressure groups, etcetera, and everywhere we heard the same thing – in response to any question about John McCain's remorseless climb back up the greasy polls, Democrats yielded to no one in their ability to marshal excuses. The polls were wrong, unregistered voters weren't counted, it was silly-season August, the American people wouldn't be fooled. Despite, or because of, its eerie similarities to the course of the disastrous 2004 Kerry campaign, no one wanted to know, or even discuss off-record, the indisputable fact that the party was failing to seal the deal. It was a series of premature victory parties, unconsciously preparing for defeat.

Now, after it looked that McCain had lost this months ago, it may be the Democrats who are now seeing the whole thing slip away. Why? Because the McCain team recovered from its disasters and pretty much changed the whole campaign around while the Democrats, after the primaries, have had no campaign. They're still defensive and reactive, unbelieving that the initiative's been taken from them. The gaffes pile up – a South Carolina Democratic heavy saying that Palin's only a candidate because she hasn't had an abortion was a doozy – and the only punch they've landed has been a ridiculous fuss over whether Obama's use of the old 'lipstick on a pig' political line was a sexist remark. And still they won't hack into the McCain–Palin ticket for the single most important thing about them: they're Republicans. Had they been attacking McCain as an enemy of ordinary people from day one, there would have been traction now. Starting from zero is going to be tough. Not impossible by any means, but tough.

And though the Palin scandals are piling up – she took per diems for living expenses while staying at home in Wasilla as governor, she campaigned for 'the bridge to nowhere', the Troopergate thing seems to go deeper than previously thought – none of it's landing a blow. The GOP has played the last six weeks brilliantly, the kiss of the whip being placards featuring a modification of the old 'Rosie the Riveter' WWII posters, with Palin's face in place. Suddenly, the historical impact of this campaign has become the way in which feminism, gender politics and all that, have been changed forever.

So when she descends tonight to farewell her son amidst the flaming trees, the drifting mist and distant blue mountains of the Alaskan promised land, in this weird cult of death whereby parents contemplate the despatch of their children to futile wars with pride, the Republicans will win this one too.

'Hey man, you're afraid to hug.'

A compact, muscly, clean-shaven dude, Bred (that was his name – it must be an Alaska thing) had grabbed me around the midriff and choked me tight. I hadn't hugged back because it was 3 a.m. and I was worried that I'd chuck all over him. He was friendly, but I thought a shoulder splurk might finish that.

He was shipping out the next day from Fort Wainwright, along with a few hundred other troops, one of them Trig Palin. He was a sniper by training, hated the war, thought it was futile, but was going back anyway. Service? Duty?

'I do one year, then I get a gig with Blackwater.'

This was at the Marlin Bar, a bunker in Fairbanks that was once a fishing club and has used the old club license to serve Alaska's ridiculously cheap booze until 5 a.m. The joy of a small- to mid-size place like Fairbanks is that there's only one place for anyone bent, dissenting or just out for a fight, and the Marlin is it. So it was where backwoods punks, lesbian singer–songwriters, 'Alaska 4 Obama' honchos and some ornery troops had gathered. Fake fish on the wall, interspersed with band posters and an old barometer stuck in a permanent storm.

Hours earlier, half the crowd had been at the airport for the arrival of the divine Sarah, Inuit goddess come from sky. Say what you like, the thing had been perfectly choreographed, with the hangar door flung wide open and Palin's plane taxiing to a set of flight steps standing like a lonely totem on the tarmac. The plane slid up beside it as a crowd of 2000, stoked by a brass band, worked themselves into a frenzy. When the door popped and the distinctive diminutive figure in biggish hair and stylish eyewear appeared, the crowd went batshit orgasmic.

'I've been telling the country about John McCain and a lot about Alaska!' she roared to the crowd, who roared back.

She didn't give much more than what's evolving as her stand-ard stump speech minus the catty remarks, and with a few local references, but she could have recited Inuit words for snow and got a killing reaction. Two weeks ago, she was a novelty governor the state was still getting used to. Now she was potentially one thrombotic-argument-with-Cindy away from the big job.

'I told them that here in Alaska it's a "snow machine", not a "snowmobile"!'

Big laughs, applause.

'Alaska is a half-socialist big government behemoth that wants your money because it won't spend its own.' I bet she's not saying that. They don't even do socialism that well. There's no sales tax on anything, so all the booze is cheap and the food is through the roof. It's like a social engineering experiment in creating one big drunk tank.

'Man, hug me back.'

What to do? I liked this bloke – he was utterly clear-eyed about the Iraq mess, a step or two to the left of Chomsky. He felt he could talk to me without being judged. But he was going to sit in a concealed place and shoot people from a half mile away. What is owed in such situations? Pure human solidarity, I guess. I hugged back.

A 9/11 deployment is a helluva PR act by the military – especially since it's mostly bullshit. Most of the troops going from here are going to Fort Dix and other bigger despatch camps where they'll cool their heels for weeks or months before going OS.

No politicising 9/11? Yeah, right. McCain's website has a huge 9/11 banner with the 'Serve something other than yourself' legend on it, the Republican Convention ran a 9/11 clip that was effectively a snuff movie (shots of falling people 'n all), and, of course, the Democrats have just let them waltz right in and do it, too pissweak to assault Republican complacency, duplicity and arrgghhhh.

It's not a 'snowmobile', it's a 'snow machine'.

Everything's coming at once today, including Palin's first TV interview with ABC's Charlie Gibson, which was basically an attempt to trap her into a foreign policy idiocy. She avoided everything but then got cornered into saying that if Georgia was invaded by Russia when a NATO member, the US would have to go to war, a shockingly consistent argument which has no place in current discussions.

There's no business like snow business . . .

Obama and McCain are doing back-to-back TV interviews on PBS, following the 9/11 ceremonies where they had walked around together giving out flowers to 9/11 survivors, firemen, etcetera, like a pair of ageing debutantes.

'Serve something greater than yourself,' McCain rasped. 'It doesn't have to be the military. The peace corps, Ameri-Corps – these are all forms of acceptable pseudo-fascistic soft power . . .'

(I made that last bit up.)

But seriously, what is all this creepy stuff about service and collective national identity all of a sudden? For a society founded on liberal individualism, it's a creep-out. The whole point of the American Revolution was to create a place whose meaning was a product of the sum total of the individual pursuit of life, liberty and happiness by its citizens, within the framework of a strictly minimal law.

Snow news is good news.

Both major parties are now collaborating on some Mussolini-ish corporatism where the meaning of your life flows from service to the state. Is this the next stage in America's fraught obsession – fleeing from exurban anomie – after a brief flirtation with ludicrous religion? To the point where a young man, signed up again to go to a war he doesn't believe in, has become the epitome of sentiment, a killing machine who needs a hug?

Snow job.

And a mother will send off her son to possible death for the assembled media ('If we hold you a little tighter, if there's a tear in our eye, please understand,' Sarah Palin told the assembled troops) as forty press photographers snap and thirty journalists clack clack a report of this tender moment down the wires. Hugs – who doesn't need them?

It's snow go the bogeyman, it's snow go the Ghandi,
All we want is a nice little war, a nice little war would be handy.
The glass is falling hour by hour, the glass will fall forever,
But if you break the bloody glass you won't hold up the weather.
(With apologies to Louis MacNeice)

By the end of the week, every aspect of Palin's life had been put on display, from her early prowess at sports – 'Sarah Barracuda', she was known as – her peripatetic tour through five 'universities' (really, tech colleges) in search of a degree, her move from the Pentecostalist Assemblies of God to an even whackier church, the role of 'first dude' Todd Palin in shaping the Alaska budgets while she was in power as governor, her inquiries as to whether she could ban books from the library during her first term as mayor of Wasilla, her refusal to support her own stepmother's mayoral campaign (she was pro-choice) after she had supported Sarah, and on it went . . .

But lurking behind it all, and getting real interesting, was 'Troopergate', the ongoing investigation into whether Palin had sacked a police commissioner who had refused to sack a trooper who happened to be Palin's sister's ex-husband, the couple now locked in a bitter custody battle. Palin had set up the inquiry before she was nominated VP – because under Alaska state law she had carte blanche to sack him without cause, in any case – but the national scrutiny meant that the Palins and the national Republicans were suddenly keen to shut the thing down damn quick. Unfortunately for them, state Republicans were supporting the Democrats in seeing the inquiry go ahead. And that's why things are starting to heat up in the icy north.

ANCHORAGE: FRIDAY, 12 SEPTEMBER

'We're going to need some more, Frank,' the dapper state Senate aide said to the beefy security guard, who was putting out another row of stackable chairs at the back of Room 200 in the Alaska legislative building in Anchorage.

'Frank, we ain't got any more,' said the guard.

It was 8.45 a.m. and the room was already full to bursting, with a dozen camera news crews at the back setting up, stealing each other's pitch. In one corner, the *Wall Street Journal* reporter had commandeered the only power outlet and set himself up a little mini-office, tapping furiously into a laptop and mumbling into an iPhone cradled between shoulder and neck folds.

'Where are you from?' I asked the guy next to me.

'*New York Times.*'

'And you?' I asked the two women beside him.

'We're all from the *Times.*'

Out the window, in 4th Avenue, you could hear whooping. It was PDF day in Alaska, when every Alaskan adult gets a couple of grand from the royalties on the oil from the North Slope – and an extra grand, courtesy of Governor Sarah Palin, who designated it an 'energy rebate' payment. More on that later. Here, something else was going on. As a dozen Alaska pols milled about making nervous small talk – men in suits last fashionable in the late '80s, women dressed like maths teachers, and a Fred Thompson look-alike in full hunting camouflage – Senator Hollis French sailed in, took the chair's chair, banged the gavel on the scrimshaw pad and announced that 'the Joint Judiciary Committee would come to order'. Troopergate was about to start a new chapter.

Troopergate is the rather unsatisfactory name for the Sarah Palin scandal that has engulfed Alaska for the last month or so, and is now spreading to the nation at large – the accusation that Governor Sarah Palin sacked Public Safety Commissioner Walter Monegan because he failed to sack State Trooper (i.e. rural cop) Mike Wooten, Sarah's sister's ex-husband, after the couple's messy divorce. Accusations about the incident swirled for months and Palin eventually agreed to a proposal from the (Republican-controlled) legislature that a special investigator be appointed to clear the whole mess up.

The investigator, former Anchorage DA Steve Branch-flower, began collecting witness statements and all was going swimmingly – until the day that 'Walnuts' McCain got up to announce that he'd selected Sarah Palin as his running mate. That afternoon, as Branchflower tells it, the hammer came down. The Palins clammed up, their friends clammed up, the state clammed up. Branchflower and the Committee chairman announced their intention to seek subpoenas compelling witnesses to testify. And that was why the world's media was assembled in downtown Anchorage for the business of a committee that usually attracted a bored AP reporter and local loons.

Juicy stuff. But 'Troopergate'? Booooooring.

'We should call it Glaciergate, it's been going so long,' I whispered to the Reuters correspondent, who acknowledged my wisdom with her total silence.

Then Steve Branchflower took the witness stand and the whole thing went spack.

Glaciergate has been dismissed as piffling by the right-wing media. On the national scale of things, it is – though not to Monegan, whose sacking the Governor attributed to his alleged incompetence. But as always, and as people never seem to realise, it is never the crime but the cover-up that has the judge reaching for the black cap. For Branchflower's quiet testimony – a list of people he wanted to subpoena and why – told a tale of small-town heavy tactics and everyday gangsterism that laid the story bare. Though by agreement Governor Sarah Palin had been excluded from the subpoena list, it extended to everyone around her, including all her staff and her husband Todd.

Most of this was expected by the local press who have been on the thing for months, and it was only at the end that there was an intake of breath when Branchflower told the Committee that he'd been contacted by a whistleblower – an insurance agent who had been heavied to deny Wooten's insurance compensation claim, but had refused. The call, the agent claimed, came from the Governor's office.

That revelation sent the whole thing spinning, because no one had known about it, not even the Democrats pushing hard for the inquiry to be concluded before the election date. If true, it's evidence of a more forthright process of intimidation than had previously been suspected. If true – and Branchflower's report will hit the public prints on 10 October, three weeks before the election – it may well paint Palin and those around her as vindictive, petty power junkies, northern exposure Nixonians.

That this may be the result is looking more likely, as further reports emerge of what exactly the Palin reign involved, in both Wasilla and the state as a whole. *The New York Times*, in particular, has managed to get half the town on record, providing a picture of Palin as someone who has filled state offices with barely or unqualified cronies, most of them former high-school classmates. Todd Palin appears to be heavily involved with the actual exercise of power, calling legislators to heavy them about hiring 'enemies' of Palin. There are also accusations of the use of the governors' office for party business, the use of personal email addresses because 'they couldn't be subpoenaed', the attempted intimidation of critical bloggers, and on it goes.

Quite possibly some of it is the tittle-tattle of disgruntled rivals and the usual small-town crap, but there's a lot of it, and a lot of actual evidence, including emails gained from FOI requests. If Glaciergate finds direct evidence of criminal abuse of power, then it will all be thrown in together and Palin's image will change from that of local heroine to village dictator.

Indeed, the gloss is already starting to come off, if just a little.

The moment currently being replayed around the traps is her stumble on an interview question of whether or not she agreed with 'the Bush doctrine'. Given that everyone, not least Bush, has been trying to work that out for five years, it wasn't a huge thing of itself. But the manner in which Palin stumbled – suggesting the whole interview was a crammed exam – would have focused many who saw it on the real proposition of a President Palin. News that she not only had eagerly sought congressional 'earmark' funding, but that when John McCain campaigned against the practice in 2001 he had singled out some of her earmarked bills for ridicule, sent the Republicans into an 'up is down' process of barefaced lying. McCain himself attempted to stonewall all such accusations during his appearance on *The View* (an all-female morning program featuring Whoopi Goldberg and Barbara Walters, among others) – forty minutes which must have had him longing for a concrete cell in Hanoi.

In response, the right has ramped up the Culture War thing about any inquiry into Palin being some sort of elitist assault on blah blah blah. (Mind you, some of the commentary has been pretty snobbish. The *Anchorage Daily News* rounded up some of the descriptions of Wasilla and was particularly irritated by the portrayal of the town as 'a small unkempt-looking place, defined by a series of out-of-town stores, a huge lumber yard, a ramshackle bar named the Mug Shot saloon with Harley Davidsons parked outside . . .', in a paper named *The Australian*. Anyone know anything about this smarmy inner-city feuilleton?) The FOX News report on the Glaciergate subpoena hearings were a classic of this malarkey, constructing it as a Democrat shakedown. They failed to mention that the subpoenas had been ordered on the vote of a Republican senator, one Charlie Huggins, the camouflage dude. The House Committee voted separately and all four Republicans voted for the subpoenas. Huggins stilled the room by observing that he had been called in from moose hunting for all of this (yeah, they really talk like that – *Northern Exposure*, by my estimation, was a studied understatement of this place) and said he wanted this resolved because he thought of 'Walt Monegan's 90-year-old mother Betty, and you know, I have looked Betty in the eye . . .'

After that, everyone adjourned to the Fletcher Christian Bar in the Captain Cook Hotel (yes, he discovered this joint too), a huge, old poo-brown behemoth with toffee wood-panelled interiors that recalled 1976. There we watched the Chivas flow as the Anchorites (?) went hell for leather to burn through their PFD cash. 'Rumours that some energy rebate may be spent on energy bills,' the newspaper headline had noted drily that morning. Ha ha, not in the Fletcher Christian Bar.

Everything comes from the oil royalties and federal grants. In thirty years, Alaska has amassed $35 billion in dividend funds – Norway in the same period has raised $400 billion and earned a bunch more from reinvesting it. Meanwhile the state has become an advertisement for public squalor, with just about the worst state stats on every social indicator from health to literacy, the result of chronic social underinvestment. Palin came late to that process but she ramped it up to a higher degree – and has made what she's done a symbol of good Republican governance.

What? Oh yeah, of course John McCain is the presidential candidate. But look, not even Republicans give a rat's. The moment Palin left his side his audience numbers went through the floor and the demographic shifted back to the God's waiting room end of things. By the time she rejoins him this week in Carson City (it looks like they may be on the road together permanently), her image will have begun to shift.

'Man, are you a reporter?' said a pale guy in a tracksuit and Russian hitman shave, to the network field producer next to me. 'I've got a Palin story.'

The producer sighed, flipped his notebook and drew angry crosses as the white Russian described an unsatisfactorily-ruled-upon petty claims court fandango, and Governor Palin's unaccountable refusal to overrule the Alaska Supreme Court.

Out the window, before a roiling grey sky, Alaskan ravens – black, turquoise and white, pure shots of colour and grace – were alighting on the totem outside City Hall, which depicts a raven god bringing the moon and stars to earth. Glaciergate may yet be a mere stoush in the Fletcher Christian Bar, or the heavens may fall. Come October, we will find out.

WASILLA: MONDAY, 15 SEPTEMBER

Mountains in the distance, bright sharp air, gleaming lakes to the west and to the east . . . God, Wasilla is a dump. Etcetera. Old wooden township swallowed by sprawl between the lakes. The bus stops in a sort of strung-out sprinkle of streets and shops.

'Which way is the centre of town?' I ask.

'This kinda is the centre of town,' the driver replies.

Strung-out is right. Like in that vampire film *Thirty Days of Night* (shot in New Zealand, but set in Alaska), there are kids with gaunt faces and bad skin sloping around town. Crystal meth capital of the state, apparently – last year forty-eight meth labs raided in the municipality. Forty-eight! No wonder Palin's so friggin' energetic – Nazi crank everywhere.

Old town at the centre and then the rest between the lakes. Everyone wants their slice of countryside, which makes the whole thing a sort of Arthur/Martha place. Big box stores and mini-malls strung out along the highway. Journos in the Mocha Moose cafe, comparing notes. I ask them if they've felt intimidated in Palin central. Palin has more enemies here than in the rest of the state, says one.

Cab driver laughs when I ask to go to the sports complex. 'We can do the whole Palin tour if you like.' We go to a gleaming new building, Palin's masterpiece, a giant indoor sports stadium – the Palindrome, if you will. It blew the city budget sideways. Fifteen million, it cost, and it's now surrounded by litigation because it's not certain the city properly acquired the land it's on. We pass back along the highway and the famous library, a dowdy place in an old house established when Wasilla was a small town of 3000 or so. The area's doubled and again in the last fifteen years, as Anchorage workers have built houses, but the library's been starved of funds. Now there's more information that Palin *did* try to ban a book, a thing by a liberal evangelical preacher called *Pastor, I Am Gay*, emphasising tolerance.

Sport versus books – pretty much the Palin pattern. The government budgets during Palin's reign show the Republican appetite for public squalor as public policy at its worst. Buckets of money for sports complexes everywhere, several half-million grants plus for Astroturf. Every budget application for classroom computers, library upgrades, slashed. This in a state with the forty-eighth worst record in education (no one will ever beat Alabama to the wooden spoon).

'We're pretty fond of Sarah round here,' the bartender tells me at the Great Bear Brewing Co.

No shit, Einstein. Cos she fought corruption?'

'No, cos of all the neat stuff she got us.'

True dat. Wasilla gleams with road improvements, airport improvements, etcetera etcetera, while the rest of the state – and Anchorage in particular – has fared less well.

Bad head. Late night at Alaska's premier strip club, the Alaskan Great Bush Company. Not my fault, that's what it's called.

'Where are the good bars?' I'd asked the Inuit trawler fish-sorter beside me on the plane up.

'Best place is the Bush Company – it's a strip club.'

Do I look like a strip club regular? I thought. Then, don't answer that, I thought.

'Seriously . . . Everyone goes there.'

True dat. An old, wild west-style saloon, with a lot of

bumping and grinding up the front, and a mixed crowd at the back. Canadian whisky cheaper than coke, and stickier. Half the girls were Russians, so, à la Palin, the visit counted as foreign-policy research.

Woke up on floor of the living room of my 'executive suite' (living room with fold-out bed) with the OJ trial blaring from the TV. Shit, finally brain damage. Hallucinating that it's 1994. No, hang on, it's an entirely new trial. 'I was selling a baseball signed by a famous corrupt baseball commissioner and OJ and friends came in with guns,' said the witness. OJ's charged with armed robbery for stealing back stuff of his that was being sold by a man described by his own lawyer as a 'hustler'.

Flick channel while waiting for cab to Wasilla. American economy apparently collapsing.

Proposition: Palin's Wasilla, Palin's Alaska, is America writ small – running on pork and privilege, deluding itself with tales of frontier ingenuity. Gleaming buildings, services downgraded everywhere. You have to pay for your own rape kit? Cash or direct debit if you think you're going to be needing one on a regular basis, a reasonable bet in Alaska.

Thinking about this, late afternoon, watching MSNBC with head on side on cool counter of ice-cream shop.

'Alright if I just lie here and buy an ice-cream I don't eat?'

'Sure honey, people do that all the time.'

The week after cheque day, but everyone's got hang-overs anyway.

The news is that Palin's not going to cooperate with the investigation she herself started into Glacier/Troopergate. No big surprise, but will Todd Palin, the first dude, respond to a subpoena?

There was a great story in *The New York Times* yesterday about Todd, and much more besides – like, how Palin basically hired all her high-school friends to run the government, including appointing someone as Agriculture Commissioner on the grounds that they have 'always liked cows'. But the real deal is the report on Todd, who was apparently heavily involved in decision-making, budget meetings, etcetera, throughout Palin's governorship.

Is the first dude two heartbeats away from the Presidency? The Palins were part of the Assemblies of God pentecostalist church for yonks, which teaches a 'surrendered wife' view of marriage; i.e. that the bloke is head of the family, as a mirror of God being head of the world. Be scared. Be very scared.

I took the train back to Anchorage. It's cool that it whistle-stops – you can pick it up anywhere along the line. Old worlde charm, long since los—WOULD YOU STOP BLOWING THAT FRIKKIN' WHISTLE.

Small-town values: I can live with trains and Nazi crank, but I don't think that's what McCain/Palin have in mind when they talk about it. How hard is it not to have a brain-dead zombie smack town with all this oil around?

Any attention the ins and outs of Glacier/Troopergate might have received on the national media was severely truncated by the apparent fact that the economy is collapsing, with the simultaneous bankruptcy of Lehman Brothers investment bank, the folding of Merrill Lynch into Bank of America and the wobbling of Goldman Sachs.

And McCain–Palin are pulling ahead in all the polls.

ANCHORAGE: TUESDAY, 16 SEPTEMBER

Down the road in the Superior Court this morning, Republican lawyers are up on their hind legs making a last-ditch plea to try and stop Glacier/Troopergate subpoenas. Since the subpoenas were issued by a legislative subcommittee, I can't even begin to understand the basis of law on which they're working, but nor can anyone else, even the lawyers.

The parties are spread out across the tables at opposite ends of the Snow City Cafe, the standard-issue funky cafe that I suspect is airdropped into remote cities everywhere, whereupon they just fold open with instant Gaggia machines, riotgrrrl waitresses and notice boards advertising spoken-word gigs and vacancies for bass guitarists.

'This is nothing, isn't it?' I asked one guy in the queue for coffee.

'Off the record . . . this is nothing.'

'I guess I should ask one of the Republicans.'

He looked tired. 'I am one of the Republicans.'

Someone showed me the court calendar. Apprehended violence order, apprehended violence order, opposed custody agreement, sexual assault deposition, apprehended violence order, ex parte injunction against special investigator, apprehended violence order . . .

Funny, I don't remember drunken gang rapes in *Northern Exposure*. Must have missed that episode.

This is a place that proudly advertises itself as nowhere. It's three days into the world financial meltdown and it still hasn't hit the last frontier, cushioned as it is by last week's cheques.

'Is that a dividend tip?' a waitress said across the counter.

'No, I want some of the twenty back.'

I'm flying out today (to the Lower 48, as we Alaskalans say) with all my exciting Woodward–Bernstein leads eaten up by *The New York Times*. They have three reporters and two stringers here, who are set for the long haul, renting apartments, or so the gossip has it.

I would like to stay, and not only because the beauty is so eerie that you could almost believe – along with Sarah Palin's loopy church – that Alaska is the promised land, the last place on earth, the redoubt for Christians during the seven years of struggle with the dark angel.

But also because here it's slightly easier to ignore the stunning, endless, utter ineptitude of the Obama campaign, and their determination to lose under any circumstances.

Consider: the damn financial system is crashing, and doing so because of the deregulation of it put in place by, among others, Phil Gramm, John McCain's economic advisor. McCain says the fundamentals of the economy are sound, that only $5 million-plus is rich and that he doesn't know how many houses he owns. His advisor says the recession is a 'mental' one, while another advisor, Carly Fiorina, says Sarah Palin isn't fit to run a company (and only later adds McCain and Obama to that list).

Yet still Obama is getting no traction on the financial disaster issue. And McCain, bloody McCain, for all his stumbles, is adding to his image as a maverick, a 'trustbuster' who's going to make trouble for the 'fat cats' on his own side.

'This has got to be good for Obama,' says Brit Hume on FOX News.

'Yes, but the Democrats should be streets ahead,' says a commentator, 'and they aren't.'

Damn right. McCain comes on gangbusters and spits bullets about sticking it to the greedy Wall Street types who are betraying the honest American worker, and hell, *I* want to vote for him. He sounds like the type of guy who can sort this out.

Obama comes on, whines about McCain, and throws some nine-syllable words around about a 'failure of regulatory oversight'.

How has this come about? Simple. From day one the Obama campaign has refused to attack the Republicans for one very central failing – that they're Republicans. That they represent the rich. That they have impoverished large sections of middle America. That there is such a thing as class.

Why did they fail to do this? Because of the same failed, stupid advice by the loser political professionals that sit at the centre of the Democratic party like heart cancer, working overtime devising new ways to lose without honour. Their thought has always been that American politics will not bear class warfare, that you have to talk in the language of false universalism – we're all in this together, we've got to find consensus.

Well, to quote Kirk Douglas from Billy Wilder's great satire *The Big Carnival*: 'We're not all in the same boat – I'm in the boat, you're in the water.'

Because the Democrats left a vacuum where a populist class politics should be, John McCain is moving into that space, marshalling a right populism last associated with Teddy Roosevelt. And he is getting away with it! He is frikkin' getting away with it!

He has more lobbyists in his campaign than . . . than a very big lobby full of people . . . and he's getting away with it!

Really, it's a retroactive judgment on Obama. I'd always assumed that he'd shift out of the 'hope-change-love-all-serve-all' rhetoric after the primaries, but that hasn't happened. There is something vacant, something absent about Obama, some sort of lack of understanding about what is required – in terms of message, in terms of sound bites, in terms of sheer fight.

Hell, what would Hillary be making of this? McCain and the Republicans would be sashimi.

Of course, the Democrats may still win. God help us, that would almost be worse. Staggering along with the same crap crowd, scraping in by one state when they should be clear by ten.

If they lose, of course, they will blame Nader.

The way things are running, these subpoenas will be over-turned and Palin will be home-free on Glacier/Troopergate.

I've had no luck in having this scandal renamed. Approaching an aide to Tony McAllister, Palin's governmental press secretary, I outlined the 'Glaciergate' case. He had time to listen cos he's got fuck-all else to do – the McCain campaign have cut Palin's Alaska staff out of all media management.

'Pal,' he drawled, 'we'd do it if anyone listened to a thing we said.'

Rain slanting sideways outside, 3 p.m. Winter is coming, but first there is fall.

7

DON'T PANIC. (OKAY, NOW PANIC)

In DC for Meltdown '08

NEW YORK: FRIDAY, 19 SEPTEMBER

'Yah, I think the whole problem is the CFMA – that was crazy,' the Ukrainian supermodel said, reaching for the seasoned almonds.

It was Friday evening and we were watching the American economy collapse out the floor-to-ceiling windows of a fifth-floor loft she was thinking of buying in SoSoHo (South of SoHo . . . okay, Chinatown).

She wasn't going to need no mortgage, but she seemed to know her onions. Seven foot eight and burnished bronze, she'd arrived out of the lift in installments, limbs unfolding like a Cubist triptych, talking about the failure of the two-party system. Part Canadian, her background clearly combined prudence with an appreciation of the nearness of mass catastrophe.

Twelve hours earlier I had been in the Anchorage airport bar trying to convince a bearded guy who wouldn't take his hood off that Obama was not a Muslim.

'Well, okay man!' he'd shouted. 'Here's my address for the politically correct squad! I just know what I know . . .'

Now we were back in the Big Rotten Apple. It was the first night of the New York Burlesque Festival but all anyone could talk of was the collapse of insurance goliath AIG, even supermodels.

God bless America.

God help it too, if this mess continues. With the first presidential debates days away, there's suddenly a whole lot of new and urgent subject matter. Doubtless by now the journalistic team have written and torn up two entire sets of questions, as every day brings fresh news of what President Nixon used to call 'the exact length and width of the shaft'.

'Lipstick on a pig'? What was that all about? 'Bridge to nowhere'? What the f—? The multiple financial collapses, with AIG the latest to call for help, and the drafting of a $700 billion rescue plan for the sector as a whole, have concentrated the mind wonderfully. Especially because, as Democratic congressional leader Harry Reid says, 'No one knows what to do about it'.

For McCain it's been a nightmare, as anything that even vaguely reminds people that the place has been run by Republicans for the past eight years is bad for business. The GOP's standing hasn't been helped by McCain's wobbly set of remarks on the matter, going from calling the economy fundamentally sound, then reversing and saying it was a crisis, then saying that by 'fundamentals' he meant the American worker – who is 'sound', presumably, because their hands haven't dropped off or something – then blaming the whole crisis on Barack Obama for having had an advisor who once worked for mortgage giant Freddie Mac, now subject to federal takeover. Then he said that they shouldn't bail out AIG. Then that they should.

Sarah Palin threw her bit in by saying that Freddie Mac and sister company Fannie Mae had been 'a burden on the taxpayer for too long', which suggests she thought they'd been taxpayer-subsidised for years, when they hadn't. But she got away with it because people remembered the recent bailout, which was on Johnny/ette Paye's tab.

With all that sort of slipping and sliding around, Obama's flat numbers couldn't help but come up, and political news site *RealClearPolitics* has him running at an average of 2.1 per cent ahead now. He's playing it statesmanlike, eschewing John McCain's crackerjack populist 'Let's reform Wall Street!' act, which is taking old Walnuts dangerously close to sounding ridiculous to just about everyone. Instead, Obama's said, 'Blah blah blah, too important for politics, will not be issuing a statement on the proposed Federal plan until I've studied the details, etcetera', which is responsible and wise and prudent and ARRRGGGHHHH! It's Team Obama again – never saw a chance for division they didn't want to pass up, never saw a vacuum they didn't abhor. Obama's holding off on a statement may be wise politically (and, you know, wisdomly), but for God's sake – sitting at the heart of the McCain team is Phil Gramm, who was instrumental in the Commodity Futures Modernization Act of 2000. The Act basically ensured that a whole lot of derivatives and credit default swaps would fall between the regulatory cracks, which is consequently where all the spare money has crowded into in the last eight years. Gramm tacked the CFMA onto a broader bill, and if he were later proved to be a known associate of Mohamed Atta, the whole thing would make more sense than any other explanation. Gramm's influence on Walnuts McCain (he was moved from view after his comment about the recession being an imaginary one of 'whiners') was clear in McCain's earlier statement about the strong economic fundamentals. Just as he relies on Joe 'douche bag' Lieberman for foreign policy details, he doesn't stagger far from the side of Phil. But his advisors must have yelled in his face until he came round to something recognising the fear and loathing gripping middle America.

Of course, Obama is limited in his ability to hack into Republican incompetence as regards the CFMA and a whole lot of other stuff because the President who signed it into law was – drum roll – Bill Clinton! Yes, after Bill rolled over and submitted to the whole neoliberal agenda, and with the 1994 Republican takeover of Congress, there's so much that leads back to him that anyone wanting to keep him in the circle would avoid any discussion of such matters absolutely.

Anyone who did want to.

'It's amazing because I don't meet anyone who would vote for John McCain,' said the supermodel. Free jazz played softly through the Danish speakers.

'That's because the rest of the nation thinks New York is

an island of Jewish Communist homosexual pornographers and . . . I kind of agree with them,' I said. Well, Woody Allen said, but I repeated.

'Thank you – I am glad someone said that,' she replied, clinking glasses with me. In the corner, her lithe boyfriend smoldered like a stick of incense, and not the good stuff.

Clinton has given Obama less than nothing in the last two months, partly because the Obama camp hasn't come a-courting. There would be a good argument now for throwing the Clintons overboard and damning the last twenty-five years of wanton deregulation from either side of the house, thus presenting Obama as a candidate of real change. But this was the week they decided they wanted – *needed* – Bill and Hillary back, to give them the oomph that their own presidential candidate can't provide. So they're running dead on any past recriminations. Either that or it's force of habit.

The truth is that the dimensions of the current financial collapse are so great as to terrify anyone who believes this system should survive and knows its vulnerabilities. There is no guarantee that the $700 billion – say that again, SEVEN HUNDRED BILLION, or $3500 from every American adult – being proposed by the Bush administration will actually fix the gaping hole in the global financial system.

But as my good friends Jim Hightower and Philip Frazer have noted in *The Hightower Lowdown*, the one thing it will do is promote a massive transfer of power from Congress to the Executive, and one that the Democrat-controlled Congress is willing to surrender up without provisions, which suddenly puts Treasury (and its sinister, robot-head-on-a-stick man Paulson) in charge of getting everyone out of the mess they got them into in the first place.

And – well, let the supermodel tell it: 'Isn't dar a whole audo industry bail oud on der way?'

Indeed there is, another package of many billions for a dying industry. Furthermore, the AIG mess opens the gate to the whole world of instantly insured swaps. Of these, as John Quiggin noted in political blog *Crooked Timber*, the largest field is interest rate swaps, with a value of $300 trillion ($0.3 quadrillion) – just to point out where we are.

Of course, this started with the savings and loan scandals of the late '80s, and shysters like Charles Keating and his congressional supporters such as, ohhhhhhh . . . John McCain.

If Obama can't get five points clear on all this, shoot your dog.

'You can see for a long way,' said the supermodel on the loft terrace.

'That's where the Twin Towers used to be,' I said, pointing randomly. 'It's amazing how nothingness is in fact prior to presence and determines it.'

She thought for a minute, then put her drink down on the Robert Rauschenberg-esque coffee table.

'I really have to be somewhere else.'

NEW YORK STATE: MONDAY 22 SEPTEMBER

Out of New York along the edge of the Bronx, taking the long route to get a last glimpse at Yankee Stadium, the venerable home of New York baseball for more than eighty years and about to be demolished and replaced . . . The way that this evisceration of a beloved landmark has proceeded has been familiar: a relentless PR effort by management and especially players to sell the move as necessary, a birth not a death, etcetera etcetera.

They need to say this because there's a mute melancholy around about the decision. Pleasure grounds, sports stadiums, Luna Park or Princes Park – they're all places we associate with simple moments of happiness, of joy undiluted in a late goal or a home run, a lightness and presence we remember before it all went horribly wrong.

Saying that the 'tradition of the stadium will live on', as one after another multimillionaire player was wheeled on to affirm, is beside the point – these are concrete objects, sacred sites, they anchor us to place and time. Like a cathedral spire, a stadium can be seen from all places in the neighbourhood, from all approaches. But of course, nothing lasts for ever. Some stadiums, like Wembley, have to be replaced because the crowds simply dwarf them. So, didn't the Yankee have to die?

No is the answer, and you realise that as you come across the Triborough Bridge and see, rising behind Yankee Stadium . . . Yankee Stadium. Yes, they've already built its replacement just behind it – a copy done in high luxe fashion, the sort of faux-Roman style beloved of instant five-star hotels and wedding reception centres.

The new Yankee Stadium has been completed before the old is demolished and it's not so much larger than the original. As m'generous NYC benefactor Philip explained, such a move, part of a wave of demolitions, had nothing to do with capacity. It is so that class and corporate power can be cemented into the architecture, with corporate boxes in the new stadium piled to the sky and a total separation between the areas occupied by corporate clients (most of whom couldn't give a shit about a ball-and-stick game) and actual fans. In the old stadium, rich and poor would have to watch the game in something approaching common conditions – and that is surely part of the meaning of sport, its universal character. The new stadium hangs behind the old, a parallax error generated by the faulty vision of the last decade or so. The faux marble – a dead spit of Nicolae Ceausescu's monster edifices in Bucharest – shimmers and seems less substantial than the air around it.

'We gotta start getting tough with the CEOs. I mean, these guys get paid whatever happens.'

Some blowhard is on the radio as we cruise into New York State.

This morning, the fabled $700 billion blow-out has been sheeted towards the Democratically-controlled Congress, for them to deal with. It's a crock, of course, with the White House, represented by Treasury Secretary Paulson, trying to stampede everyone into signing a blank cheque without any provisions for re-regulation, social equity, an inquiry into how the whole damn mess occurred, limits on golden parachutes, etcetera etcetera. There's no time for that. Indeed the situation is so dire that Treasury really needs some elbow room to work.

Here is section eight of the plan: 'Decisions by the Secretary pursuant to the authority of this *Act* are non-reviewable and committed to agency discretion, and may not be reviewed by any court of law or any administrative agency.'

You have to wearily admire the chutzpah. The most immediate aspect of this crisis came about because oversight and regulation was removed from a key sector of the finance market, because, according to its advocates, the West's economy needed increased liquidity and velocity if it was to compete against the East. And now the solution is to abolish checks and balances altogether.

As New York City gave way to the drab and dilapidated towns of New York State – old diners with pink paint flaking off the windows, gas stations with signs for oil companies that no longer exist – reports on the radio had the bailout getting richer still, like the *Cloverfield* monster fattening itself on whole cities. By Tuxedo Junction, foreign banks were lining up to be part of the bailout – UBS, which pays Phil Gramm, making the loudest noise.

By Woodstock, Goldman Sachs and Morgan Stanley had turned themselves into commercial (rather than investment) banks, merely by saying so, and will thus be afforded greater guaranteed protection in return for reduced scope of operation.

This was . . . there are no words for this. It's like the scene in escape movies where the prisoners make inch-perfect uniforms from a grey sock and a tin of nugget and pass themselves off as the German general staff. Will they get away with it? It depends if they've got someone on the inside, like say, former Goldman Sachs partner and current Treasury Secretary Henry Paulson.

Yet even here in the heartland, passing farms to which nothing ever trickled down, the Democrats were still failing to sock home what to any half-effective political outfit would be the greatest gift of a decade.

'Well, I've always voted Democrat,' said one radio caller, when the tuner switched stations as we travelled between towns. 'But I just don't know if Obama has the experience. I mean what's his solution for this?'

I DON'T KNOW! I DON'T KNOW!

The Democrats are still on the defensive. Rather than piloting some ludicrous, populist bill called the *Flay the Rich Act* or something, they've given us a beautiful, responsible alternative bailout bill which makes them the Republicans' bitch again. Again.

We hit Burlington around evening. I bought a Coke, a local paper and a copy of the free state secessionist magazine. The paper had a Yankee Stadium story.

'That's sad,' the cashier said.

I looked up. She was wiping away a tear.

'They've built another one,' I said.

'It's never going to be the same,' she said.

Indeed it ain't. Indeed it ain't. All that looks solid is melting into air.

VERMONT: TUESDAY 23 SEPTEMBER

Heading towards the middle of the last week of September, with the first debate only days away, it suddenly became clear to everyone that America was lurching towards genuine crisis. Not a problem, not a dilemma, but crisis. As fall – season of death and tragedy – came to the northern half of the country, the Senate Committee on Banking, Housing, and Urban Affairs assembled in Washington to hear evidence from Fed Reserve chief Ben Bernanke and evil disembodied floating head Treasury Secretary Hank Paulson.

In the days prior, Paulson made a few preparatory noises about how there was no alternative to this move, dire consequences, etcetera, and in his testimony to the Committee he really dialled it up to eleven. After a few preparatory remarks by Committee Chair Chris Dodd, Paulson basically said that if the plan wasn't voted in, the whole American economy would immediately grind to a halt, as major corporations wouldn't be able to make the short-term loans they need to cover week-to-week payroll demand surges, and so on.

If he was hoping that this would stampede the Committee, he was direly mistaken. One by one the committee members put themselves on the record as to their 'frustration', 'desperation' and 'anger' at this desperate and hastily put together measure.

'We don't want to be stampeded,' Dodd said. 'There is no second act.'

'I'm going to have to answer to the people after January 21,' said another. Jim Bunning, Republican Senator from Kentucky, said, 'This is financial socialism. This is un-American'.

This was rather more than the token resistance than either Paulson or Bernanke had counted on and you could see the consternation in their faces. You could also hear in Paulson's voice, unless I am mistaken, genuine fear, as he detailed the cascading process by which the whole economy would fall apart.

The whole thing came wrapped off the airtubes midmorning, with everyone suddenly realising that this bailout wasn't a done deal anymore. As the full cost began to focus people's minds – a four-person American household is paying $10 000 for this thing, with no guarantee that it's the last ask – the sort of zombie drift to passing the thing was halted. What were we really getting for this?

Such thoughts were interrupted by a live cross to the UN for the opening of a General Assembly week. Suddenly there was Dubya, talking to the leaders of the world. It was really jarring, like one of those moments when a disappeared character is reintroduced into a soap by means of a dream sequence. A hundred million people were thinking, who is this trembling, grey-haired guy talking about America's role in the world in defeating extremism, when the auto-parts supplier/Starbucks/airline/lap-dance club I work at is just about to close?

Outside, a whole flank of New York had been shut down

to allow five hundred black limos to shark through the streets, and a big anti-Iran demonstration was underway in anticipation of President Ahmadinejad speaking to the gathering later in the afternoon.

'We shouldn't even let him into the city,' the demonstrators yelled, not really understanding the principle of hosting the UN. But they seemed to be getting a lot of support from passers-by.

'Damn right. I can't get to my car. Why do we have to have this thing at all?' said one man, taking a leaflet.

'Look, that's not what we're talking about AT ALL!' yelled an angry woman, but the guy was gone.

It was entertaining and on any other day it would have been the lead story, but this was a day when too much news wasn't enough and by midday we had a gazumper, though almost no one noticed it.

But all this, all this palaver was superseded by a single comment from Defense Secretary Robert Gates. On Tuesday, Gates cautioned against a rapid US military expansion in Afghanistan, stressing instead the need to build up the Afghan army.

'I think we need to think about how heavy a military footprint the United States ought to have in Afghanistan,' Gates told the Armed Services Committee, meeting down the hall from the Banking Committee, in the corridor of crises.

Note that? Seems innocuous, but this was the day that the US gave up on Afghanistan. Gates will be out in January, but he's basically saying that an Afghan surge ain't going to work. This comes a week or so after a vote in the French parliament about whether the country should stay there. It was lost, but the fact that it even got to a vote can be taken as a harbinger.

Europe will be out of Afghanistan in two years. The US may linger a little more, but Gates' testimony today was a quiet reminder that there was no point making a big commitment to it because it was a done deal. The Afghan army couldn't be stood up because the state doesn't exist beyond Kabul, and barely even there. President Karzai (who met Sarah Palin today, looking as always like a failed auditionee for a Merivale and Mr John commercial) is a useless pashmina horse.

Each crisis doubles the other, of course. The sudden collapse of the American economy has made the continuance of two wars practically impossible, and their leaching effect on liquidity would exacerbate any attempt at a genuine recovery.

By early evening everyone was back on the bailout plan and how it was a crock and probably wouldn't be enough. No one had a clue whether it would work or not but, as Senate Minority Leader Mitch McConnell said, 'it would pass easily'. I mean, who was really going to st—

APNewsAlert

II minutes ago

WASHINGTON (AP) — Sources say FBI investigating Fannie Mae, Freddie Mac, Lehman Brothers and AIG.

Omigod! That flashed onto my screen the same time it came on the networks and surely it must be the moment – about 7.17 p.m. EST – that the Paulson plan died.

There isn't much more information than that at this stage, but I would suspect it's enough. Every congressional member is saying they're getting calls ten-to-one against the bailout without conditions – will it even be possible to vote for it with this outstanding?

You should mark this day in your memory, folks. There are no planes flying into buildings, but this is the day when America was officially flipped over. Lost in a war with no solution, in a financial crisis that goes to the root of its system – crisis in the literal, medical sense, in that there is no way to tell whether the cure will save it or hurry it on to burial.

By evening I was lying flat out in the jet spa of the Days Inn Burlington with reddish trees tapping the window in the wind as I watched Larry King interview President Ahmadinejad, an event that othertimes would have got banner headlines but today seems like a tepid line-up. Hilariously, Ahmadinejad sounded like a San Francisco Democrat on Palestine and like a Southern Republican on homosexuality ('It's a health problem, but we don't care what people do in their homes'). Give credit to that old goatfucker King – a man with more wives than any given Muslim – it was a breakthrough interview, if only because President A sounded four times as intelligent as most US politicians ('America should limit its political influence to its immediate geographical region and use the money for the people's health').

Amen to that. Earlier in the day I'd become a de facto provider in the American health-care system. The woman in front of me in the pharmacist's queue was crying (Americans cry a lot these days). She had had her insurance card refused – some rock-bottom scheme she joined, maybe after seeing it on a 2 a.m. infomercial, not realising it only covered New Jersey. She was ineligible for Medicare and so was exposed to the full cost of the anti-seizure medication she needed – 130 bucks, which would have been about $40 under the Australian PBS.

She had her own meltdown, pure tears of despair. If it was a scam, it was a better performance than anything in the New York Burlesque Festival, that's for sure. I gave her thirty bucks, another bloke gave twenty, the pharmacist knocked down the price, and we scraped it together. She had never asked any of us. She travelled for some online services company, but mostly on commission. Her business suit was cut-price, her car was ten years old.

I would venture to suggest that this is not a world-standard health system at work.

History is hard to feel when it's happening, but, hell, this is it. Whatever this country comes out as from this, it won't be the place that went in around 2000 – the giddy world of irony and dotcoms.

It was amazing to our ancestors that the world died in the fall. They made burnt offerings, cut the throats of their enemies, their weak, their children, in some effort to stave it off. But die it did. And when the next spring came, not everyone was there to see it.

WEDNESDAY, 24 SEPTEMBER

Tonight, George W Bush emerged for the second time in two days – a little creepy, like something out of *Sunset Boulevard* – to address the nation on the gathering crisis. God knows what his staff are pumping him full of, but it's keeping him upright at the price of eating him away from the inside. Has anyone ever looked less like they wanted to be addressing the nation at the time? Has anyone ever wanted more to be on their ranch at Crawford, clearing brush?

> BUSH: Many Americans have felt anxiety . . . I understand their worry and their frustration . . . We are in the midst of a serious financial crisis . . . I urge Congress to provide much needed money.

My God, can you imagine how Clinton or Reagan would be eating up this moment, to reassure the nation, to shine, to lead (even if Ronnie would have thought he was addressing a March of Dimes rally in 1943). (Google it.)

It was another bizarre day, a situation military strategists describe as fluid. In the morning, apparently, Barack Obama had called Walnuts McCain and suggested they put out a joint statement on the economy. By 2.30 p.m. Walnuts had called Obama back and agreed. He also confirmed his statement of the previous night that he was going back to Washington and suspending his campaign, i.e. continuing his campaign in Washington.

> BUSH: How did our economy reach this point? . . .For

more than a decade a massive amount of money flowed into America from investors abroad because our country is an attractive and secure place to do business . . . (microphone bumping hilariously)

HA!

McCain also suggested that Friday's debate (which is on foreign policy) be postponed so that everyone could deal with this crisis. Senate Leader Harry Reid then called McCain to say that he wasn't actually needed in Washington and would stuff the whole thing up in any case. By late afternoon, Obama had told McCain he wasn't suspending his campaign, no way no how, and Ole Miss, the university hosting the debate, had said it was going on even if neither of them turned up. Which was odd.

> BUSH: How did this financial crisis come about? . . . That's not a rhetorical question. I have no idea . . .
> *Here's how it happened. Once upon a time there were two bad bears called Fannie Mae and Freddie Mac . . .*

What was Walnuts thinking? This was a velly velly strange way of doing things, making him a plaintive petitioner to Barack Obama. Obviously it was an attempt to build on the theme of 'country first', but it simply looked like cutting and running. Is the McCain camp genuinely worried that, without Joe Lieberman by his side, he will simply screw up too much, talking about the defence of Formosa from the Teutonic Knights, etcetera? Maybe they're simply working on the idea that the man needs his sleep before such an event and that he just can't get that while having to focus on the economic stuff.

> BUSH: With the situation becoming worse by the day, I faced a choice . . . hide under the bed or go to Crawford. But they found me and put me in front of the microphone . . .

However, by far the worst result of McCain's move may have been pissing off David Letterman, on whose show he had been due to appear tonight. McCain cancelled this afternoon's taping and Letterman, after paying credit to the Republican's heroism, proceeded to tear him apart.

> BUSH: Ultimately we could face a long and painful recession . . .
> *Depression*, George. Depression.

LETTERMAN: Okay, he's a hero, but don't you think if you cancelled you'd send your second in command along – but where is she? She's nowhere.
PAUL: She's hot.
LETTERMAN: She's driving around in the white van waiting to pick him up.

> BUSH: Under my plan $700 billion will be given to the financial market . . . Wow, am I fucking doing this?

Letterman then cut to pre-feed of CBS where McCain was having his cancers dusted by a make-up girl before talking to Katie Couric.

BUSH: Over the years there have been various proposals to update our 21st century economy from its 20th century . . . And I have shit on them all . . .

Where indeed is Palin? The previous day there was a press revolt (and to get the pusillanimous American press up and yelling, you gotta be really obnoxious) after they were refused entry to Palin's meeting with various leaders, save for photographers. Today we got the word from the Pakistani president regarding the Republican vice-presidential candidate. She was 'gorgeous'. Doh.

Where is Palin, indeed? As the crisis has proceeded apace, she's just been ignored for the joke person she is. Team McCain don't want her anywhere near a microphone, although she already had an interview with Katie Couric, which is frikkin' hilarious. Here are the best bits:

COURIC: You've said, quote, 'John McCain will reform the way Wall Street does business'. Other than supporting stricter regulations of Fannie Mae and Freddie Mac two years ago, can you give us any more examples of his leading the charge for more oversight?

PALIN: I think that the example that you just cited, with his warnings two years ago about Fannie and Freddie – that, that's paramount. That's more than a heck of a lot of other senators and representatives did for us.

COURIC: But he's been in Congress for twenty-six years. He's been chairman of the powerful Commerce Committee.

And he has almost always sided with less regulation, not more.

PALIN: He's also known as the maverick, though, taking shots from his own party, and certainly taking shots from the other party. Trying to get people to understand what he's been talking about – the need to reform government.

COURIC: But can you give me any other concrete examples? Because I know you've said Barack Obama is a lot of talk and no action. Can you give me any other examples in his twenty-six years of John McCain truly taking a stand on this?

PALIN: I can give you examples of things that John McCain has done, that has shown his foresight, his pragmatism and his leadership abilities. And that is what America needs today.

COURIC: I'm just going to ask you one more time – not to labour the point. Specific examples in his twenty-six years of pushing for more regulation?

PALIN: I'll try to find you some and I'll bring them to you.

'He's also known as the maverick, though . . .' Oh, magic. It's almost as good as the YouTube video that shows Palin being protected from evil spirits by the laying on of hands by her crazy Kenyan pastor in Wasilla. Frik, what a day this was.

With McCain hanging from a twig like the 'Oh shit' kitten, Obama stepped in for the kill. I'm joking, of course. He didn't. Though it may make no difference, the lumbering Obama campaign was blindsided by McCain stealing the initiative on the economic meltdown. That barely worked for Walnuts, but then Dubya helped him out by summoning both to a Thursday meeting at the White House, which Obama agreed to.

Here's what Obama should have said:

'Today, John McCain suggested we suspend the first presidential debate on foreign policy because of the financial crisis. Well, I am happy to change the topic from foreign to domestic policy, but let me make it clear: I will be in Oxford, Mississippi on Friday night, whether Senator McCain is there or not. And if he is not, I will take any and all questions on any matter from the audience for two hours, and the networks can broadcast that, or not, as they wish.

Whoever becomes president will be dealing with this crisis for some time to come, and the American people have a right to hear what we think about these vital matters. It should be easily possible for both the Paulson plan and the debate to be attended to – these are, after all, the sort of multiple challenges a president would face. Senator McCain seems to believe that debate between the two candidates for the highest office is not important, which strikes me as pure contempt for the American people and the democratic process.'

Here's what he said:

'Ah, well, you know, I've been on the phone with Nancy Pelosi and Harry Reid and, you know, this is exactly the time we need to hear from the person who will be, uhhhh . . . leader in the next forty days, and uh, I think you should be able to do both things at once.' Whine, whine, whine. Besides, I called first.

That last bit was his aides, not Obama, but fuck, if these people don't win, they need to put up against a wall.

Man, I'm getting that crossroads feeling again. It's been with me ever since I started this gig. You know, the myth of the crossroads . . . Robert Johnson, who pretty much invented blues and rock'n'roll, was famed in his Mississippi hometown as a bad guitarist. He went away, came back and played like nobody had ever heard a guitar played before. 'Course, everyone said that it wasn't just a matter of hard work and talent. They said he'd sold his soul to the devil, and sooner or later the devil would come to take his due. Johnson was poisoned by a jealous husband at twenty-seven . . . But really, who's Johnson in this metaphor? And who's the crossroads? Is Obama the guy who's thrown it all away? Or is he about to be the road less travelled?

> BUSH: This is our opportunity to show the world that Americans are . . . a nation with ADD, incapable of anything other than two speeds: backwards and panic.

I made that last bit up, I made that last bit up, I made that last bit up . . .

THURSDAY, 25 SEPTEMBER

By the time John McCain flew into Washington today, having told David Letterman he couldn't appear on his show because he was flying out last night (and thus prompting Letterman to deliver a show's worth of baiting that may well cost McCain the campaign), the House had already cut a deal on the bailout. It wasn't a great deal, indeed it was pretty crap, but a deal it was. His flacks tried to make it look like he'd been there all along saying that McCain had spent 'most of the day in the office getting the lie of the land'. Pure lies, of course, but that's the stock in trade of the campaign these days.

The deal had been agreed upon even before McCain was wheels to the ground in DC. That was the last thing he needed, or wanted, so he spent a couple of hours sniffing around for an alternative – a proposal by conservative Republicans for a mortgage insurance plan that doesn't involve the government buying up four large investment institutions and trying to flog them off later. McCain could care about which plan went ahead. He just needed something to screw the whole thing up and put the place in turmoil, so that he could look like he was coming to the rescue – and maybe, as an added bonus, swing into the debate tomorrow at the last minute, the hero returning.

He can do this because he knows that Obama won't respond by attacking him directly. He won't go on TV and say: 'If you don't get paid next week, blame John McCain. He screwed up a deal in place that would have guaranteed that the Wall Street crisis didn't spread to main street. Those crucial forty-eight votes may cost us financial stability. John McCain is playing politics with your future.'

Yes, I'm writing campaign ads again. So are half the journos on this. Roland Martin was reduced to it on CNN today too, saying: 'If he doesn't show up, I'd just turn it into a town hall meeting. That's what I'd say if I were running the campaign, but I'm not.' It's the same frustration we all feel at this lack of assertion, this vacuum, this wimpiness, every time McCain pulls another fast one.

'Senate Majority Leader Harry Reid said he was "a little stunned" when he heard talk at the White House about a completely new plan drawn up by House Republicans.' – Reuters

Gee, amazing. Harry Reid was blindsided – that blinking Mormon moleperson, part of the lame Democratic leadership who seem to like getting hit again and again and again.

It was again, as the saying by now goes, a helluva day. Washington Mutual (WaMu) was seized by US regulators and is now to be purchased by JP Morgan, pretty much the last man standing. The bank had basically had a run on it since 15 September and had been tottering before that in any case. The slogan of their ghost ads, still playing: 'WooHoo! We got you covered!' Well, you were covered, but their arse was hanging out.

Rumpled Congressman Barney Frank was at least coming out fighting, saying that McCain had flown in and wrecked the deal, and comparing it to Nixon wrecking the peace talks in '68. Kudos to him for that, but Frank is an amiable, owlish figure with a lisp and it doesn't really have the force.

The B theory of McCain trying to delay the debate has been because he wants to knock out the VP debate and have it replaced by the first presidential match-up. As more snippets of Katie Couric's Palin interview appeared – Palin's rambling answer when asked to explain her claim that Alaska's proximity to Russia counts as foreign policy experience is just deliciously excruciating – you can see why. I reckon Team McCain is genuinely worried that she will fall apart completely on stage. Though she did answer four questions shouted over the jetwash today.

By the time all this was being digested (and a lot of it is still going on, with no one really having a clue where things are at), news came that the Pakistani military had fired on American troops and planes trying to cross the border from Afghanistan. Man, oh man, what is needed now is the killing blow. Choose one, Obama:

a) John McCain is acting politically and tactically, and putting the economy of this country at risk;

b) I respect John's sincerity, but these manoeuvres show poor executive judgement just as we're trying to work together here; or

c) To be frank, I'm a little worried about John. I really don't think he's thinking very clearly on this and that is cause for concern.

Pick one Barack, any one. Sheet it home, for godsake.

FRIDAY, 26 SEPTEMBER

'We don't meet foreign leaders with preconditions . . . When Nixon met Mao, he didn't . . . I mean, there had been meetings before . . .'

Halfway through the debate in Oxford, Mississippi, it looked like McCain was losing it. He'd been attacking Obama's statement that he would meet with foreign leaders without pre-conditions, and he'd suddenly wandered into a trap – for of course, Nixon's meeting with Mao had been assailed by many as a legitimation of a regime that, at the time, did not even sit at the UN. Suddenly his eyes looked wild – oh no, he was about to crash another expensive Navy jet. Would Barack Obama nail him – show him up as a fool? No. Instead, McCain went into more waffle about what he had actually said, and no, of course he wouldn't meet without preparation, etcetera etcetera, and once again he avoided the killing blow.

It was like that all night, a game of cat-and-mouse, a slow bicycle race, whatever metaphor you like for a debate in which neither candidate was willing to set out a whole encompassing philosophy, a whole approach to government. Days earlier, in New York, during a discussion – actually a drunken shouting argument – over politics, I had been reminded of a Kate Jennings poem that goes something like, possibly wildly wrongly: '*Blood on the Tracks*, dinner and an unsatisfactory fuck . . .' Never was there a better summary of the first presidential debate of 2008. It was the single most mutually unsatisfactory political consummation of modern times.

9.03 p.m. First question: Where do you stand on the financial recovery plan? Obama giving general spiel and then into his four-point response to the financial plan. 'This is a final verdict on the Republican party of eight years.' Tails off nicely.

McCain sucking up to Kennedy being in hospital, Republicans and Democrats sitting down together tonight – is he actually going to claim credit for people sitting down together? A bit cowed and calm. 'I went back to Washington . . .' He's rambling a bit. He sounds tired . . . rambling and unfocused.

Chair returns them to the plan – what do they think?

OBAMA: 'We haven't seen the language yet . . .' NOOOOOOO, don't go all technical. But then he comes back into claiming some credit for himself.

MCCAIN: 'President Eisenhower, before the '94 Normandy invasion . . .' The '94 invasion? Must have missed that. McCain rambling again, with no focus, no shape to his answer.

HA HA, McCAIN IS OBAMA'S BIYATCH, FOR THE MOMENT.

Obama passes up the opportunity to really sink the slipper: 'Ten days ago John said the fundamentals of the economy are strong . . .'

MODERATOR: 'Tell him what you really feel . . .' Jesus, this is like some sort of marriage counselling shtick.

Second question: Are there fundamental differences between your approach and Senator Obama's approach? McCain: 'Spending is the problem – we spent three million studying the DNA of bears in Montana . . . A criminal issue or a paternal issue . . .' Can't get his own gags right. Slates Obama for earmarks.

Obama slates McCain for the three hundred billion on tax

cuts for the rich, but he's wobbly and fey . . . McCain comes out stronger on the waste thing, then wanders into anecdote. Obama comes back strongly: 'I don't know where Senator McCain gets his figures from . . .' Slams him effectively. Go 'Bama.

McCain comes back pretty strongly with specific policies and ends by saying that people might be interested to hear what Senator Obama thinks of as rich. Obama should come back swinging here ('Well, you think that over $5 million is rich'), but he doesn't. He goes into specifics.

Obama started strong and is getting wobbly; McCain started weak and is getting stronger, feeding off Obama's energy. Jesus, Obama, fight back. This really is old material, very boring. Pick up the pace, guys.

We're off domestic policy now and back onto foreign policy, which is where McCain can get a few donkey punches in. Obama failed to really lay a few gloves onto him as a friend of the rich, etcetera, complicit in eight years of Bush.

The Iraq question – the weird thing about this is that McCain can bait Obama about the surge and land some points, but the American public don't really care – they just want out. A strange crossover. Obama starts to punch back and actually gets a bit of passion in, telling McCain he was wrong on the war, on WMDs, on etcetera etcetera. Then he stumbles. Arrrgghhhhhh.

It's running about even by my assessment, McCain getting a slight edge on the Iraq stuff. Question gets on to Afghanistan, and Obama really knocks a few out of the park about the failure there. McCain comes back saying that Obama is being too bellicose about Pakistan. Obama sounded presidential on this stuff, which is what he needs to do. McCain sounds very plaintive about his record voting on whether we go in or out, but then he gets back on to the military shtick and the voting worm goes up. Stuff about the bracelet a mother of a dead soldier gave him out at the airport. Obama: 'I've got a bracelet too.' We'z all got bracelets. 'No US soldier dies in vain.' Well, they do, but it's a good get.

10 p.m. One hour in and we're on Iraq. McCain gets into the usual shtick pitched to the Florida vote: '. . . an existential threat to Israel, blah blah blah'. Obama signs on to most of this. Goddamit, wouldn't you love him to say, 'Go Hezbollah! Victory to the revolutionary cadres!' But he won't. McCain gets into the 'won't talk to dictators' and then gets on to Nixon talking to Mao and nails himself badly.

Why doesn't Obama say, 'What are you so afraid of? What are you so afraid of? Aren't American interests paramount?' But he doesn't. And McCain nuts him.

Then we move on to Russia. I missed a bit of this because I was getting ice. When I came back McCain was banging on about Georgia and Ukraine. Here's what Obama should say: 'ARE YOU PLANNING THE NEXT WAR, JOHN? WOULD YOU GO TO WAR WITH RUSSIA FOR SOUTH OSSE-TIA?' But, of course, he doesn't. Wimp. He mumbles on about Russia etcetera, and then moves on to energy. Senator McCain has voted against alternative energy funding twenty-three times. HAMMER IT HOME! HAMMER IT HOME! Say it again: twenty-three times! Twenty-three times! But he doesn't.

Final question: '. . . the possibility of a 9/11-type incident?' McCain goes into a rambling thing about his involvement in the 9/11 Commission. Here is Obama's chance to shine, to clear the pack, denounce the whole last eight years. What does he say? 'We've improved supervision of chemical sites.' Why not, 'We've taken our eye off the ball in Iraq'? But he doesn't, but does, sort of, and ohhhhhhhhhhh . . . But hell, the viewer worms are going up and up and up. 'We have weakened our capacity to act around the world', etcetera etcetera. Then a general spiel about, well, everything, and he seems to sum things up. McCain really sinks the slipper – Obama does not have the experience.

OBAMA: 'Let me make a closing point – my father came from Kenya. He wanted to come to the US . . .' YES, YES . . . BUT WOULD YOU FUCKIN' ATTACK MCCAIN PLEASE? ATTACK HIM! He goes too long, then McCain gets a final bit in, but it isn't that great.

Wheeewwww. Neither nailed it. McCain got some shots in, but it was pretty much a draw.

In general the candidates kept themselves to narrow details and tried to catch each other out. You couldn't really have great hope for the health of the republic from either contribution to this encounter.

The times we're in demanded a bold statement about what America is and what it could be. We didn't get it here. There were obvious reasons for McCain to avoid doing that, after eight years of Republican domination, but what was Obama's excuse? Even if Obama wins in November, the story of this election – played out yesterday – will have been the failure of the Democrats to stake out a claim as the party of bold change, of moral politics, of a party on a mission. And if they lose, they will simply implode, and deserve to. Whether this is because Obama has been persuaded to act against his own political instincts by cynical and deadened professionals, or because it is an expression of his diffidence, only history will tell.

VERMONT: SATURDAY, 27 SEPTEMBER

Round Burlington, Vermont, the leaves are starting to turn in the first days of fall. Downtown, past the Ben & Jerry's store and the poet who writes verses to order on an old Underwood for a buck, there's a small demonstration taking place. There's no more than a dozen people, a mix of the newer, young urban types who've refashioned this old farming town over the past years, and the shaggier mountain types, descendents of the fiercely independent Green Mountain folk who made this state the only one that never voted for Franklin Roosevelt and his 'big-city socialism'.

Today they're united in a single objective: opposing the $700 billion bailout, which the Treasury Secretary has been trying all week to hustle through Congress. The day after it was announced, demonstrations erupted all over the country, including one on Wall Street, as people began to realise what was being proposed – that, with no guarantee of equity, social control, executive payout limits or capacity for public oversight,

Congress was seriously proposing to buy four major investment bodies at an average cost of $10 000 for every American
household.

As the seriousness of the financial crisis began to become
clear to many people over the past week, and the McCain and
Obama teams tried to pin the other by the shoulders, what was
most remarkable was the way in which the crisis seemed to be
changing the positions in one of the key debates of the election – the question of experience. Abstract notions about what
sort of CV and life experiences qualify someone to lead began
to yield to more concrete concerns, about what each of these
candidates would or could do in the teeth of this real and una-
voidable situation. Perhaps as importantly, it made visible how
much of the campaign to date had been based on an essential
unreality, a struggle for identity-defining and framework-setting
moments. As one of the youngest-ever presidential candidates
faced the oldest, much of the back and forth centred on the
question of experience.

From the moment he made clear his intention to seek the
nomination of the Democratic party, it was clear that one major
question hanging over Barack Obama's head would be that of his
relevant experience for the job. When he was selected to give the
keynote speech at the Democratic National Convention in 2004,
he most presumably thought that this would put him in position to be a prominent senator (at the time he was running for
the Illinois junior senate vacancy) and a presidential candidate
in sixteen, twelve or, at the earliest, eight years' time. If anyone

senior thought that he would begin his presidential run two years into his first senate term, they didn't mention it. And you have to go back a long way in the presidential campaigns – to Wendell Wilkie, the Republican candidate who lost to FDR in 1940 – to find someone with no significant record, either as a governor, a long-time senator, a cabinet member or a military commander, someone with as little on the meter as far as actually running major enterprises goes. And even old Wendell had been CEO of a power company.

When talk of a 2008 Obama campaign began publicly in 2005, it was a 'what if' sort of thing, a dream. After all, not only was he young and inexperienced, he was also black – and half-African black to boot, with some weird Swiss Family Robinson background. Hillary was the main candidate and it was still going to be seen as a big ask for the liberal wing of the party to get her up, against whichever white Southern male governor the party machine would be able to find.

Katrina changed all that, of course; or rather, a series of events that Katrina capped off – the big whammies of emerging failure in Iraq, the Abu Ghraib scandal, the Guantanamo impasse, the Enron collapse, the . . . well, there were a lot of them. But it was the combination of cronyism, incompetence and above all perceived indifference in the face of the destruction of New Orleans that put a hole in the floor under George W Bush, plunging him into a basement from which he never managed to climb. The perception of many liberals was that the slot of government was essentially vacant.

For many, Obama was a more attractive candidate than a de facto coronation of Hillary Clinton. The Obama team knew that lack of experience would be a major charge and they had an answer – change. Change became the one-word mantra of the Obama campaign, its aleph word, meaning everything and nothing at all. Faced with this, and with Obama's stunning early successes, the other Democratic candidates had no choice but to lean on the issue of his junior status.

Here's early primary contender Joe Biden:

'You know, he's a very smart guy . . . [But] I watched several presidents come in and they're smart as the devil, and they get here, and unless you already know when you get here exactly what your foreign policy is, it's awful hard to hit the ground running and not to make serious mistakes the first couple of years.'

And Bill Richardson, after the fact:

'It was change versus experience. Obviously I ran on the experience mantle. It didn't work out too well.'

And, when it got really tough, Hillary Clinton's would-be killer zinger:

'I have a lifetime of experience that I will bring to the White House. Senator John McCain has a lifetime of experience that he'd bring to the White House. And Senator Obama has a speech he gave in 2002.'

Similar and harsher stuff – insofar as one can be harsher than Hillary – would come from the McCain campaign, at least for a while. The Obama campaign largely countered by emphasising different themes, accepting that some independent and

Democratic voters would depart based on their fears of putting the White House in the hands of such a young and relatively untested man. Yet what neither they nor the media did was unpack the notion of 'experience' that had suddenly emerged. What exactly was it? What were the assumptions that underpinned it? Why did it matter so much?

'Experience' came to the fore in the 2008 campaign not merely because of Senator Obama's candidacy, but because both candidates were trying to run on anti-political notions, both arguing that politics per se was a problem, rather than a process by which solutions were arrived at to other problems. For Obama, it was themes of consensus, of getting beyond 'red' and 'blue' America, of hope. For John McCain, once he'd defeated other Republicans on national security questions, it was 'country first' and being a 'maverick'.

Any notion of a struggle between two world views, two moral frameworks, two ways of running things, fell to the wayside. 'Lack of experience' had been fired at poor old Wendell Wilkie too, but it was way down the list – the struggle was between the Democrats' social liberalism at home and internationalism as a moral obligation, and the Republicans' small-government tilt towards isolationism. Hitherto, even the greatest crises have not met with such a characterless appeal to experience for its own sake. Churchill's selection by the English parliament in 1940 was not due to his experience. Most members of the parliament were half-terrified of his judgements. It was in support of his ends – unconditional war and total victory – that a majority were persuaded to select him over the more conventionally 'experienced' Lord Halifax.

When faced with the volatile and precarious situation American finds itself in currently, the more important question might be not what a candidate has done in the past, but what they think a certain event – an invasion, a financial collapse, a bombing – actually means. What use is experience, after all, if all you've seen for forty years is the same thing – illegitimate challenges to American supremacy and to a set of universal values. Witness John McCain's attempt to transform the complex and particular situation of Russia's brief incursion into Georgia into nothing more than a repetition of WWII – that last moment of alleged moral clarity – with the phrase 'We are all Georgians now'.

Had they wished, the Obama campaign could have attacked all this head-on. They could have pointed out that the intangible qualities of a good politician – judgement, knowledge, reflection, the capacity for prudence and audacity and the wisdom to know when each is appropriate – are acquired from many sources. And that someone who has taught constitutional law, worked with the poor, and written extensively about the sort of transformations required, may have a acquired a reflective clarity that would put him in good stead to take over a country. Better stead than the extremely experienced people who over the last eight years have unquestionably run this country into the ground.

The Obama campaign could never go there, of course, because the whole topic of experience was not open to all comers. Though the idea purported to be about the wisdom of accumulated years, only certain types of experience were acceptable. The term had a measure of anti-intellectualism and anti-urbanism about it, hence the celebration by the Republicans of John McCain's result at the Naval Academy – fifth from the bottom in a class of nine hundred. Experience was running a business, being a governor of a state (and not one of them gay coastal states either, a heartland state), or military experience. McCain's dose of the latter mostly involved crashing expensive aeroplanes (he never commanded men in action) but the gloss of that was enough to separate him from that pointy-head community organiser (a *what?*) Barack Hussein Obama.

Indeed, the one weapon he hasn't deployed in the maverick role is Cindy McCain. Now, she could turn out key demographics, but only if they put front-and-centre the thing they tip-toe around – her painkiller addiction in the '90s, a jones so fierce she would steal pills from her own medical charity. Given that prescription drug abuse seems to have replaced basketball as American youth's number-one sport, that seems to me the Republicans only conduit to the 18–25s. 'Hey kids – I treated an international medical charity like it was Aunt Flossie's bathroom cabinet. I'm clean now, but I really liked those pink ones. Will someone put on some Cat Power?' Three weeks of that and Barry Obama would look like a gutless hippie dopehead priss.

The McCain campaign surprisingly didn't take this route. Instead, they thought they could pull off the ultimate audacity, by nominating Sarah Palin to the vice-presidency. Palin was an arguably more exciting candidate than Obama, but by any reasonable measure she was even less experienced than Obama in dealing with the global matters a president would need to attend to.

Palin had become governor off the back of eight years as mayor of a small town that serves as a dormitory suburb of Anchorage (and a stint as chair of the Alaska Oil and Gas Conservation Commission). Her campaign against the entrenched corrupt network that ran the Republican party catapulted her into the governorship. This happens from time to time in small states, where most other dissident political talent has long since left town. Nothing in her CV could welcome comparisons of leading Alaska with leading America – the jump is a simple category error, as many American conservatives have subsequently observed. McCain's team thought she could be celebrated in the very manner that Obama could be caricatured. She hadn't sat around reading boring old books about the Constitution (the *what?*) or grappling with the social problems of the country's second-largest city – she'd shot moose and raised five kids while cutting taxes. That was real experience! In the service of identity politics, Palin's experience was who she was, not a guide to the capabilities she might have.

That was fine, as long as the VP could be kept tucked away. With this week's financial crisis being called a '9/11 equivalent' it was all hands to the deck. Suddenly, people's minds were really, really focused on who was going to be running this show when the concept of leadership was reintroduced to America in

January 2009. Whatever Palin's chops were, her minders didn't think much of them – they kept her under wraps even though such treatment generated ridicule. And when they let her out to do an interview, with Katie Couric, this ensued:

> PALIN: The interesting thing in the last couple of days that I have seen is that Americans are waiting to see what John McCain will do on this [bailout] proposal. They're not waiting to see what Barack Obama is going to do. Is he going to do this and see what way the political wind's blowing? They're waiting to see if John McCain will be able to see these amendments implemented in Paulson's proposal.
>
> COURIC: Why do you say that? Why are they waiting for John McCain and not Barack Obama?
>
> PALIN: He's got the track record of the leadership qualities and the pragmatism that's needed at a crisis time like this.
>
> COURIC: But polls have shown that Senator Obama has actually gotten a boost as a result of this latest crisis, with more people feeling that he can handle the situation better than John McCain.
>
> PALIN: I'm not looking at poll numbers. What I think Americans at the end of the day are going to be able to go back and look at track records and see who's more apt to be talking about solutions and wishing for and hoping for solutions for some opportunity to change, and who's actually done it?

Wow. In selecting Palin, the McCain campaign never really counted on a categorical event like the current financial crisis, which potentially threatens the continued functioning of the US economy. In such situations consciousness changes rapidly and things become their opposite. The virtue of experience becomes the vice of complicity, and that is how McCain's campaign is now being coloured. Americans are pretty sure that things won't be the same again, and all indications are that they're looking for someone who projects an air of calm and good sense.

Fall is, after all, traditionally the season of tragedy, when the hubris of summer yields to the realisation anew that nothing lives forever. Or to put it another way: 'Fool me once, shame on you, fool me twice, you . . .uh . . .shame . . . uh . . . well, you can't fool me twice.' Or, put yet another way: after innocence, experience.

VERMONT: SUNDAY, 28 SEPTEMBER

On Sunday, after untold hours of negotiation, House Speaker Nancy Pelosi and Senate Banking Committee Chairman Chris Dodd emerged to front a press conference, announcing that they had come to an agreement on a bailout bill to be put to a vote on Monday.

At one hundred and ten pages, (immediately available on the internet), the bill is a substantial transformation of the Paulson/Bush three-page plan, which had basically consisted of 'Give us your money . . .erm . . .that's it'. It includes several severe, and almost entirely useless, strictures on CEOs' golden parachutes, etcetera, but it also has a provision whereby the government has a right to buy back into the shares of the companies its taken over, at a preferential rate, and then sell them back on, thus generating an overall profit on the deal.

The significance of the deal is that it's been negotiated with Republican Senator Judd Gregg, senior member of the Banking Committee, behind it, and he will now be charged with rounding up his party colleagues to get behind the thing.

There's a whole lot more back and forth about what was given up – the Democrats sacrificed some provisions that would have helped out low-income defaulted mortgagees, for example – but both Obama and McCain have given their cautious endorsement to it.

So now only one question remains: will the House Republicans go for it? If all the Democrats are onside the House GOPs aren't required for a simple majority, and the Senate Republicans are onside. But if 'conservative' Republicans – the term for those renegade fantasists who believe the US is somehow based on free enterprise, and its success built on those values – can form a sufficient block to vote against, then they will have a chance to transform themselves into the 'representatives of the people' bravely resisting Wall Street socialism.

That would be a big gamble. People are now sufficiently panicked by multiple organ failure in the financial sector to be persuaded that delaying a bailout might have serious consequences. The collapse of WaMu, a bank that had presented itself as the cuddly, friendly people's bank, really focused minds. Recent polls showed that despite the noise of the anti-bailout crowd – and hey, I'm one – three quarters of Americans support the idea, so coming out against as the pillars of the temple crash around us could be a really bad idea.

On the other hand, if the House Republicans can destroy the notion of a consensus and present the Democrats as thieves and fools, they may well be able to take some political capital away with them from the whole experience.

The Democrats know this, which is why they have been so desperate over the last days to get some sort of bipartisan 'all go down together' thing going, to share the blame. The strategy may well work. Pelosi, Dodd and the redoubtable Barney Frank have emerged of late as the de facto leaders of the country, in the vacuum created by, well, the vacuum of Bush, and the bizarre antics of McCain. The projection of Democrat authority appears to be paying off in the polls, with Obama now leading by a 5 per cent average across all polls – and that's including obviously fixed stuff like the FOX News poll, taken chiefly among the blonde airheads who comprise its on-air staff.

Despite the fact that Obama has still failed to really sell a narrative of what he would do – i.e. that he would not be a Republican and fuck things up – the bad odour of the GOP is attaching to McCain like shit to the proverbial. That's why McCain's been trying all these loony 'game changers' like suspending his campaign, blah blah. He and his team basically agree with the Obamist argument that Mr Change has another 3 per cent or so in newly registered voters, thus pushing his lead up to around 8 per cent and delivering around 330 electoral college votes.

For Team McCain there's potentially nothing but pain on

the horizon. Thursday's vice-presidential debate is being contemplated with nothing but pain by Republican loyalists. Neo-con hack Bill Kristol said he wouldn't be watching it, because he didn't enjoy humiliation comedy, and conservative columnists like Kathleen Parker are already suggesting that Palin should resign for the good of the ticket. That may be a systematic lowering of expectations, of course. Joe Biden is quite capable of fucking things up with his prolix lovable Irish bullshittery, and if Palin has been properly drilled she could undercut him effectively. But if Biden is on form, he may well destroy her.

If there's a real Palin meltdown, then this is 98 per cent over. I've met three McCain sympathisers in the past week who say they've changed their vote because of Palin. The McCain campaign couldn't have anticipated just how monumentally stupid this woman is. I mean most of what she's been tripped up on is stuff she could have learned by rote in the past three weeks. She's got a bad case of the Andrew Landeryous – she's even dumb at being dumb.

The Katie Couric interview, released in instalments by the liberal media at its best, showed her as just not up to it. And then there was that most amazing thing, a second *Saturday Night Live* sketch with Tina Fey as Palin, in which a significant chunk of the hilarious dialogue was actual transcript of the divine Sarah herself.

But hell, it's Sunday in Washington. Tomorrow, when the bill goes to Congress and the whole circus starts up again, anything could happen. Obama could still, with his diffidence, his professoriality, his shrinking from the killer blow, could still lose this. He could lose Ohio by 10 000 votes and fail to gain enough Southwest states to offset it. And if anyone can, it's he.

Nevertheless, nevertheless, nevertheless. Nevertheless.

MONDAY, 29 SEPTEMBER

The final act of today (Black Monday? Greyish? Houndstooth Black-and-White Monday? It's like picking Cindy McCain's Nazi mistress wardrobe) was a press conference by Walnuts McCain himself in Des Moines, Iowa. He'd put it off for a long time – so long that CNN just played footage of a tech setting the white balance by holding a piece of paper up to the cameras, as they droned on about the day's events. It had a weird performance art quality, as if Laurie Anderson had taken over the airwaves. Eventually he hustled on like he was power walking, flourishing a single sheet of paper, and began:

'I worked hard to bring everyone to the table . . . We improved it greatly . . . Our leaders are expected to leave partisanship at the door . . . Senator Obama and his allies in Congress infused the process with partisanship . . . Now is not the time to fix the blame, now is the time to fix the problem . . .'

Good old John, the chutzpah kid – now is not the time for partisanship, especially from that partisan cunt Obama – the old showman's still got it. He gave the statement and then he hustled out as fast as he came in, not taking a single question. So the whole Republican ticket is now off limits to actual scrutiny.

He had no choice but to say all that because the silly boob had made a statement practically claiming credit for the whole bailout, just before jumping on a plane at the exact moment the bailout went kablooey. He'd landed to find that his last statement zinging around the wires was claiming personal responsibility for the failed deal that may have killed America.

Obama didn't do a specific press conference, but he didn't need to. He gave two great speeches with a half-dozen zingers in each that the cable networks were more than happy to excerpt. It was old stuff ('I think John McCain just doesn't get it') but delivered with more authority than there'd been for a while. Most importantly, politically, he took on the presidential voice, urging everyone to 'stay calm' and work through it – pretty much the stuff the President should be saying, if America currently had a president.

For those who missed the morning news: EVERYTHING IS FUCKED! CONGRESS DIDN'T PASS THE BAILOUT BILL, DEFEATING IT 228 TO 205, AND THE MARKET FELL NEARLY 800 POINTS! NO ONE KNOWS WHAT THE HELL'S GOING ON OR WHAT TO DO NEXT!

Okay, where were we? Ah yeah, the collapse of America. People thought it could be over as night came down. But of course we live in a global society, so nothing is insulated. It was morning in East Asia and everything started tanking there too, falling by the requisite 5 per cent. This fed back into the evening news shows to create a fresh round of panic, disguised as earnest discussion.

By that point, any hope of sensible discussion had departed as the evening discussion shows took over. It is the particular tragedy of the US that its TV discussion programs have become dominated by a particular type of telepopulism, in which various hosts – Lou Dobbs and Glenn Beck are the most prominent examples – present themselves as the unmediated voice of the people against a monolithic political class. This has always been tiresome, but now it's starting to look ridiculous and noxious. It's part of the dominant political fantasy of American life – that government is, in the last analysis, not a part of society but a necessary evil, like an annual colonoscopy, to be despised, loathed and feared.

This mood took hold of America in the late '70s, with Ronald Reagan humming the tune, as everything was going wrong for the country. Reagan and his supporters, taking up the themes of the failed Goldwater campaign of 1964, suggested that government was 'the problem' and linked that theme to the American Revolution, effectively portraying the founders as a bunch of anarchists.

But the whole point of the American Revolution, at least in terms of ideals, was not minimal government per se – it was virtuous government. The core of it was that there were good and bad governments, and you could judge them based on the principles they were founded on.

The weird thing is, that thought survives to a degree. Watching Congress today, I didn't see caricatured, crony government, even though it was obvious that those voting the bill down would be members from both sides in danger of losing their seat. I saw complex, detailed arguments, the clash of ideas about what should be done, about what was happening, about different models of reality. The TV pundits were the least intelligent thing going on, with their failure to get behind one idea of what is going on.

Man, oh man, this ain't the dumper – that will be the next one, in around 2017 – but it's starting to feel really, really big. What anyone in the know in the US is scared witless about in the developing stock-market tank, is the 401(k) situation. Basically, 401(k)s are super funds built evenly by employee and employer contributions, as in Australia. Unlike in Australia, employees still have little control over their 401(k)s, which can be regularly raided and ruined even though hundreds of millions depend for their old age on them utterly.

The 401(k)s are all invested by various pension funds in the stock market – not in crazy stocks, of course, in stable blue-chip things, like Washington Mutual, or Wachovia or . . . So the short point is that if the market tanks to the degree that 401(k)s slide through the floor, then this economic crisis will become a social and political one as, faced with the prospect of lifelong penury and no reward for decades of work, people will simply be disabused of any notion that the system has any legitimacy whatsoever.

That is already starting to happen and, to a degree, the general political cynicism is the beginning of a more mature political push-back. But it's likely to be nipped in the bud by the Democrats and Republicans' acceptance of a deal that everyone calls 'rotten', 'the worst possible deal', 'something I would normally never vote for', etcetera.

But what is really important to understand about this current event is that this is not merely a financial system crisis – it is a mere ripple of a much deeper problem. Desperate to gain some political capital, the right have been suggesting that the problem is over-regulation, which is mad. But no less illusory is the centre-left assertion that the problem is simply one of lack of regulation, and that if a proper framework could be put in place everything would be alright.

The great truth of this mess is that the folks who designed the deregulation were, in a narrow sense, correct, if their goal was to give Western capitalism another lease of life. What the market faced in the US at the end of the '90s was a crucial lack of things to invest in with the free money sloshing around the markets. By 2001, the dotcom bubble had burst and you couldn't shove $X billion into Ewidgets.com, so there was a desperate need for another object that would keep the circus going. Mortgage-backed securities was it – bricks and mortar. But what looked like the most concrete investment was actually the most abstract: the notional capacity of people with no-deposit mortgages to repay.

Crazy, but what could you do? For the bitter fact is that without these pseudo-investments, the West is running on fumes. As China and the East roars ahead in classical 19th century high-capitalist mode, the West runs on financial services, rents (such as intellectual property), and debt and debt and debt.

For twenty-five years, the US has been starving its public sector of investment – investment that would have created jobs and real growth and lowered overall costs – and allowed the rich to shuffle money into luxuries and useless services and waste, as the society decayed around them. To keep that running there was no choice but to keep coming up with increasingly unreal financial instruments, to give the illusion that a real economy was at work.

But there is no way to avoid what is now obvious to many people – the big sectors of the economy are not private products, they are social products, hence the need to keep them going even when the morons who run them screw it up. The great result of this crisis is that hundreds of millions of people have now begun to understand this. Effectively what we have seen is the first glimpse of the shores of socialism. It may take another decade or two to get there – and another two crises each worse than this – but we are on the way.

In the wake of this crisis, blame is being sheeted home to the average person, who is apparently running up too much debt. Well mercy, what a surprise, it's the people's fault. Let's face it, people only consent to this crappy society because of what they can rack up on debt. If you're going to spend forty years of fifty hours a week – your whole, single life on earth – in the same office, doing crap you don't want to do, damn right you want a frikkin' flat screen TV at the end of it. And to eat out. And drink stupid overpriced cocktails in awful resorts. The short point is that if we close down easy credit, the rationale for western capitalism collapses instantly, because the rest of it is so god-awful that without rewards no one would put up with it. Hence the need, over the last eight years, to keep it all bubbling, at any cost.

This is not an economic crisis, this is a political and cultural crisis of capitalism, and if you don't understand that, well, you're a financial journalist.

That's the meaning of what happened today.

Ya es de dia!

8

COME ON UP FOR THE RISIN'

The Debates

America woke with a heavy political hangover and took a look around the proverbial living room. Boy, they thought. We really wrecked the joint, didn't we? It was fun at the time, but now . . .

President Bush addressed the nation at 7.45 a.m., a clever strategy to make sure even fewer people tuned in than would normally do so. He said nothing but the standard platitudes about wanting Congress to work together on behalf of the blah blah . . . At least, that's what he said according to the reports. Waking up, or staying up, to watch George W Bush at 7.45 a.m. is, as the man said, a bit above my pay grade.

Though Congress was technically in session, much of the day was taken up with meetings between various factions, often across party lines, with the bailout forming two temporary de facto pro and anti parties. Left Democrats such as Dennis Kucinich, who want to load in tens of billions' worth of protection for defaulted mortgagees, are working with Republicans up for re-election, who want to strip the bill down, or replace it with a mortgage insurance proposal and a capital gains tax holiday, or abolition.

It's a weird game of chicken. While the pro-bailout party can work together on a common proposal, the antis are working together only so far as they can strike the bill out. After that, it's a free-for-all open season.

To forestall this, the Senate – where the bill has broad bipartisan support – has brought the thing to the vote as an amendment to another bill. The idea is that Senate support will bolster the House to do what allegedly needs to be done. But it's hard to say if anything will persuade Republicans in marginal districts to come in, because the whole issue has become a very interesting game theory model. Consider this – if the bill passes, the economy is kick-started again (they hope) and the panic is over. But for many Republicans, voting against it will nevertheless make them local heroes, standing up to those Wall Street fat cats, elites or (south of Nashville and east of Santa Fe) them rich Jews.

However, if they vote against it, it fails and the economy really tanks. People would ask whether it might not have been a good idea.

So it is in the political interest of House Republicans for the bill to pass, but in the interest of no actual Republican to vote for it. Delicious, *n'est-ce pas*?

No one really knows what the hell is going on, again. If the bill passes the Senate on Wednesday and then fails to pass the House Thursday, then . . . [insert picture of cartoon man tearing out hair and shouting the top line of the keyboard, shifted]. Effectively, both sides will have to come up with substantially different models and put them to the House floor.

From the left (and it may gain support from sections of the right) there is a scheme to establish a public holding company to take on the mortgages bundled into the traded securities and ensure that no one except the most dilatory defaultees (the 1 or 2 per cent who never intended to pay a cent of their mortgage ever) lose their shirt, which might be acceptable. The problem is, of course, that there is no longer a hard-and-fast division between the share-owning class and the rest of us – overwhelmingly because trade-union pension funds are invested on the open market.

So on it went. But the great event of the day was the continuing unravelling of Sarah Palin, a show that may run longer than *Cats*, and the return to the punditry circuit of James Carville, the Lizard King, reminding us once again how politics is done. While other talking-points hacks do the full lung-burst (trying to get a hundred words in, hitting six issues including Obama's friendship with Bill Ayers, his dope-smoking and his kindergarten essays, when the question was 'Is your microphone working?'), Carville sits back like a sensei master, or a cottonmouth rattler, waiting to strike with a few words. He'd hit on a simple but killing line, which he used on the Campbell Brown show, *Larry King* and elsewhere. After Republican pundit X had banged on about McCain the maverick coming in to help this and that, etcetera, Carville leaned in and said, 'And what does Sarah Palin think of this bailout?' – and suddenly his opposite number was mortally wounded. Bay Buchanan, Palin's greatest defender (and before that a stern critic of mothers working full time), tumbled out of the sky like a peppered partridge, going: 'Well, uh, erm . . . we'll find out on Thursday, but I know whatever she thinks she will stand with the American people.' Buchanan knew that Palin was on tape standing against the bailout, but she knew she couldn't lie and say she'd spoken to Palin and she had told her she was now for the bailout, in line with her presidential candidate John McCain – because no one's spoken to Palin for the past three days, except those who are drilling her furiously about, you know, how a bill becomes law, that the separation of powers is not an episode of *Heroes*, etcetera. It's bloody marvellous to watch because no one expected it – Carville clearly held it back to use it on one single day.

Simple? Obvious? Of course. But that's the supreme art of this sort of politics. Remember Hawke's 'You can't put your money under the bed – that's where the Reds are', Keating's 'I want to do you slowly', Reagan's 'There you go again' and Clinton's 'It's the economy, stupid'? Oh, that last one was actually Carville, and if Obama had managed to hire him, and if Carville had agreed to work for him, I reckon he'd be eight to ten points clear of Walnuts and the Warrior Princess, across the board.

But man, the McCain–Palin thing is now officially in deep

shit. The conservatives who have now come out against her include Charles Krauthammer (uber neo-con), David Frum (Bush's speechwriter), most of the *National Review* and, most recently, George Will, a true conservative elder. But the death-blow went to middle-of-the-road (okay, liberal) journalist Fareed Zakaria, who pointed out that it was not that Palin didn't answer very well in interviews, it was that: 'She clearly didn't understand the questions. This is a level of incompetence we have not seen before.'

Goddamit, the woman can't even do *Saturday Night Live* properly. When she was booked to go on the show, everyone expected it would be some sort of encounter like the Hillary Clinton–Amy Poehler classic, the two Hillaries firing off each other. Inevitably, it wasn't. It was the sort of half-assed, dithering bullshit the Republicans specialise in these days. Palin was in a cold opener sketch in which she and show producer Lorne Michaels discussed her appearance, before Alec Baldwin turned up and presumed she was Tina Fey . . . Anyhoo, we never got what we all wanted, which was a Tina Fey–Sarah Palin double act. They simply passed each other awkwardly on set and she later appeared in the news gag section, saying she wouldn't do a certain act – a rap – so Amy Poehler did it while she bopped along. It was lame-o, and the desperate, unfunny way it which it was all handled suggested to this old sketch comedy producer that it was all about last-minute chaos, refusals to do certain things, etcetera etcetera, and desperate fix-ups to put something, anything, together. Kinda like the whole campaign really.

All this makes Thursday's VP debate just about the most important in history. If Palin can somehow hold her own and be effective, then it will be one of the most stunning turnarounds in history, and the whole anti-elitist thing will be ratcheted up, like, a billion notches.

It would be good to give back McCain another three points. But if she fails, it's all over, and an announcement will be seriously on the cards next week, that the duties of caring for a special needs child are more than I etcetera . . . and thus with regret I am withdrawing from etcetera . . . And Romney or, fuck, Huckabee, will be on the ticket.

You wouldn't hold out much hope if you were a conservative. The most recent clip released from the Katie Couric interviews (which has now become a cruel process, like getting body parts of a kidnapped child through the mail in instalments) is Palin on what she reads. The answer: pretty much nothing at all. As Celine Dion once said, 'I don't need all that extra information in my brain'. God, it's cruel. God, it's funny. If they put these interviews together on a DVD, damn, that's my Christmas list nailed.

WASHINGTON DC: THURSDAY, 2 OCTOBER

So there I was in the John Hoban bar on Dupont Circle, yukking it up with a bunch of bright young DC things, waiting for the 'debate watch' party being hosted by Elizabeth, who bills herself as DC's only Wasilla resident! It's an Obama fundraiser.

Rolling the golden, free Chivas slowly in my mouth, thinking that before I start filming I better check the camera, and . . .

Mofo. The damn thing isn't working. I checked it yesterday, and it worked when I was shooting a Swedish tourist in a 'Vote for Pedro' T-shirt, which had clearly been given to him by someone who hates him, and it worked then. And now . . . there's just a white flash in the screen. Narrggghhhhh.

Following a dash to Radio Shack and back, I was reloaded with a forty-dollar special which may or may not work. It's strange, sailing through the heart of DC, because the feel of the core of the city is so . . . well, European. It's the centre of a great behemoth but it feels like a French froufrou, with the race relations of Alabama.

Over on the hill, Congress is hammering out the House version of the bailout bill, which has now grown to four hundred pages after the Senate process of loading the thing with thousands of earmarks for everything under the sun. It was all blatant sugar for stray House members to go back to their districts and pose as heroes. It's a pretty insane and decadent way to run a damn railroad, much less a financial crisis.

Back at Dupont Circle, the joint was heaving with about three different watch parties – two Dem, one Republican – but everyone had a Sarah Palin drinking game card. Much hubbub before the thing started about the issues discussed during the day; i.e. frantic attempts to spin Palin up by the Dems and then spin her down by the GOP. Mostly people said the prospect of the thing was almost excruciating off the back of her disastrous interviews with Katie Couric. Cuts were also played in the media from Palin's 2006 Alaska governorship debate, in which she was alleged to have been a sharp performer for answering two questions competently. Lowering the bar? They were burying it.

So when it finally began about a half hour ago, it wasn't surprising that Palin, having been drilled for days by most of McCain's staff, came out sounding surprisingly competent, laying out the McCain position on tax cuts, etcetera, pretty well, if without killer flair.

Fighting almost immediately began to break out between the various parties as to how much noise there should be. 'Stop SHUSHING ME!' someone yelled. 'We're all TiVo-ing it anyway.' He was a Republican.

One early answer of Palin's had the drinking gamers pretty quickly smashed – a bravado hit of 'hockey moms', 'oh golly', 'yada yada' and 'betcha'. Four more pints please. And shooters. 'Hockey mom' is a shooter.

Biden got Palin onto rough territory by talking about McCain's whacky health plan, and Palin countered by talking about energy. Biden went back on to tax breaks for big corporations and Palin went back onto energy . . . 8tcfvvvvgvfhvuughg—

That bit occurred while I was moving location and I missed Palin answering on Iraq – I'll probably find it was the classic of the evening. And then we were onto Iran and Pakistan. Biden got the first bite on that and rolled out the whole of Middle East policy. Then the headlamps went on to Palin.

Palin pretty much threw the question back about meeting

with foreign bad-guy leaders, such as well-known vaudeville act the Castro Brothers. She trotted out the line about meetings giving people PR victories and Biden got tangled a bit on defending Obama on the nature of the meetings. Will Israel, the next question, tangle her up? Does she know what a two-state solution is? She gets back onto the Iran baddies thing, then a good bit about Israel's heat-seeking— sorry, peace-seeking. Biden comes out even more hawkish, portraying the Republicans as wimps.

We got our first Palinode on the question, 'In what situations would nuclear weapons be usable?'

'Well, gosh, nucular weapons would be the be all and end all of too many people and too many parts of the planet.'

Biden fumbled in the response, his prolixity getting the better of him. Palin has held up well so far and even seems to be drawing a lot of energy out of Biden.

Back at the hotel, the CNN repeat of the whole thing was just starting, which gave one a chance to reflect upon it. The latter part of the debate didn't see any great departure from the dominant style, although Palin became increasingly snappy at Biden's heels as she gained in confidence, and he clearly had to restrain himself from a more cutting comeback. On foreign affairs, the problem for both of them was that, Iraq aside, the fundamental philosophy towards the rest of the world is so similar – a vigorous dose of exceptionalism, which allows the

US to step into everyone else's sovereignty while regarding its own as inviolate. Though the Democrats put a spin on 'ethical' interventions and the Republicans on pre-emptive ones, the core approach is identical. Hence the effort, as someone noted, of each candidate to climb over each other in their effusive praise of Israel, though of course the Florida vote is also in play.

As the topic came back round to domestic things, Palin started to reach for the populist outsider tag both for herself and McCain – talking about the view from Wasilla Main Street, and about John McCain as the maverick, and both of them as a pair of mavericks, and etcetera etcetera. This put Biden on the defensive but he came back very well, demolishing the idea that McCain was a maverick, refuting the idea that he didn't know the struggles average Americans were facing and mentioning practically every town he'd ever lived in – the old steel town of X, the slurry works of Y. It was the only point at which there was the slightest hint of friction when Palin brought up being a mother of a special needs child, and Biden choked up when he noted that you don't have to be a woman to be worried about your kids and whether one of them will make it (his son, who was critically injured in the car crash that killed his first wife and daughter). By the end of it, Palin was leaning too heavily on the folksiness and the few key points the McCainistas had drilled into her (hit the maverick, the raising taxes, the selling out our troops, etcetera etcetera). But Biden's ability to have concrete examples at his fingertips, while also by and large avoiding the temptation to go all prolix (though one classic example was talking persuasively about having spent as much in three weeks in Iraq as we've spent in seven years in Afghanistan . . . well, six-and-a-half years . . . and you could see the possibility that he would spin into ten minutes of clarification). Palin's final gambit ('Oh, there you go again, Joe, looking into the past') was an attempt to grab some sort of phrase like, almost exactly like, Reagan's 'There you go again', but it didn't work. Biden had made the argument that a McCain–Palin administration would be a continuation of Bush, and that kinda stuck.

In the end, not only did Palin hold her own, but there were more 'mavericks' in her contribution to the debate than at your average cattle rustlers' convention (which was bad news for anyone in the John Hoban going to work the next day – 'maverick' was valued at a shot). Together with 'energy', 'outsider' and 'Joe Sixpack', these formed her go-to phrases every time the questions got difficult or, you know, pertinent. Did she succeed in calming Republican fears about her basic presentability? Undoubtedly. Did she reassure any fair-minded viewer as to her competence? Not for a second.

But by the end of the evening, Republicans had reason to feel, if not blessed, at least relieved. The debate format – allowing neither cross-questioning between candidates nor a panel throwing in follow-ups – allowed her to trot out a series of set-piece answers, and pretty much not answer questions she didn't like. Her lead arguments were that she and McCain were a team of mavericks, that tax cuts were the key to prosperity, that Iraq withdrawal would be 'a white flag of surrender', that she knew oil because there was a lot of it under Alaska, etcetera. Whenever a question was the least bit challenging, she simply switched the topic – challenged that McCain didn't support new proposals to ease pressures on people declaring themselves bankrupt, she said, 'That is not so . . . but I want to talk about energy again', and went on to remind us that she knew oil because there was a lot if it under, etcetera. On foreign affairs she got away with a question about an Israel–Palestine two-state solution by going off in effusive praise of Israel, making it pretty clear she didn't know what a two-state solution was. By the end of the debate, she was running out of material, and the 'mavericks' and the 'you betchas' and the 'our fragile freedoms' came pretty thick and fast. But aside from a major gaffe – suggesting a degree of equality between same-sex relationships and marriage, which the Christian right will make her retract – she was home.

If Palin had been universally urged to be herself, Biden was widely encouraged to be someone else. Biden was focusing on McCain in any case, but the concern was that nailing Palin's lack of knowledge about her own candidate's program would make him appear hung-up on those elitist liberal fetishes of, you know, 'knowledge', 'command of detail', 'judgement' and so on. Whether this was good advice or not, he largely stuck to it, assailing the general Republican record and correcting remarks on Barack Obama's policies.

Though the perception was that Palin had won by not losing, and professional Washington cocktail circuit right-wingers went into new backflips about 'anti-elitism', polls universally declared

Biden the winner – about 50 to 35 per cent on average. What will be keeping Republicans up at night is not whether her performance got in independent voters, but whether it convinced a section of moderate Republicans that she really was capable of leading, should John McCain take one accidental Viagra double-dose too many. Her candidacy satisfied the religious right – who would still vote for her if she had fallen to the stage and frothed at the mouth – but the number of Republicans who think she's unprepared to lead has shot up 17 per cent over the last weeks. There's also the wider blame on Republicans for the financial mess and concern over McCain's repeat kamikaze performance of 'suspending his campaign'. It's the departure of these voters that has prompted the McCain campaign to wrap up operations in a potential swing-state like Michigan and pile into Florida and Ohio, in a desperate attempt to hold the line of 2004. With McCain's spending limited by his acceptance of public funding, the Obama team is now in a position to swamp swing states with wall-to-wall advertising. They didn't get the meltdown sound bites they wanted from the vice-presidential debate, but if they string together twenty 'mavericks', then liberal drinking-gamers might not be the only people getting a hangover from the event.

NASHVILLE: MONDAY, 6 OCTOBER

'Once you pass this line you must – repeat must – continue exiting,' reads the sign at Nashville airport baggage check. Why the emphasis? Well, there's a big screen TV playing standard awful alt-country immediately outside, so maybe they'd had a few too many travellers coming to the sudden realisation of what being in Nashville involves.

At the taxi rank, the good ol' boys in their body-hugging shirts and heavy jewellery roll past the black valet.

'You have to wait in line for a taxi, sir.'

'That's alright, little fella, we'll just take this one.'

Little fella. The man is in his thirties and if he's doing this job, he's got a family. Jesus god, we ain't in Kansas anymore. This is worse.

With tomorrow's debate at Belmont University, Barack Obama is stepping into enemy territory, politically and culturally. Though Nashville, to be fair, is a centre of culture and learning with half-a-dozen pretty solid universities, beyond the guitar-shaped pools and the Grand Ole Opry, Tennessee will go 20 per cent for McCain in November, unless he . . . well, to be honest, I can't think of anything he could do to turn this state blue.

Root a mule on stage? This is farm country, that's nothing they haven't seen. Say 'Most of you people are office workers, you look like dicks in those faux ten-gallon hats'? Scream during verse two, 'Could you people shut the fuck up until you've learned a fourth chord'? Maybe, but most likely Tennessee will stand proud against the n— nice man from the Democrats, who is surely right smart, but just ain't our cup of tea, no thankee.

That's unlikely to be reflected in the town hall meeting-style debate tomorrow night, if the organisers have done their job and got a properly diverse crowd.

With the financial bailout/rescue in place, Americans returned to work today to find that the market was continuing to dive, falling 800 points in one day, before recovering to an overall 300+ point loss and sitting just below the important 10 000 mark as the closing bell rang.

The day's recovery would appear to be a simple rebound – there is no reliable forecast on whether it will continue to fall for the rest of the week, or where it will bottom out. But the fact that the passage of a bailout hasn't given an immediate lift is a worrying sign, since 90 per cent of it is about restoring confidence, rather than keeping an actual industry spluttering along (unlike, for example, the simultaneous $25 billion auto industry bailout).

The Wall Street dive continued to feed the widespread feeling that a change of leadership is needed, and on national polls Obama is now leading by a clear 8 per cent averaged across the Gallup, CNN, CBS and Rasmussen dailies. Indeed this is one of the first times they've been moving in lock-step. In state polls, most of the swing states that McCain had brought back into his camp have now slipped away – Pennsylvania, Minnesota and Michigan, blue states the McCain team thought could be turned against an 'elite' black candidate, are now running 7–12 per cent for Obama, as is New Hampshire. Of the 2004 red states, the Democrats are leading by around 5–8 per cent in New Mexico, Colorado and Nevada, and 3–5 per cent in Virginia and North

Carolina. In the key swing states of Ohio and Florida you can get whatever numbers you want, but they're mostly leaning towards Obama, from 1–8 per cent.

The Democrats had high hopes for North Dakota and Montana, but they abandoned those once Palin was selected – she was good for a 5–7 per cent swing back to McCain (Why? A lot of Alaskans are from the northwest states and they identify with her style). But the economic meltdown has given them renewed hope in Indiana and Missouri.

There are, in short, half a dozen pathways by which Obama can get a win without getting Ohio or Florida. There's only one path for McCain and that is to hold just about everything, though he could survive losing two or three small states if he kept Ohio and Florida.

Unfortunately for McCain, he's fighting with funds limited by his acceptance of public money, while Obama can now simply open up multiple fronts of crushing ad-buys. And the McCain camp agree with the Obama team's conclusion that there's another 2 or 3 per cent of never-before-registered support out there unmeasured by the current polls. If so, and if the figures don't come in, there's the possibility, as Pat Buchanan noted, of a thirty-five- to forty-state victory and a thorough Republican rout.

For the McCain campaign, the fact that they've gone back to the Bill Ayers material, stuff flogged to death during the primary season, is a sign of utmost desperation. Like the moment in a stand-up act when the hapless tryout does the, 'You don't have neighbours in Kings Cross/Footscray/Cabramatta, you have witnesses'. Hear that scraping sound – it's the bottom of the barrel.

Ayers, for those who missed it, was one of the 'Weathermen' group, or the Weather Underground, which set a number of bombs at the height of the anti-Vietnam war movement. Since the '80s, he's been a Chicago community activist, academic and so on, and has since described the Weathermen thing as deluded and wrong. Obama had a few contacts with him during the '90s in various community organisations, including those run by the eminently conservative Annenberg Foundation.

The first time round, during the primaries, this stuff came up in tandem with the fuss about the Reverend Jeremiah Wright. But Hillary and Obama's other Democratic rivals didn't pick up the Ayers connection, cos . . . well, cos Bill Clinton pardoned half-a-dozen Weather Underground folks serving long sentences, during his famous all-night pardoning session on the last day of his presidency.

FOX News has been running with the Ayers thing incessantly and Sarah Palin has now been given the job of taking it out for a walk, telling a Florida crowd today in that whiny fake singsong voice of hers that 'Barack Obama thought the country so imperfect that he palled around with domestic terrorists who had attacked their own country'. Big booing. Presumably it was a north Florida crowd – south of Daytona Beach, half those old Jews sunning themselves in Miami are ex-members of the Irgun, who know a thing or two about terrorism, as does the ageing Cuban Bay of Pigs veteran next to them on the sundeck – but I digress.

This strategy is beyond risky – it's a last roll of the dice, a way of keeping in the game, having something to say in the hope that something that might happen. That something has narrowed to: 1) an attack on Iran, following 'horrendous new information about blah'; 2) a terrorist attack in the US, either genuine (Al-Qaeda would prefer a punchy McCain administration, to add to the chaos) or homegrown; or 3) the assassination of Barack Obama.

By far the most likely of all these highly unlikely possibilities is the third. For McCain the most advantageous time for it to happen would be after the ballots had been printed – since people are still free to vote for a dead candidate and the electoral college members in states Obama won would be free to choose whoever they wanted to replace him – in other words, an unknown quantity. Would some enraged 'patriot' be so motivated by the increasing likelihood as to take the ultimate step? Some sort of redneck, suicide pick-up with a fertiliser bomb? (Yes, I know fertiliser bombs take hours to go off.) Yelling 'Yeehah!' while driving towards the podium at a million miles an hour, playing this awful music for Dutch courage, dreaming of redneck heaven, franks and beer and seventy-two close female relatives? Does that count as an unknown known, or an unknown unknown?

Well, who knows? That's the thing about the double unknown, dark energy clustering around the edge of the real. What seems unthinkable before it happens, appears inevitable in retrospect. Whatever the case, we're into the final days, and the McCain campaign has crossed the line and must, repeat, must continue exiting.

NASHVILLE: TUESDAY, 7 OCTOBER

'Man, you got the best stall.'

On Belmont University's main drag where hundreds had gathered for the second presidential debate with their wares, their literature, their arguments and their crazy shit, a young Obama kid was going into ecstasies over the right-to-life stall.

'That is so beautiful.'

He was spot-on too. The anti-choice crowd had really made an effort, with window boxes full of bright marigolds and large-headed daisies festooning the site. You could see their intent. 'We really care about all life, even pretty flowers,' they seemed to be saying. 'When it comes down to it, abortionists are just slobs.'

They were on Tory row, just between the McCain–Palin official stand and the Lamar Alexander for Senate site, which was much as the name suggested. It was an island of conservative resentment in a sea of Obama hope, rolling and crashing to both ends of the campus. In red-state Tennessee, and red-city Nashville, Belmont is one of four universities pretty much next to each other, which form a sort of force-field.

Fair go, though, Americans can take anything as an opportunity to sell shit. Is this a good and great thing, a relentless spirit, or is it why everyone's hanging from the end of the Dow as it shrieks around the rollercoaster rails of obsolescent capitalism (to use Samir Amin's phrase)? Who knows, but I reckon a lot of Americans are questioning the very basis of their life at the moment, as the recession widens and deepens across the world. Monday's stocks dive really hit people hard, after the hope that the bailout would act as some sort of shazam moment. It made it clear to everyone that they were heading for a grinding recession at the very least, and probably something worse.

The Dow dipping below 10 000 was another such moment, because the first time it crossed 10 000 was in 1999 at the height of the dotcom boom. Remember that? The new economy, the weightless economy? The problem of cycles had been busted and things were just going to rise forever and ever?

The dotcom boom was the bubble *de choix* at the time – finance capital so desperate to keep the merry-go-round going that it was willing to pour billions into a website and a ring-binder business plan. Before that it was savings and loans; old, cautious institutions juiced in the blender and poured into the mix. When the dotcoms tanked, mortgages were pressed into service.

Why? Well, because mortgages are the last big and sluggish asset. There ain't nothing else. And they look so solid, their value written down in bricks and mortar. But they're not. The value of real estate is dependent on occupancy levels – once those start to go backward, housing values can fall off a cliff. In the US, multiple occupancy – moving in with your parents or your kids, or sharing, or sleeping in your cousin's living room – has risen by 45 per cent in the last three years. The latest estimate is that by the end of 2009 40–50 per cent of mortgagees will be paying more out than the house is worth, and there seems no likelihood that Australia will be much different.

Down Debate Alley came the 9/11 Truthers, marching lockstep until the cops dispersed them. They seem to have taken up a uniform verging on self-parody – raincoats and trilbies, like Gene Hackman's character in *The Conversation*, that prescient masterpiece of postmodern paranoia.

'You're not being told that Barack Obama and John McCain are the same,' yelled one as he was thrown out.

Behind them, presidential look-alikes were gathering near the Bono-influenced 'One' movement, a cult worthy of an investigation itself. Bill, Dubya and Sarah in attendance. No Hillary, or Monica, though she may have been in the trailers.

'You didn't ask a Bill Ayers question!' I yell at the FOX News reporter doing voxpops.

'We're FOX local. I don't have anything to do with that crap,' she yells back.

Fast footwork may re-liquify the West, but I wouldn't bet the house you suddenly own a lot less of on it. There are a lot of reasons being given for the current crisis and the looniest, most dishonest one I've seen has currently been taken up by the Oz press in the form Gerard Henderson and La Albrechtsen. It's the right-wing argument that this was all the fault of excessive regulation. But it seems finally to be coming clear to people that this is not a mere bubble, but a reflection of a deeper crisis in the world economy – a lack of useful production in the West, under-consumption in the East, and vice versa.

To base global growth on the West borrowing money from China to buy crap from China was a short-term solution at best, and what we are now hearing is the same noise you hear when glaciers calve, the sort of awful/wonderful sound of what's going to happen happening. In that respect, Albrechtsen and others are right in slating the blame on 'greed' as asinine. If greed was corrosive of capitalism, the thing would have collapsed long ago. Your average Wall Street banker is a pussy compared to the thugs and murderers who built the railroads and steel mills of the 19th century.

Whether this will make an appearance in the debate at that sort of level remains to be seen; i.e. no, it won't. But Americans are thinking a lot more seriously than other people (certainly more than the likes of Henderson or Albrechtsen) about what's happening at the moment. They can but do little else.

That's bad news for McCain, who has played the most recent economic crisis so, so wrong right from the start, going from 'the fundamentals of the economy are sound' to 'the greatest crisis since 1929 when I entered the Senate' in a week. He pfaffed around with the campaign suspension while Obama consulted and then came to a measured course of action, the process suddenly reversing the presumption of experience and not. Now, via Sarah Palin, the McCain campaign has simply abandoned the economy altogether and gone back to the question of character, via the obscure personage of Bill Ayers. Obama supporters watched this renewal of trash politics – the new accusations of Obama's disloyalty has moved McCain supporters to call out 'Traitor!' at rallies – with trepidation. Would they do a Kerry yet again and stay on the high road?

Crowds thickening at the entrance where the candidates will arrive. Academics and guests gathered on the balcony of the University Club looking down. Medieval, like a seething carnivale waiting for the saints to bless the buboes.

A 'green jobs' demonstration marches through a gas station forecourt and a few peel off to buy snacks from it.

'Fixed News!' yells someone as the FOX News local comes into the Bongo Java cafe.

'I don't . . . ah, screw it,' she says.

Fortunately the Dems would not do another Kerry, bringing the character issue round with an attack on McCain's record as part of the late '80s savings and loan scandal known as the 'Keating Five' (what a crap doowop group that was), and as a twofer, digging up an old bunch of Nicaraguan contra thugs and murderers who McCain palled around with at the time. The Alaska Independence

Party stuff is still there to be used – the party that Sarah Palin told to 'keep up their good work' at their 2008 Convention was founded by a man who said that 'Fires of hell were glacial compared to the burning hatred he felt for the American flag', and who was buried in Canada so as not to rest under the Stars and Stripes (after he was murdered by a man from whom he appeared to have been buying plastic explosives). Man, they've got to hit that. There's also Troopergate, the report due to hit the streets on Friday. McCain–Palin may regret opening up these fronts.

Yet what else could they do? They're lost on economic issues, and only 15 per cent of Americans rate foreign policy as the number-one concern, should the GOP consider turning focus abroad. Some have been talking about McCain's undoubtedly superior skills at the one-on-one joust in front of a town hall meeting audience, but that may be less commanding than it once was. For one thing McCain sounds tired, as you would expect him to be, and simply erratic, contradicting himself one sentence after the next. The suspension brouhaha knocked him around and Obama suddenly sounded more aggressive and energetic. That faded somewhat, but McCain's ability to growl him down is much diminished.

Yet Obama can be terrible in answering questions from the audience, unable to find focus, hitting the wrong note. If McCain had a great alternative approach to the economy, now would be the time to show it. That his erratic behaviour may have become terminal seems to have been demonstrated by his announcement that he would get tough on Medicare spending (state health insurance for the over sixty-fives, paid by levy on income). At the same time he's campaigning hard for Florida and has just shifted a bunch of his former Michigan workers there. South Florida is one long Medicare ward. It doesn't make a blind bit of sense. I'll regret saying this, but I sure hope McCain has one shot still in his locker to make this interesting.

Well the Bongo Java is full now, with four big screens in three rooms, every local freak, Dem and Obamaite gathered in the one place. I come back through Debate Alley one last time as everyone's packing up – is that all there is to a circus? I turn the camera on an essential oils stall ('FOX News – fuck off' over my shoulder), with a young black alt woman who looks like she does her colour chart.

'If Obama was one of your products, what would he be?' I ask, hoping for some dippy answer.

'Calendula, because it's for hope.'

And dammit if that's not an answer. So beautiful.

8.15 p.m. central time: Fifteen minutes in, and McCain is clearly winning because Obama seems to have forgotten everything he learned over the last four weeks. McCain's already snapped out one new idea (or a new spin) – a direct state buy-up of bad mortgages; i.e. pure socialism from the shameless old coot. Then he says that Warren Buffett would make a great treasury secretary – Buffett being an Obama supporter. He sounds rackety and old, and he's doing the same lines. But he sounds like Lady Day belting it out at the Blue Note compared to Obama, who's already playing catch-up, defending himself against McCain's charges. Yeah, yeah, play the mature one, focused on the issue, but man, nail this guy on the economy. Repeat it.

McCain stumbles on the answer to: 'Why should we support either of you when you got us into this mess?' His sentences start to fall apart. 'This is the most liberal voting record . . .' If he means Obama's, he doesn't say. 'I have fought against excessive spending and outrages.' What outrages? 'I know how to do that, I know how to do that,' he keeps saying, hitting all the energy buttons.

8.27 p.m.: The two styles are starting to diverge now. McCain is continuing to try and jump on Obama's corns, having found a new earmark – a $3 million overhead projector for Chicago, or something – with which he can hit Obama. And he does it again and again. Obama takes the discussion higher and higher, talking about sacrifice and a revival of the Peace Corps and getting to the moon, which gets a roar from the crowd.

Then McCain gets onto taxes and talks about how Obama wants to tax everyone, and 'My friends, we shouldn't increase taxes on anyone.' The worm measuring audience reaction absolutely flatlines, then goes into negative territory. People really hate this, really hate it. Obama clarifies his tax policy and how 95 per cent of people won't get an increase, and the worm goes through the roof.

8.41 p.m.: 'Look, it's not that hard to fix social security . . .' McCain opines. I reckon that's a bum note and the worm agrees, faltlining again. Wow, these folks don't like him and they don't like his stories anymore. Again, 'Senator Obama has never challenged his own party'. He's well into the territory of just rearranging his clichés and his charges, like Obama having raised taxes ninety-four times.

God, they're both pretty duff. McCain is attack attack attack, but he's tumbling over basic sense to get to his lines, like another mention of nuclear power. I should listen to the arguments – I would if there were some – but I can't stop watching the worm, which McCain can't get off the floor. Only when he starts to talk really, really green (the hybrid car, etcetera), does he start to get a lift.

Obama comes back, talking reasonably again. He seems more relaxed now, more focused. He gets back to how McCain says we've been doing nothing about alt fuels for thirty years – and he was in Washington for twenty-six of them. A great cogent answer on energy by Obama, the best of the night.

8.51 p.m.: We're onto health care. Divergence is now complete. McCain doesn't need conjunctions, just lists of things that Senator Obama did or didn't do. Obama knocks McCain out of the park on his $5000 rebate plan, which goes straight to the insurance provider and makes your health care taxable at the point of provision by your employer, who will then discontinue it. Obama gives the best and most cogent explanation of his plan I've heard to date. McCain hits the whole 'government is bad' thing – which flatlines. That Reagan stuff is so over. People are so shellacked by the market in health care, they would join the Moonies to get a secure plan. There's a huge gender split in the worm when Obama talks about children's health – women go through the roof, men couldn't care less. Obama's got this nailed and then . . . ohhh noooo, he refers to health insurance relocating to one slack state, like banks do to Delaware – which Joe Biden made possible.

9 p.m.: McCain managed to flick the thing onto foreign policy. Smooth move. He's getting big ups on this, though it's old material. Obama steers onto actual economic constraints and the disaster of Iraq, and then pays obeisance to the whole 'America is the greatest nation in the world' thing.

9.05 p.m.: Maybe it's not necessary to mention it, but Obama's answers on the question 'When would America intervene?' sketch him out as virtually identical to McCain in effect. Perhaps it's a pose, but it doesn't sound so likely as far as, say, Darfur is concerned. Would he be a 21st century Woodrow Wilson?

9.09 p.m.: The Pakistan question (would we trash its borders to pursue Obama Barack Osama bin Laden . . . hang on, that's wrong) comes up. Obama fails to answer it magnificently, there's a long delay and then the usual thing about 'we can't coddle dictators'. Then he lays out what he'd do, and still ducks it with the 'We would take them out'.

9.11 p.m.: I must not watch the worm, I must not watch the worm . . . but if anyone in an ICU was getting McCain's ratings they'd have electric paddles over their chest. He's spent more of this debate on the floor than I have. His Iraq stuff produces a flatline. His Pakistan stuff – flatline. Even namedropping Petraeus doesn't do it.

9.13 p.m.: Obama comes for a follow-up on Pakistan. Why? Bad mistake. He'd won that. Now he's losing it, I think.

9.16 p.m.: From Pakistan to Afghanistan. The moderator refers to the British ambassador, who was quoted last year saying that Afghanistan was a decades-long strategy of democratisation, now saying that what's needed is an acceptable dictator and a quick exit. Obama refers to getting out of Iraq as crucial to progress in Afghanistan. McCain refers to General Petraeus and then hits Obama with the surge – and promptly flatlines again. When he gets a question on Russia he does much better. Talking of Tiny Georgia? Midget hooker? Oh, the country. Why the big ups? It's appealing to Americans' better sense of themselves, without promising an invasion. Maybe it's just relief. It's tricky for Obama to come back in here, and he stumbles around trying to find a significant difference. It's mostly waffle about 21st century challenges.

9.24 p.m.: Yes or no – is Russia the evil empire? A dumb question. Why doesn't anyone say it's a dumb question? Both waffle.

9.25 p.m.: From Russia to Israel, of course. Would US troops defend Israel against Iran? McCain dodges the question, going into a big geopolitical rave, and then arcs over into Obama's no preconditions thing, and finally his superhero-like League of Democracies. Obama dodges the question by going into generalities, and then splits off from the McCain answer to go into diplomacy, which gets a huge up from the audience, as does the 'direct talks' routine.

9.29 p.m.: Final question. From New Hampshire: 'What don't you know and how will you learn it?' Oh God. Obama starts with the 'Ask my wife' gag then to the unknown unknowns thing, and finally the set piece he was always going to deliver . . . and nails it, perfecto. It's a hard act to follow, and I'm not sure Walnuts is going to get there. 'I don't know what the unexpected will be.' My God. A sudden realisation – he hasn't used the POW thing once. It must have tested really badly. He's doing well, and gets the 'country first' thing turned around. Not too shabby.

So there it was. After a shaky start, it looks pretty likely that Obama won that one handily, partly because he got better, more focused and more outward-looking. But mainly because people just hate hate hate Republicans and everything they stand for, and McCain is – as Jesus himself would be – beyond doing anything to change that.

BETHLEHEM, PENNYSLVANIA: WEDNESDAY, 8 OCTOBER

'Sarah! Sarah! Sarah!' they chanted in Bethlehem, Pennyslvania, in the basketball stadium of Lehigh University, as the travelling Republican circus – the divine Sarah, John McCain, wife Cindy and now daughter Megan – entered the auditorium. If McCain was a jealous type (and he is, he's an angry, fizzing, perpetually punchy old goat) this would be killing some big part of him.

I can't imagine he's the type who's being willing to accept his sudden eclipse with equanimity, especially to a young woman. Dammit, can you imagine what the strategy sessions are like?

'Sarah, you have to go after Obama's Weatherman connections.'

'Sure, well, I was a sports journalist, so you betcha, I know . . .'

'No, we're talking about the Vietnam War, about the time of the Tet Offensive.'

'Offensive? It's outrageous!'

'Somebody give her a cue card.'

Argggghh. Courage, John. Grit your remaining teeth and get on with it.

The McCain team was forty minutes late getting onto that stage. Their warm-up act, just like Palin's warm-up act in Florida the day before, had returned to using the full 'Barack Hussein Obama' nomenclature, and it was alleged that Team McCain was taking a pause to try and work out what to do about it. Or taking a pause in order to give the appearance of doing such. Three hundred and fifty-one years ago, during the primary struggle between Obama and Hillary, McCain had condemned a shock jock who had thus introduced the Illinois senator in Cincinnati. Now the question is purely tactical. The McCain team has no qualms about opening up a whole descant of dog-whistle politics, but the last three rallies have had stray creeps brought to the pitch of emotion yelling 'Traitor!' whenever Obama's name is mentioned – and even 'Kill him!' – and the situation puts McCain in a difficult position.

Condemn the comments and you kill the mood of identification you need to make the rally a success. Ignore them and it looks like consent – or worse if you can't hear it and you're caught grinning while the news networks play it back and with subtitles, just so it can be really clear. It's ugly stuff in a country where one in four presidents has suffered a serious assassination attempt, successful or otherwise.

But it is also worth the risk. Like the Democrats, the Republicans have on staff their cognitive psychologists and their politico-psychosocial-linguisticians (George Lakoff is the most prominent on the Dems' side), and the Hussein reference is part of a double strategy, the other part of which is the Bill Ayers connection.

Trying to explain the political context of the Weather Underground in the 'zeroes is like teaching Chinese to a lungfish, but the GOP don't need or want to do that – all they have to do is connect 'domestic terrorist' to the 'Hussein' name and hope they can create an unconscious identification in a certain type of voter. It's part of the whole culture of the talking points, focus groups, fifteen-second ads and the debate worm – essentially post-politics, the bypassing of the human subjects to connect instead with a series of impulses and affects.

In that vein, John Murtagh, who alleges that the Weather Underground tried to firebomb his family home when he was a child, is due to do the media rounds tomorrow, with a neat line: 'Obama says he was eight years old when Ayers was active. Well, I was eight years old when he tried to kill my family.'

Sadly for McCain, the sort of people who will salivate at this on cue, do not appear to extend far and wide into independent voters at the moment – and they're not even that keen on John McCain. For the first time in memory at a VP and presidential candidate roadshow, people have been reported leaving these events after Palin has finished doing the warm-up.

The old Oz blues band Madder Lake, if memory serves, used to get this. Hired occasionally to open for a poppier overseas act, the promoter would be gobsmacked to see three hundred people leave as one on the last note of '12lb Toothbrush'. Why leave something you already paid for? Because, as an old blues-man – actually, redman – said, it's voting with your feet. Ditto in Bethlehem. They never liked McCain and a lot of them came for a glimpse of the divine Sarah, for the identification, for the sense that the values they hold are incarnated in someone, somewhere.

Nothing that they heard in last night's debate will persuade them that McCain is that someone. The reaction in the morning was like an Advokaat hangover, the pain made worse by the memory that the actual drinking itself was a deeply unpleasant act.

The rules for this pseudo town-hall–style debate had been agreed by the candidates' teams so as to prevent nasty surprises – to whit, no follow-up questions from petitioners (their mics were cut off after they'd finished their question). Nor was there any opportunity to pose questions to each other. *Politico* nominated it the 'worst debate ever' and as the US meltdown started to play through world markets – a CNN debate repeat was interrupted by a switch to their Asia feed so we could watch the Nikkei lose 10 per cent in a day – the disconnect between the 'dinner theatre' debate, old tired lines endlessly repeated, and the real challenges the world and America faced became total. Obama was widely picked as the winner, but only in the sense that McCain had to, I dunno, glass him or something to get a win.

After a terrible start, Obama's ability to actually answer in cogent paragraphs suggesting a degree of thought about the issues, started to come through. McCain stuck to his script of short punchy promises and hacks at his opponent – much of the fuss focusing on his reference to Obama as 'that one', which, tiresomely in the American context, has been worked over for possible racial motives. But it simply sounded, as all campaigns eventually do, like a bickering couple ('I said semiconductors were a good investment but *this one, this one*, wanted a rumpus room. A 4000 per cent yield!' 'Frank, for chrissake, that was thirty years ago.')

The Palinites would disagree, but it seems clear that America likes the calm joined-up thinking better than the scattershot attacks. Everyone's suddenly realised that the rules they apply to choosing a lawyer or a financial advisor – damn right you want someone smarter than you, not as was famously and ironically said of Dubya, 'someone you could have a beer with'.

As Obama's campaign gets more streamlined, once again seeming to become as quasi-anorexic as its leader in what it actually proposes, the McCain campaign becomes more like *The Price is Right*, desperately looking for something the public will buy. The latest? A $300 billion direct government buyout of mortgages – on top of the $1 trillion bailout – that seems to mark the final collapse of the McCain campaign from any sort of minimal free enterprise probity into crude right-wing populism. I'm not against a mass state buyout of mortgages (indeed, a larger one, as a substitute for the bailout, would be the go) but it has to be recognised for what it is – a piece of genuine socialism, an acknowledgement that the capitalist system is simply unable to sustain a way of life.

The mortgage buyback – which McCain, seeming only half-enthused, didn't hit enough during the debate – marks the final schism between McCain, the business-class Republicans and associated classical liberals, because it is, effectively, the white flag of surrender. But McCain is past caring. Indeed, he's starting to fall apart. Everyone is. To go back to that old politico-psychosocio-linguistics again, the slips are getting bigger.

Obama said, 'I can take four more weeks of John McCain's insults, but the country can't take four more *weyars* of . . .' etcetera. He meant to say 'years' but his brain crossed it with 'weary' to come up with a finneganism expressing his fears about the campaign. McCain had a better one, trying to refer to keeping his eye on others in the Senate, which came out as 'my fellow prisoners'.

Prisoners of what? Of the evil zombie march his campaign has become? Of the process by which he has shredded his repu-tation for a campaign he'll lose? Of Cindy? Her contribution today was to damn Obama for voting against funding the troops (just as John McCain did), which she said, 'sent a chill through my body'. Or, as Republicans call it, an orgasm. 'I want Barack Obama to spend a day in my shoes.' So do I. It would be more entertaining than the debate.

Now, in the evening, after the rallies have finished, the teams reappear on the cable shows – Michelle Obama on Larry King, and Palin and McCain on a FOX News interview that would shame the news director of TV Pyongyang.

Even with Sean Hannity feeding her Bill Ayers questions, Palin can't get her lines out. And even McCain baulks at going the full-court press. 'Well, I think it goes to the truthfulness of Senator Obama. It doesn't so much matter about an unrepentant terrorist and his wife who incidentally was worse than he was . . .' He snorts and laughs, and the old McCain emerges – because the old kamikaze can't keep a snicker of approval for the bomb throwers, especially the chick. Better than the stiffs he's hanging around with.

Be calm, prisoner. Soon the Vietcong will be at the gates to liberate you once more.

NASHVILLE: SATURDAY, 11 OCTOBER

'I believe that diplomacy should be the cornerstone of any foreign policy,' a simmering Hillary Clinton said.

'And I can see Russia from my house!' squeaked a perky Sarah Palin.

Was this *Saturday Night Live* sketch, featuring the uncan-
nily Palinesque Tina Fey, the moment of the 2008 campaign
that everyone will remember? Despite the historical import of
the Barack Obama candidacy and the body blow of the global
market crash, you wouldn't want to bet against it.

Fey's Palin and Amy Poehler's Hillary Clinton (and even the
show's portrayal of 'Irish' Joe Biden: 'John McCain – and I can't
stress this enough – I love him like a brother. I'd take a bullet
for him. But he is bad at his job and mentally unbalanced') have
been so dominating that the show has budded off a Thursday
night edition to put itself firmly in the centre of the political
process. It is far from the only comedy outfit doing double duty
in this presidential election

Towards the end of every weeknight, British and American
viewers gather around the TV to get a summary of the day's
news. Americans do too, but it isn't shows like *Lateline*, *Nightline*
[RIP], or the BBC's *Newsnight* they turn to – serious forensic,
critical encounters around the issues. Notoriously, a significant
portion of Americans now get their snapshot of the political
day from Comedy Central's *Daily Show with Jon Stewart*, or
its spin-off, *The Colbert Report* – in which a former *Daily Show*
reporter plays an 'in the tank' FOX News-style presenter, giving
his right-wing spin. Or they watch the opening monologues of
David Letterman and Jay Leno. Or, if they're really hardcore,
they stay up for *Red Eye*, a FOX News panel show that sounds
like Radio National's *AM* would if *The Footy Show* ran it.

None of these shows set out to be politics central. They

became such because nothing else was doing the job. Ever since the rise of the three 24-hour 'news' channels – CNN, FOX News, and MSNBC – mainstream American political coverage has lost about 90 per cent of its critical intelligence, ceding the ground to endless panels of party hacks with their 'talking points' – lines they want to trot out regardless of the context.

Where UK and Oz politicians take a deep breath and turn up for *The 7.30 Report* or BBC Radio's *Today* program, knowing they will leave with their flayed skin hanging off, US politicians know that the 24-hour news cycle makes them a scarce and much-needed commodity, with favours that can be withheld. When CNN reporter Campbell Brown repeatedly asked McCain spokesman Tucker Bounds to specify some of Governor Palin's hands-on foreign policy experience – a mere four out of ten on the Kerry O'Brien scale – the Republicans responded by yanking McCain from an appearance on *Larry King* and speaking of Brown's impertinence. Impertinence?

Though Campbell Brown refused to apologise, the station clearly pulled its head in, mindful of the five nights a week that King has to fill. But when the McCain campaign was similarly high-handed with David Letterman – canceling an appearance so McCain could fly back to Washington to 'solve' the bailout crisis – they discovered where the true power lay.

Letterman went for McCain in a way that the American news media has long since given up its license to do ('You know, the guy's a war hero, but someone's been putting something in his Metamucil'), and then went on to pull McCain apart for ten minutes, culminating in a switch to a live feed that showed McCain having make-up applied for a CBS news interview, still very much in New York.

In myth and tradition, the fool can say anything by virtue of his status as a non-player, a non-threat to the King. But when, in order to say anything, one has to take on the fool's motley, then you have a cultural problem. Politics is about the contestation between different worldviews and the relentless contestation with the enemy. If you don't genuinely believe that the other is a threat to the world you want to bring into being, then you ain't doing politics.

SNL's portrayal of Palin is an excoriating satire of her Alaska faux-ksiness – but it also lets her off the hook in a way that a genuinely searching interview does not.

The continuum of 24/7 cable news with entertainment networks in a society dominated by discontinuous and decontextualised images tends to make everything float-free. If America's news media were doing their job, and talking back to the professional spinmeisters, then comedy – whose function is to release tension and dispel contestation – would not have to do the sort of heavy lifting that has suddenly been required of it. After several hours of watching these – and crossover news-polemic shows like *Countdown with Keith Olbermann*, which come to the news-comedy mix from the other direction – you feel like you've been entertained for hours.

And for a country with two wars and a depression on its hands, that's no laughing matter.

IN TRANSIT, JOHNSTOWN, PENNSYLVANIA–RICHMOND, VIRGINIA:
SUNDAY, 12 OCTOBER

I got a job working construction for the Johnstown company
But lately there ain't been much work on account of the economy
  – 'The River', Bruce Springsteen

'Man, this is the most corrupt town in America . . . No one wants to know.'

Yesterday, in the only bar on the shuttered main street of Johnstown, Pennsylvania, Jackson, a one-time major league football player, was holding forth to the assembled Saturday afternoon crowd, which was three barflies, plus me and fellow Aussie journalist James Norman.

Every fifteen minutes he halted his disquisition on small-town Pennsylvania stand-over crap – the cops chase people away from his bar so they can knock down the price and buy it – to hug his wife/girlfriend/chiquita, a hispanic mama with a memorial tattoo on each arm (literal portraits of a dead, usually murdered, loved one).

She was an ample woman, with generous bye-byes under the arms, which, as they shook, made it look like her dead tattooed sisters were laughing. Possibly that was intended.

That morning James and I had been at the Sarah Palin rally at the Cambria County War Memorial Arena, a brick bunker soon to host Frankie Valli, according to its bitmap electric sign – can that be possible? – as well as other ghosts of the recent past, now consigned to the small-town circuit, the endless whistlestop, playing the old hits.

Johnstown likes the old hits, which is why there were a thousand people queuing on a frozen Saturday morning to hear a forty-something energetic airhead speak in a week when the American economy teetered on the brink of collapse, and the only way to save it was part-socialisation. But forget that. They were here for a laying on of hands.

Over the other side of the street, about two hundred pro-Bama protestors had gathered, most of them with union T-shirts. The chanted slogans flew thick and fast. Eventually a phalanx of McCain supporters came over to get in their faces and yell 'Get a job!' at the protestors. 'Frank – come on,' one said to the other, before the police slid a car between them and chased the Palinites back to their side of the street.

Yes, years ago some of these people had known each other, worked together, been part of the same world. The town is pure *Deer Hunter*, made by eastern Europeans (Croatians and Bulgarians in this case) going west from the slums of Philadelphia.

On the riverbank beside the town, massive brick warehouses, masterpieces of construction, hang empty, their mouths gaping open. In the scumble of old row houses, the onion domes of the Orthodox houses point at the sky. As the Springsteen song suggests, even thirty years ago, the place was work and life.

Now it's rust, and men circling in cars, revving them at the traffic lights, and bars in lean-tos, where you have to buy food to get a sixpack. On every table the corner of an uneaten pizza slice droops off a paper plate, like a dozen tongues hanging out, wanting something.

Pennsylvania, as James Carville once noted, is Philadelphia and Pittsburgh with Alabama in the middle. The churches are lined up on the main street, and in the motel room there isn't a 'What's On' guide but a 'Directory of Places of Worship'.

Yet Carville's theory was oversimplified. Thirty years ago, religion was a quietly held and traditional thing. Now the fundamentalist outfits can build garish tabernacles where the downtown used to be, on the strength of local donations. As the jobs went, the union membership fell, and when it was clear that the jobs weren't coming back, the churches went up.

'Men must have legends lest they die of strangeness,' as the man said, and this one-time stronghold of American socialism was now the place Barack Obama had in mind when he had foolishly talked openly of the bitterness that drove them to guns and God, when everything else had quit the field.

Palin, of course, drives them wild. McCain, not so much. For a long time they'd never heard of him, or if they had, it was as that senator who was willing to work with Democrats on bills, the ultimate insider. His reinvention as a 'maverick' is a measure of people's desperation to think that the party they believed in hasn't got it terribly wrong and become a European socialist party overnight.

'McCain and Palin will fight for us,' yell one couple, holding a 'Nobama' sign. 'He turned that bailout bill into a rescue bill.'

Thus do myths of healing by touch start and propagate.

Inside, Palin, her hair down from the sexy librarian bun, is giving the audience what they want. The Bill Ayers stuff is on hold, after John McCain (rebelling against his own advisors, it would seem) started to talk his audience down from the tower on the question of Barack Obama being a terrorist. When a woman in one deathful town-hall meeting broke down in tears saying she was scared that 'Obama was an Arab', McCain talked her and his audience down, saying they had 'nothing to fear from Barack Obama . . . I just disagree with his vision for America'.

Well, big ups to him – and that is not meant sarcastically. Commentators are suggesting that this extraordinary statement by McCain, while his campaign is still going around with the baby-eating stuff, is a measure of how badly it has played in the polls. If that were true, he'd simply leave it alone.

I think his sudden Damascus road turn is a sign that he thinks he's lost the election and he doesn't want to be remembered as the one who hammered the wedge deeper into America at a time when it could do with a bit of common purpose. He is now thinking of his reputation, and of the dark, dark thought that he could be the guy who tempted some wing nut to pop off the first black president.

There is clearly a core of decency in the man that he has tapped back into – much to the chagrin of the nihilists surrounding him – and that may well be the greatest contribution he has made to the republic in his long chaotic life.

Instead of Bill Ayers, Palin talks about abortion and 'life'. The audience, most of whom have five to ten years shaved off their life because they don't have universal health care, applaud wildly. This unique incommensurable issue (abortion) has become for them what the gold standard is for the Ron Paulites – some solid measure of value, against which everything will be guaranteed.

Later in the day Palin will use her kids like chattels, taking them out to an ice hockey game in Philadelphia where the working-class crowd booed her to a turn. 'I thought there'd be less of it if I put Piper [her 8-year-old daughter] in a hockey jersey,' she said later. What a great mother she is.

But what craziness this is. Palin runs a state that is as socialist as Norway in all but its achievements and she's lecturing this deprived crowd about free enterprise. And if the people of Johnstown lived in Sweden, the empty warehouse would have a hospital and a social centre and three high-tech companies housed in it. Instead there is . . . rust. Rust and God.

My colleague James, sporting a clubbish pilgrim beard and with bags under his eyes from overindulgence, gets yelled at at the stoplights. 'Hey, Osama!' they shout.

'Was he yelling at me?' Yes mate, he was.

Springsteen's song had rivers as some sort of life force; the rivers that flowed through the mill towns, heavy with metal, occasionally catching fire.

Then I got Mary pregnant and man that was all she wrote
And for my nineteenth birthday I got a union card and wedding coat

I typed those lines from memory. What Springsteen sang of as deprivation, Palin et al have elevated (via her hapless daughter) to the level of myth and good. What greater sign of failure could there be that the grim life of a mill town can be looked back on with nostalgia?

Palin is here, and will be elsewhere, because the McCain campaign believes their only chance is to tap into that nostalgia for certainty of any sort, and to find it in this political odd couple, this senatorial insider and Jesus-freak sports reporter. Bruce, help them.

Is a dream a lie if it don't come true or is it something worse
that sends me
down to the river . . .

And still after four hours, the queue kept waiting.

RICHMOND, VIRGINIA: MONDAY, 13 OCTOBER

'Look, I can't go down there,' the driver said.

We were on our way to another Palin rally, out in the back-blocks of Richmond, a city that appears to be all backblocks. The brutalist concrete stadium loomed high above us as we circled in closer, the familiar carnie fringe of T-shirt stalls, button sellers and home-school kids pushed into service selling cups of warm soda.

'Not there, *there*,' James said in frustration. 'Follow that van.'

But the guy was a timid gentlemen. He looked like he'd had

some sort of real job before being consigned to the twilit life of taxis, and cops waving wildly at him had got him mozzed. Silly bugger, we thought.

We persuaded him round eventually, street by street, until we found an entrance that was open near the main car park, full of trucks of a size that wouldn't have seemed out of place in an open-cut mining operation. The crowd was already being warmed up and whooping as we made our way in, and found out that the driver – even now squealing away – clearly had some voodoo good sense we should have tapped into. The place was scary.

'Wear red,' the invitation had suggested, and thousands of participants had been happy to comply. The red/blue swap over in American politics has been a source of humour before ('Keep Alabama Red' type signs on highways, suggesting that a revolutionary committee sits in Little Rock, sending out fighting girl brigades to extend the revolution to Chattanooga), but this was something else.

Skeins and veins of scarlet ran through the crowd, like blood was pouring from the stage with a bit of splatter. There was a touch of Maoist opera about it in everything but the mood, which was less exuberantly fixed on the radiant future than just downright mean.

With camera in hand, James and I had hit on the hilarious gag of using my passing resemblance to Lenin to address the crowd from behind and have them turn in bewilderment and anger, as if it were the may days of Petrograd. We pretty quickly abandoned that after observing that: a) people were not in the mood for our funny, funny jokes; and b) there was no easy escape route. Resorting to the last refuge of the scoundrel, we tried direct journalism.

'Few words for the Australian media?' By and large, they had two, and one of them has a dash in the middle.

Pity really, but you can't blame them. Republican politics are so tied up in knots at this point that any belief can only be sustained by keeping yourself clear of the process of reasoning. With the US Government now proposing to take a larger stake in the banking sector than the Venezuelan Government has in its, the final sense of legitimacy and identity attached to the 'American way' of doing things has completely collapsed.

Attempts to blame the Democrats are half-hearted at best, as the US scrambles to nationalise a key sector of its economy, like one of those little bitch European states it used to like to punk so much. So a gruesome triage has been performed, pivoting on McCain's 'maverick' message. For the crowds gathering in the coal towns and NASCAR tracks of the swing states, it is the *Republicans* that McCain and Palin are going to Washington to sort out. The Democrats barely figure in the narrative, save for Barack Obama, who is less an actual politician now than a distilled symbol of everything that negates them: bookish, exotic, inner-city, thoughtful and, of course, bl— . . . For a long time they weren't paying much attention to the national race, or to the possibility that Obama might be their president. When they started to watch, McCain had pulled ahead. Now the reality of an Obama victory is starting to sink in, along with the anticipation of pain, that awful crunch in the stomach as you contemplate total loss.

As always happens in such circumstances, Team McCain and friends have formed themselves into a circular firing squad. With McCain refusing to stay with the strategy of damning Obama as a mysterious, dangerous friend of terrorists, hardcore conservatives such as Jonah Goldberg of the *National Review* hacked into McCain for not having the guts to stick with the scorched earth policies his Karl Rove coterie of advisors had developed.

Now Bill Kristol, the *New York Times*' house conservative who's been using his column as a series of gentle memos to the campaign, has advised McCain to sack his campaign, stop running the attack ad, and use the money to run televised town-hall meetings where people can see him and Palin for the great campaigners they are.

This is fantasy (and also a pre-emptive strike against being blamed for helping lose Washington to the GOP for a decade or more). McCain is too exhausted to do great town halls these days, and he spends half of them getting ambushed by his nastier, crazier, or simply more spooked, supporters. With the bitterness rising, they're becoming increasingly uncontrollable.

This week, for example, one jerk had brought along a toy monkey with an 'Obama' headband on it. McCain would never have even seen it, but it doesn't matter. Had he suggested letting North Korea run the joint prior to a return to barter, it couldn't have got more viral than that one guy with a ten-dollar toy and a sticker, disgracing everyone else.

But if the 'show the real McCain' push is fantastical, then the idea of 'unleashing Palin' is equivalent to thinking that the lap dancer really liked you. Though she's made a couple of stonking speeches, Palin's abilities on the stump, as judged by today's blood-red rally, are third-rate at best. Short of flying in the whole of Wasilla, she couldn't have had a better crowd, yet hell, they were doing all the work in getting up an atmos today. Even given a stump speech crafted by experts and touching all the bases – maverick, pro-life (with markedly less interest in their lives), yada yada – she can't breathe life into it, can't get it to the next level.

This is the sort of occasion where lack of experience shows. US politics, more than any other, demands that you master the art of the stump, which is to make boilerplate material sound like it was something you had just thought of, a sudden and instant formulation that you were communicating to you, yes you, Joe/Joan Sixpack/Lunchpail/Hockeymom.

You take out or put in a para here or there, but the art is really to sell the same material. Palin can't do it because she never really had to in Alaska – her campaign for governor was a series of informal chats and coffee meetings around stuff she knew about; i.e. Alaskan municipal–state relations. She sells it like, well, like she was still in a Miss Congeniality competition talking about world peace.

'Gosh, doggone it, special needs kid, special needs love, maverick, clean up Washington . . .' she schlepped through, the crowd never really energised. At points, chants of 'U-S-A!' started up from the crowd's fringes and she took up the chant.

When the audience is giving *you* the energy, your act is in trouble. Whatever the advantage of Palin's candidacy – and it has undoubtedly delivered – she can't get it to the next level, which is to get the base out to convert their friends and neighbours, to get that wavering vote, to be viral.

That's the sort of thing a Huckabee (now with his own FOX TV show) or, godhelpus, even a Romney could have done, tag teaming with McCain. Joe Biden is doing this across the northeastern swing states, rounding up Ohio and Pennsylvania and quietly talking, more in sorrow than anger, about what a tool his good friend John McCain has become.

God knows, McCain could have used that. Today, ahead of the debate, Obama released an expanded financial plan, guaranteeing tax credits for small businesses who employ extra workers and a bunch of other stuff, turning the focus onto grassroots economics. Poor old Walnuts, doing a one-on-one interview on CNN, had to concede that two of the proposals were 'good ideas'. Having spruiked his wasteful mortgage guarantee plan – a profligate version of earlier Democrat plans – he could hardly bang the 'government is the problem, not the solution' drum. Never seen him so tired. Bradley effect, Schmadley, um, feffect.

He thinks it's over and he's thinking of his reputation, of history. And also that he will have to spend a lot of time with himself in the coming years, and he wants to be the sort of person he would want to hang around with.

The crowds at the raceway, the Palinites, the NASCAR folk,

the bikies and angry vets and whatever – this dynastic Navy man is as alien to these people as Obama is. He's repelled by their ressentiment, their exuberant know-nothingism, their worship of complacency. Deep down, they know it too. At the stalls, as we leave, Palin-only buttons are outselling all others three to one.

We call a cab from the local McDonald's. It's the same driver, who takes us through the backstreets of this southern town, the houses and porches unchanged for a century that seem to be contemplating great change now.

'I thought you were scared,' I say.

He shrugs. 'There's no other work.'

Forty states. He'll get forty states.

VIRGINIA: TUESDAY, 14 OCTOBER

No knives or sharp objects
No liquids or gels over 3 fl.oz
No weapons
No jokes
    – sign on door of Richmond International Airport

Well, with the McCain and Obama teams out at Hofstra University on Long Island, measuring the height of chairs and the size of water glasses ahead of tomorrow night's debate, the remainder of the campaign is looking like a toe-to-toe slog with increasingly concrete proposals being deployed to increasingly diminishing returns.

Following Obama's unveiling of a plan allowing for people to tap their 401(k) retirement funds for emergency needs without penalty tax, ending the tax on unemployment benefits (a weird thing in itself) and jobs grants for small business, McCain came out with his, which involved, erm, ending the tax in unemployment benefits and a cut in the capital gains tax from 15 to 7.5 per cent.

The go-around was advantage Obama again, who has gained traction repeatedly by going against political wisdom and holding back a move until McCain has had time to announce three contradictory things in a morning and be contradicted on two of them by Sarah Palin. Obama then slides in with a more comprehensive plan and strengthens the impression that he is, in fact, already the president, and the bloke yapping around his heels is just some crazy old guy.

So if this really is an Obama strategy, rather than the campaign's general air of laidback, cool knitwear-wearing blitheness yielding unintended political benefits, big ups to them for knowing their business.

If, as I said, the toe-to-toe slog continues, this campaign will play out in a mood of grinding boredom. There seems to be some human rule that things run out of steam just before they actually conclude – a sudden ennui hits you in the middle of the last act of Chekhov or Pinter (or in the case of Williamson, in the queue for tickets), and we're in it now. Couldn't we have an October surprise with no casualties, but a lot of Sturm und Drang? A neat little invasion, an empty plane crashing into an empty building, summat like that?

That's what the McCain campaign wants most of all, of course. Anything, anything at all. Because they keep striking these flints on the ground – Bill Ayers, alleged voter fraud by ACORN, etcetera – without even beginning to strike a spark. It may even be counterproductive.

You can't go broke underestimating the stupidity of the public, etcetera, but the Republicans are really testing this on the Ayers case. Obama had most contact with Ayers under the auspices of the Annenberg Trust, established by a former Nixon cabinet member. ACORN has been signing people up left right and centre – as have hundreds of groups from all sides of politics, including the NRA and Right To Life – and they are required to hand in every voter registration form they receive, whether they believe it's fraudulent or not.

If there is an open and deliberate attempt to persuade people to vote fraudulently, that's a different matter, but the main evidence at the moment appears to be paid canvassers padding their registration quotas. It's not enough, it would seem, to change the terms of debate, and all it serves to do is make the Republicans look plaintive and petitioning and outside the main game.

That would appear to be the conclusion from the polls, in any case. Obama is really racking up some impressive leads here. There isn't a single 2004 Democratic state in play now – New Hampshire, Wisconsin, Michigan and Minnesota are all showing double-digit leads for Obama.

Of 2004 red states, leads in Iowa, Florida, Colorado, New Mexico and Virginia are all clear of 5 per cent for Obama as an average across all polls, and second tier gains such as North Carolina and Missouri are showing a tie–2 per cent lead. Even North Dakota, from which the Obama campaign withdrew a fortnight ago, is showing a 2 per cent lead. If Obama can win a campaign in which he's had no one on the ground for a fortnight, then ask him to stroll out for a drink on the yacht sometime.

The great enigma is Ohio, on which you can get any poll you like – from 5 per cent for Obama to a 2 per cent McCain victory. But the point now is that McCain must have Ohio, while Obama doesn't need it – he has a number of paths to victory. This may be the election that busts the Ohio mythology for all time.

Of course, the hidden element in all this is money. The Obama campaign has $80 million to spend in the last two weeks, which is the entire amount McCain has been able to spend in the period since the Convention, after accepting state funding. Obama suckered him big-time on that – he said he'd agree to public funding if McCain would, and then double-crossed him magnificently.

Indeed it was a double-doublecross, the Obama team relying on the Republicans' fear that they wouldn't be able to get their base to cough up for Walnuts, coupled with their belief that the decent old Democrats would line up like suckers to receive their priss-slap. Not this time, baby.

The Obama campaign is now negotiating to buy a half-hour of prime time for the days before 4 November, a type of campaigning once common but not used for some time. That would be on top of the wall-to-wall thirty- and sixty-seconders, which in some areas – Northern Virginia, for example – are out-numbering McCain spots by ten or fifteen to one.

Now, in the lead up to the debate, the focus has turned to McCain and 'what he must say'. He's taken the underdog role ('We're six points behind in the polls, the media has written us off [big booing] . . . and Obama is already measuring the drapes in the White House') and then paused before slipping into self-parody: 'We've got him right where we want him.' With McCain having exhausted every strategy in the book, the Right has descended into fully magical thinking, with a new demand to 'unleash the real McCain'.

Oh come on, the real McCain? Really? Who is the real McCain? From the mid '70s onwards he was naval liaison to the Senate (i.e. a state lobbyist), before becoming a congress-man and then a senator. Hilariously for a party grooving on free enterprise, the dude's been a lifelong public servant. Including a five-year junket in Hanoi. The real McCain is a professional politician with a bunch of social liberal policies (and other conservative ones). His achievements are written in a series of bills – McCain–Feingold is the most prominent, the other half of which is a prominent liberal democrat. He's an insider and deal-maker, the sort of person who wants to be a 'chairman of the board' Republican, not a values warrior.

We've seen the real McCain. Then we saw the fake McCain. And the public doesn't want either of them. The chorus of 'unleash the real McCain', including today from McCain's brother Joe, is simply fantasy – his supporters cannot believe that the real McCain has been seen and is being rejected. Which is funny, really. For a group whose love of the life and works of Winston Spencer Churchill borders on ancestor-worship, they seem particularly unaware of the 1945 election.

What the 'unleash McCain' crowd want is for the nation to be obsessed as *they* are about the connections a left-liberal person might make on the rise to a position of national power. Just as any right-winger will at some point come into contact with the lower depths of their own political tradition (especially in the US), so too on the left you meet some strange folks along the way.

The weird thing is that Americans understand that more than most. With 12 000 homicides a year and a prison population of two million, well, everyone knows bad boys. Violence is in the air in American life like petrol fumes in a servo forecourt. People are less shocked by its appearance in everyday life than elsewhere.

The whole twisted story of Ayers et al's violent campaign against US imperialism is like a story about theological difficulties in the early church, a list of dead bishops.

But no evidence to the contrary will disabuse them that this matters. Let's face it, the McCain campaign is surrounded by people living off his life story – insider sybarites who never went near a recruiting office, talking about 'country first'. As a Republican President socialises the economy, what can they do? Where can they go? Nothing holds their ideology together anymore.

The collapse of this hybrid Republican ideology is total. And the Obama campaign is eying the possibility of the ultimate prize – making sixty Senate seats, a filibuster-proof majority. That was out of the question two months ago. The Dems were hoping for a five-seat gain to give them 53–54 seats plus two independents, smegma stain Joe Lieberman included therein.

Now races like Minnesota and, migod, Alaska, hitherto written off by the Dems, are opening up, and it's those four or five races which might on the outside deliver the Dems total control of the legislative and executive branches – and thus, de facto, the judicial branch. It's a once-in-a-century opportunity to remake America. That should have been enough to scare the base back to the GOP. That they can't get there is a measure of where we're at.

CNN Live keeps cutting back to the Hofstra Universtity debate site – an empty room being set up. It has a Warhol-esque, compelling quality to it.

And, as we head into the last act, please – no jokes, no sharps, and godhelpus, no guns.

LONG ISLAND, NEW YORK: WEDNESDAY, 15 OCTOBER

Low-slung suburbs and ratty convenience stores give way to long fences and fields; the black faces give way to white; brick and wood and verandahs become stone and porticos . . . If Long Island suggests to you big houses in the Hamptons and trading quips with Dorothy Parker over a bath-tub martini, think again. It's a lotta lotta 'burbs, with Hofstra University – site of tonight's final debate – in the middle.

Like most universities attended by those Americans who get to attend university, Hoftsra is a middle-sized campus with a few old buildings and a bunch of lumpy modern ones, a not particularly exciting union building, a sense of quiet innocence. The sense of overwhelming size, both crushing and liberating, that you get with Melbourne U or UNSW or UQ or whatever sort of thing LaTrobe is now, you don't get here. It's all gentler, more verdant, a feeling emphasised by the fact that there is nowhere to buy alcoho—

'There's what!!?' I think I hit an eight on the Richter scale. Students milling in the forecourt turned round. I had a bunch of gear in the bag and had been planning to unveil our 'Drill, baby, drill' campaign to encourage teen pregnancy – a big picture of Bristol, Levi, Sarah and Bristol's first daughter on the poster. And even in this proBama gathering there was no way in hell I was doing it on Red Bull.

'Yeah, well, you gotta be twenty-one to drink,' the girl at the union information counter said. 'So it kinds makes sense.'

Makes sense. Nothing about American drinking laws makes sense. You can get killed before you've legally had a beer. There are twenty parents currently in jail for buying booze for their kids' party. But this is where a lot of Americans, especially white Americans, live.

'It's a long way from Brooklyn,' my colleague James said, settling for a bowl of nachos, which looked more like a Mexican food milkshake than anything resembling a meal. James is currently using the online couch surfer service to find accommodation.

His kip in Brooklyn is a large apartment offered by a guy who likes to walk around naked and needs people there to see him do it. It takes his mind off his work, which is playing a lead role in an all-naked theatre company.

I was staying in the Waldorf Astoria, on free points, where a chicken sandwich is twenty-four dollars and you can call up an escort service whose staff are all PhDs. Four hundred bucks gets you a screaming argument about Lacanian psychoanalysis at the Four Seasons and a 3 a.m. hysterical overdose in the slate-tiled bathroom. Great town, New York.

But this was Long Island, and as dusk was gathering, the carnival of the debate was roaring into full force. It was mostly white kids for Obama, with a lot of black students and staff, as well as a few huddled McCain–Palin masses, including one brave soul who was also running a pro-marijuana campaign, and a bunch of dorky looking boys dressed as giant squirrels to highlight the alleged ACORN vote-registering scandal.

God, that was hard yards. On a hot Indian summer evening, there you are, turning up ready to do whatever needs to be done for the party for that internship – hell, you'd even do Larry Craig in a bathroom – and someone hands you a giant orange rodent and tells you to go and annoy a six-foot off-duty security guard with a 'Change' button.

'Where can we watch the debate?' we asked the 'bar'tender, while sipping ice teas.

'Well, there's a mock debate by the young leaders of the future society in the main theatre.'

'What else have you got?'

'There's a debate party . . .'

'Party? With booze?'

'No, but there's ice-cream.'

God help us.

So anyway, as the debate got underway we found a TV in a ratty old pool room that looked like somewhere in Macquarie Uni in 1976, with people who'd been there since then. Whatever happened in the debate, we weren't going to get a great reading of its public impact here.

So it proved, for in the opening minutes it quickly became clear that McCain had a new shtick that involved 'Joe the plumber'. Joe was the guy who Obama told he wanted to 'spread the wealth' around, but that 98 per cent of small businesses would get a better deal. McCain took the initiative to talk to Joe directly down the barrel of the camera.

Obama took it back to more general issues. McCain talked to Joe again. He was becoming a sort of porn character, forever appearing at the door.

Wow. By the half-hour mark McCain is really going in hard and direct. But there's no new material: it was the $42 000 tax hike, it was 'sending money to people who don't like us very much', it was 'poor me, people called me a KKKer', and so on.

Obama's comebacks are in his usual airy manner, but since McCain is spitting and hissing like one of those planes he used to crash, that approach may work – the whole well-formed sentences sort of thing.

Twenty minutes in, there's no new light thrown on things but a lot more heat.

'John, even FOX News says your $42 000 line was untrue,' says Obama, and that got the biggest laugh so far.

'Isn't it exciting?' a bubbly kid in a 'Hope' T-shirt said.

Somewhere in Brooklyn a man on a stage in an old butter churn factory is doing 'I Sing the Body Electric' with his dong hanging out. Man, if this is exciting, get out of Long Island, kid. Or get some drinks in here.

9.55 p.m. So we're forty minutes in and there's something resembling a new encounter. McCain hacks into Obama's alleged antipathy to free trade, slating his failure to sign the Colombia free trade agreement. Obama notes that this was because killing trade union leaders was standard business practice in Colombia and there was no attempt to modify that. Senator Obama has never gone south of the border, McCain says, so he doesn't know about free trade.

There was a great comeback to that for Obama ('I've been to Ohio, I know all about free trade'), but he doesn't use it.

10.01 p.m. Then we get onto health care and McCain talks down the barrel to Joe the plumber again about Obama's plan to fine 'small businesses' for not providing health care. God, Joe is coming to be like the guy in the TV movie *Recount*, the one vote who's going to decide the election.

Lots of argy-bargy about the details of health care, which clarifies things, but not much. McCain sticks to the big government thang and Obama decides not to rise to bait and say that government has a role in it, and sticks to employers' care.

First weird misspeak – McCain calls Obama 'Senator Government'.

10.10 p.m. Roe vs Wade comes up. McCain says he would never apply a litmus test to supreme court justices and that might mean a pro-abortion judge. That will get some strife from the right.

Obama defends Roe vs Wade on privacy-rights grounds and steers off the court thing into the issue itself, pushing for support on a right to choose.

McCain comes back round on Obama's Chicago votes. We've heard this all before. It gives Obama a chance to clarify why he didn't support those laws about late-term abortions and partial birth, talking about the health of the mother.

10.14 p.m. McCain replies with air quotes around 'the life of the mother' – that's been stretched, he says. It sounds brutal and will play badly. May even have been his gaffe of the night.

10.17 p.m. Final question, on how crap US education is. Obama gets onto the issue of college costs and I couldn't hear the rest of it for whooping. Gives a very wonkish answer about early childhood, etcetera. Constrained about talking about charter (i.e. private) schools by need to keep teacher unions sweet?

10.21 p.m. McCain comes in hard on charter schools and then gets onto government being the problem . . . Then says that you don't need teachers to have all these fancy certification degrees, which is very weird . . . Teechers shuld be dumberer . . .

Obama gets off a couple of good but old shots about 'no child left behind . . .' and 'they left the money behind'. 'Senator McCain's advisor said college funding was pandering to interest groups . . . I don't think America's youth are an interest group . . . I think they're our future.'

Closing remarks come up.

McCain lost the coin toss and goes first. Blah blah, guff about government and spending (I just don't think that government stuff works, it's the market they're worried about) . . . and service of his family . . . and he'd quite like to serve again . . . can I please be president?

Obama sounds much better right from the get-go, talking about the serious problems we face and what we have to do, the way America has to be reconstructed, and how we can all work together on this and believe in the American people again. It's much, much better and sounds presidential.

The score – McCain was punchier but more scattered, and he commanded the rhetorical field with his 'Joe the plumber' stuff, before Obama started to get it back onto more general matters. Obama passed up every opportunity to punch hard, which, yes, in this context seemed wise.

Once again Obama won by not losing. McCain lost by getting a draw, or even a slight win. And I reckon the 'life of the mother' air quotes are good for another tranche of female voters moving to Obama, as well as that thing about teachers not needing training. He's hitting wrong notes, I suspect, the old Navy flyer fighting the last war/campaign but two or three.

9

CLOSING TIME IN THE MONARCH BAR

The Final Weeks

With the final debate over, and the election entering its final three-week stage — it is worth remembering that there have been entire British and Australian campaigns of not much more than three weeks in toto — discussion and debate has focused all day not on whether McCain won the debate, but on whether he has anything left to campaign on.

That he lost the debate is without question. Sixty per cent of respondents on all polls have declared Obama the winner to 30 per cent for Walnuts, and even when that is adjusted to allow for a 40/30/30 Democrat/Republican/Independent vote, it still turns out pretty well for him.

Having blusteringly promised on radio that he would 'whip [Obama's] you-know-what' — what a great phrase to apply to a black man in a former slave society — McCain came out punchy as ever, while Obama, like an earlier candidate who knew about ass whuppings, floated like a butterfly and stung like a bee.

While McCain grunted, grimaced and interrupted, and, whenever attacked, wrote huge notes on a big pad like a bad schoolkid drawing an enormous cock and balls, Obama leaned back and smiled, wasn't afraid to reply to McCain's questions (on Bill Ayers, for example) and in general was so smoooooth, brother – because he knew it was driving McCain's prostate so far back up his ass that he was choking on it.

McCain needed to roll out something new and he did – the now famous Joe the Plumber, the Ohio self-employed single father, who expressed his concern about Obama's tax plans. McCain turned him into a small businessowner above the quarter-million threshold of Obama's tax cuts, and made him a reasonably effective centrepiece cum sock-puppet for his arguments that Obama's tax plans would harm job creation.

The only crimp in the whole higher-taxed small businessman Joe the Plumber thang is that the business doesn't come near the quarter-mil earnings threshold, Joe doesn't own it (he's thinking of buying it from his employer), and he isn't even a plumber, never having taking the contractors' test. Oh, and as the kiss-of-the-ass-whip, his name isn't Joe, it's Sam.

Sam/Joe the un-Plumber has been besieged with media attention since the debate, though to his credit, he's refused to say who he would vote for. If he could vote, that is – he's not registered. His few statements indicated a straightforward blue-collar Republican ('Why should people who earn more pay a higher tax rate? Stop hating America . . . Iraq has made us safer . . .') and he refused to reveal how much he earned, though the *Toledo Blade* later established it as $40 000 a year.

The conclusion was, though, a bit of a boofhead who didn't have a clue about his own economic best interests, Sam/Joe was a decent bloke. Even that judgement came to be revised when, in reply to a question about how well Obama had answered the question he put to him, Sam/Joe, Mr Average White Guy, answered, 'He danced around it like Sammy Davis Jr'.

Great answer. Great. Answer. God, what a PhD thesis there is in that answer. Sam/Joe's thirty-four. He was sixteen when Sammy died in 1990, so memories of his work are really a sort of postmodern folk hand-me-down, old clips on TV and suchlike. But they survived because Davis represented the last example of that strange mid-century phenomenon, the 'acceptable negro', the last all-round entertainer before the James Browns and Sly Stones came along. Offstage, Davis was no patsy, even though he made considerable accommodations to the time, and his great triumph was (with Frank Sinatra) finally desegregating the entertainment world by boycotting venues with a colour bar – but for the public eye, he was the frenetic, all singin', all dancin' good boy, willing to take the borderline jokes of the Rat Pack and the Dean Martin roasts. (Remember them? Weren't they great? I watched some again recently. They weren't.) No coincidence that tap dancing was the thing they loved most about him, the grinning, jittering, slight-bodied figure never still in the quest to please Massa. Tap has a sense of the old cottonfields about it, but it is the type of dance that looks most like work, and its rhythms are that of the machine, of capitalism and pure domination. It reminds some people of how things used to be, race-wise (the opening scene of *Blazing Saddles*, in which the dance emerges from the black sheriff getting his feet shot at).

For the past half century, two types of black people have been on offer to whites – Sammy Davis Jr on the one hand and Martin Luther King on the other, Leslie Uggams versus Jesse Jackson, Eddie Murphy against Oprah Winfrey, the former half of each pair the negro who is never serious, the latter (despite their utter differences) the black who is never not, whose very existence means that the world is changing. Sammy D was Sam/Joe's go-to happy place when you knew that any famous black man, by virtue of being an entertainer, was still subject to your desires.

He needed it, of course, because Barack Obama confounds the latter category completely. He's deadly serious, but he's relaxed and smooth. He's a black politician, but he doesn't have that physical solidity, the militant past and the peacocking – the expensive suits, etcetera – that tend to characterise black political leaders. He's no Don 'No Soul' Simmons, but you wouldn't be surprised to find him doing your taxes at H&R Block. And, above all, he only has to speak for thirty seconds for you to realise that he's smarter and more in command than you will ever be. The Sam/Joes of America aren't KKK racists, or even just Southern good ol' boys. They can accept powerful, rich black people.

What they can't accept is a black person who is continent and complete, as integrated as Obama is, who is neither ceaselessly emotionally performative ('Hot damn! I'm gonna hit me some of that,' said a black guy in the cafe where I'm writing from, while he was looking at some lasagne in the bain-marie, is what I mean) nor angry and threatening, and who, from the same standing start, did a lot better than them. This free radical has to be bound back to a larger, safer entity, and before you know it, you're singing 'The Candyman', a song which, were it to be performed today by the Young Talent Team, would have the police called.

Where the Christ in hell was I? Ah yes. Sam/Joe's heartfelt belief in the fairness of America and that reward is somehow related to effort, must have the country club Republicans he votes for laughing till they hoik up their epiglotti. With his encounter with Obama, it appeared as if he had done them another fine service, giving McCain a motif he needed for the last part of the contest – if not enough to win, at least something to talk about.

Now, McCain is in a right bind. With various Ohio trades boards investigating where and when Joe may have done work he wasn't certified to perform, Team GOP may have endangered his livelihood – and exposed the business he works for to legal liability problems. With Joe himself a media figure in his own right, how can McCain ventriloquise him for another three weeks? The nightmare would be that Joe would rightly get irritated, turn round and say that John McCain doesn't speak for him, and that whole tranche of remnant Nixon/Reagan/thick Democrats would be lost to the GOP.

The problem is all the more tantalising when you consider what a gaffe Obama's 'spread the wealth' remark was, in the US, in Ohio, in the 2000s. Old Barry couldn't have sounded more European if he'd said it in French, while sucking on a Gitane. 'Oue er geweng tur spreeed yer owulth lak menn yure fur ze – ow you say – leetle piggies.' Slap slap. 'Owure eez yer wayfe owur meestress? Ai wuld laike tur impregnate, etcetera . . .'

With the whole Democrat party having had drilled into them the 'language framing' argument – how about 'We're going to make the tax system fairer for everyone'? – now is not the time for the Obama campaign to return to the sloppiness and lack of focus of late summer. Joe may not be as useful (oh, he also owes a grand in unpaid taxes too) as even twenty-four hours ago, but it's some sort of crack McCain might be able to haul himself up on.

But McCain's going to need that because whatever advantages he's gained, it's now being generally argued he'll lose double on the other stand-out moment of the night, which was his wrapping air quotes around 'the health of the mother' when talking about partial-birth abortion, this numerically tiny and fraught practice that has become some sort of gold-standard for acceptability to the American right.

'Pro-abortionists have expanded that so much . . .' McCain growled. Quite possibly they have, but what is McCain suggesting – that laws should be passed that make it illegal to save the life of a woman who may die from carrying to term, or going into labour? The Christian right does believe that, of course, which is a measure of the cruelty and misogyny that lies at the base of their abortion obsession. And McCain seemed to give that remark a brutal heft coming from somewhere else, deeper and more private.

For anyone sane, it was a nasty moment. For anyone who's had, or loves someone who's had, a sudden heart murmur, a haemorrhage, or half-a-dozen other things during pregnancy, that weren't serious but could have been, it's suddenly personal – John McCain would have voted to kill me/my partner/my daughter, etcetera. That's going to decide a bunch of waverers right there.

But above all, what could be worse than air quotes around 'health of the mother'? *Saturday Night Live* would think twice about putting that on any conservative character. Is there a more contemptuous gesture, a signal staged twitch around a phrase expressing an ocean of pain, fear, guilt and more for millions of people directly or otherwise?

I very much doubt the Obama campaign will use it – their post election ads focused on McCain's pro-Bush voting record, and they'll stay on the economy and health care – but you would have to believe that 527 groups, MoveOn et al, will consider running hard on it. The only downside would be the possibility of scoring a few more base votes of McCain, but Palin would appear to have guaranteed those already.

Though the debate was widely held to put McCain out for the count, Obama has already started leaning on his supporters to keep up the pressure, warning a New York fundraiser 'not to be complacent' and 'remember New Hampshire', i.e. the in-the-bag primary which, 230 years ago, he lost to Hillary.

The battle in a US election at this stage is to get out those registered – Mickey Mouse, the Dallas Cowboys, the kid who signed up seventy-two times 'n' all – both to actually get them to follow through, and/or to make sure they know that registering is not, in itself, voting. Though the numbers are very good for Obama, they have to be to defeat any residual Bradley effect, Florida-style November surprise, etcetera etcetera.

McCain's last chance – and it is more than a merely formal one – is to use the 'share the wealth' argument as a key point of difference between himself and Obama, and portray that as the American versus un-American divide.

ATLANTIC CITY: MONDAY, 20 OCTOBER

Now there's trouble busin' in from outta state and the DA can't
  get no relief
Gonna be a rumble out on the promenade and the gamblin'
  commission's hangin' on by the skin of its teeth
Well now, everything dies baby that's a fact
But maybe everything that dies someday comes back
Put your makeup on fix your hair up pretty
And meet me tonight in Atlantic City
  —Springsteen, 'Atlantic City'

There weren't no problem getting to Atlantic City. There are whole cities in America marooned without a bus let alone a train service, strange burgs forever frozen at the moment when the Greyhound depot was shuttered for good. Atlantic City? The buses leave on the half hour from NYC, on a Friday afternoon stuffed to the gills with people desperate to get to the craps tables and slots, but too poor to afford a car that will make it there.

Get a four-day return-ticket at the NY Port Authority bus terminal and you get a twenty-dollar voucher for the Tropicana Casino. They're all there in this long queue shuffling to the coach's luggage hold: the black women in Sunday best and the white women in the sort of elastic-banded slacks they'd wear to install wall insulation, the Long Island guys in sports shirts and the rolled-gold crucifix hanging outside them, and the older white guys in da uniform – white open-necked shirt, grey jacket, slacks of a colour that is not grey.

Grizzled, slender, aged, but not gin-pickled – who'd waste two bucks on a belt of rye when you can bet – thrumming with energy, waiting to get there, to the tables, to the floors, to the life, and the chance that it might all turn around.

Atlantic City – man, if you're going to gamble, go there, not Vegas, at least first – may be many things, but the American dream it ain't. More like the American acid flashback, some nightmare snowcrash of past and future into each other making a present. Wooden row houses with bay windows greet you as you roll over the bridge into town (the place is built on an island), tired, sagging, waiting to be knocked over. And then the casinos rear up before you like enormous concrete waves.

Famed as a seashore paradise for much of the 20th century –

the original Monopoly board is based on its streets, with the wooden beachside Boardwalk getting pride of place – no city suffered more from the increasing ability and willingness of Americans to go further abroad for their holidays from the '60s onwards. Cancun rose as the Jersey shoe fell and by the mid '70s, the place was bankrupt and wrecked. The New Jersey legislature responded by legalising gambling – the only state outside of Nevada to do so – in 1976.

Well I got a job and tried to put my money away
But I got debts that no honest man can pay
So I drew what I had from the Central Trust
And I bought us two tickets on that Coast City bus

That move was just ahead of the roaring '80s and perfectly placed to take advantage of the sudden flood of easy money. And one man in particular made the new AC – Donald Trump, whose trio of casinos dominate the place. As the old resorts along the Boardwalk were imploded one by one, the place generated one great movie (Louis Malle's *Atlantic City*) and one great song (Springsteen's 'Atlantic City'), and seemed ready to ride the wave of newfound fortune forever. Right?

Well, erm, wrong. Saturday night the casino puffs up from the Greyhound crowd like a snake that swallowed a pig, but the rest of the week it's dead, and you can, like your correspondent, get a four-star suite for forty-five bucks a night. What happened? In a word, Injuns. In 1987, the Supreme Court ruled that 'native American tribal entities' enjoyed a weird quasi-sovereignty that meant they couldn't be controlled by state laws banning gambling. Now, there's an 'Indian casino' in nearly every state – Foxwoods on Connecticut is one of the biggest, a short hop from New York – and they learned from the Vegas renaissance, turning them into family resorts (drugs and hookers kept well away) so that boring people in SUVs and bum bags could have a flutter on a roulette wheel while the kids play on the organic wood playground, etcetera etcetera.

Atlantic City became a self-selecting place, where you go to do gambling as it should be done, amidst surroundings of sleaze and despair. Vegas has been knocked down and rebuilt twice since the old cow town and crossroads (Spanish for 'the meadows') became a place for the Italian and Jewish mafias to put their Mexican heroin money. Atlantic City still has its layers, the old houses, the stone churches, the '50s motels ('Color TV in rooms!') and its grand civic hall, with the legend chiselled in stone across its portico: 'Dedicated to the ideals of Atlantic City'.

Well, the ideals of Atlantic City now are a hooker with her own blow who's willing to be paid in casino chips, which was probably not what the founders had in mind. And the city runs off addiction. Addiction of the gamblers piped in from New York and Philly, who buy their return tickets, gamble anything they've got away, live off free OJ and bar snacks, and slink home on the Monday morning red-eye; the hookers who service them when they get lucky; and the drugged populations those hookers feed with money. Atlantic City's dubious achievement is to have the highest HIV/AIDS rate in the country, around 7 per cent of the population infected.

Now our luck may have died and our love may be cold but with you forever I'll stay
We're goin' out where the sand's turnin' to gold so put on your stockin's baby 'cause the night's getting cold
And everything dies baby, that's a fact
But maybe everything that dies someday comes back

Out front of the liquor stores and the go-go bars housed in old row tenements with black-painted windows, the thin men shuffle up to you, their purple karposis shining in the sun. 'My name's Duane, man, I need eight bucks, I need six bucks, my name's Curtis,' one guy said to me in a single sentence, decomposing mentally and physically before my eyes.

Atlantic City is a giant mausoleum of American hopes and obsessions, its ghastly casinos un-remodelled since the '80s (why waste the money?), still in the livery of salmon pink and grey, the fat stylish lettering – a whole city designed on the aesthetic of a Devo film clip. The fat years were ten, before the Indians took over, and nothing was invested for the winter.

As the campaign enters its final fortnight, I am here to try and wrangle some of this work into the chapters of a book, happy to be holed up in such a place because I am blessed with an immunity to games of chance. A child of two problem gamblers, I can float by the tables with not the slightest temptation, which is pretty funny, being addicted to everything else.

But you can't avoid meaning anywhere. And Atlantic City offers itself up, if as nothing else now, as a metaphor – an addiction far more powerful than mere gambling – for the American dilemma, and the Western dilemma in general.

Here, after all, is a city that was founded on modest ambitions and the ideals of puritan virtue. Not for nothing were its neighbourhoods named after English health resorts, Ventnor and Margate. The puritan ideal behind it was that sea air and water was somehow spiritually refreshing as well as physical, that it was virtue rewarded by virtue. And it is still weird that in a casino resort – usually designed to exclude nature altogether – it's three minutes' walk to the beach, and the wild Atlantic pitching itself against a continent, waves and wind howling, reminding you of a force larger than yourself and your desires.

The new Atlantic City reversed that entirely and in that reversal you can see the enormous cultural reconstruction that the West underwent in the last thirty years. For a century, capitalism had been built on encouraging self-denial among its working class – the 'frugal comfort' of the Harvester decision, of the idea that a good reward for a year's work was a one-week holiday of sea air and salt taffy in Atlantic City. But when overproduction became a terminal problem for the economy, in the post-WWII years, wages were allowed to rise to create a consumer economy. When that got into trouble in the 1970s, everything else was tried – hedge funds, derivatives, the dotcom economy, legalised gambling, mortgage floats and so on. Atlantic City is the crust of that wound, a city based on the pure waste of gambling.

Well, everything dies, baby, that's a fact, and that is all over now. The bourgeois economists are desperate to not recognise it, but the current squeeze is the end of the West. It will take decades more, but this was the year that economic power and initiative shifted to the East, crucially. When your economy is based largely on services and rents (financial services, IP, etcetera) then, at a global level, you are purely a consumer, and the bell was always going to toll. In thirty years' time much of the West, and most of the US, will look like Atlantic City – a crust of ageing luxury on squalor.

The problem for any president and Congress coming into power is that they are going to have to own this crap, and make hard decisions. In case anyone hasn't noticed, the solution proposed by all the governments of the West – lower interest rates – is inflationary in the context of no real growth, which is what we'll face for the next three years.

What we, and President Obama, face is dealing with a period of old-fashioned stagflation – remember stagflation? It's like hearing 'Fox on the Run' again, isn't it? Ahhh, you hadn't thought of that for years either? It's where the economy is flooded with cheap money in an attempt to restart the economy, but which only succeeds in inflating it, without growth. Indeed, there's a good argument for losing this election, to let the GOP take the real brunt of the collapse.

If Obama wins, as he almost certainly will, he will have to summon the spirit of FDR to lead the nation by not sparing it of the dangers and hardships ahead. As the week began he was buoyed by the endorsement of Colin Powell, but having to deal with various garrulous Joe Biden comments about Obama 'facing a crisis within six months', and the McCain–Palin team hammering home the 'socialism' message, coming off the Sam/Joe the non-Plumber encounter.

What he will have to deal with is the overwhelming mood of America at the moment, which is one of what Heidegger called 'forlornness' – a sense of departed being, of what had once been being no longer, of the no-present, haunted by the past. That's what makes the Springsteen song so powerful – this place of small, failed promises, the buses coming and going from the transit centre, the junkie shivering outside, the hookers piling off the 5 p.m. for the weekend shift, and on and on – because it reminds us that the challenges of America, of the West, of the world, will be here sooner than we think, and all our illusions, measured in gilt and towers, will be tested.

You better hope that whoever is in charge of the world's largest nuclear arsenal is a reasonable man or woman when that happens, or it is all over, and within the lifetime of your kids. One way or another, we have to leave the 20th century, and in the US that means leaving the people who think the country has some special virtue in the world. Who gets the White House this time will determine how your children's lives pan out, so you better, you better, pay a little attention . . . And over to Bruce, who wrote one of the few pop songs in pop history that reads as a poem, as spare and tight as fellow New Jersey native William Carlos Williams:

Now I been lookin' for a job but it's hard to find
Down here it's just winners and losers and don't get caught on the
wrong side of that line
Well I'm tired of comin' out on the losin' end
So honey, last night I met this guy and I'm gonna do a little
favour for him
Well I guess everything dies baby, that's a fact
But maybe everything that dies someday comes back
Put your hair up nice and set up pretty
and meet me tonight in Atlantic City
Meet me tonight in Atlantic City
Meet me tonight in Atlantic City

Strange and wonderful days, and they've only just begun, but we will get no good out of them.

ATLANTIC CITY: WEDNESDAY, 22 OCTOBER

Now Princess is talking 'bout how she/he's going to be a star
Warming up her pasties, dragging on a Silk Cut low tar
Rain on painted windows, 'Freebird' on the PA
Tonight I'll bet on black, see if I can get a place to stay
Off the boardwalk, off the boardwalk
  —Jacqueline Lee, 'Off the Boardwalk' (Rykodisk, '83)

Three p.m., and halfway through trying to knock a couple of chapters together, trying to remember where, who or indeed what, I was in March. Shuffle out of the Tropicana to do some shopping. Zen art of surfing the four-star hotel, never buy any-thing there, not a sandwich, not a Snickers from the minimart, not an in-room movie.

The foyer is 'the Quarter', a faux Cuban place centred around a bunch of Spanish restaurants run by the Maltese mafia, the walls painted in lurid colours, with an arcade of shops that includes a 'spy store' selling body armour. Close to the till, cos that sort of thing, here, is an impulse buy . . .

Outside, you're among the row houses as soon as you leave the climate-controlled environment, which most of the guests never do. Add the smell of urine and disinfectant and these hotels would get nursing home funding.

The row houses are half-boarded up – 'For Sale $500 000', one reads in a handwritten sign of desperate hopefulness – wait-ing for the next casino, the one that never came. Public transport here is Jitneys, small ten-person buses that stop every fifty yards and never bother to close their doors. 'Since 1915', they read. They must have been horse-drawn once, hence the bucolic name, trotting past the Tropicana guest house, the Bel Air, etcetera etcetera.

No logic to the small convenience stores here – they seem to have split up basic foodstuffs as a way to make a profit. Cheese slices in one, crackers in the next. The third sells ultraviolet light bulbs and pregnancy tests.

Everyone on the street makes eye contact, but nothing much friendly about it, they seem to be keeping their eyes on your hands. In the 24-hour Atlantic City international newsagency and peep show, I buy a copy of the *National Review* and *The American Conservative*.

'Sarah Palin, hmmmm,' says the large woman, cashing me up. 'You want a bag, honey?'

'Maybe I should buy some porn to put the *National Review* in.'

She laughs so hard she spits tobacco juice over me, her chest growling and bubbling like the waves against the Steel Pier. The place is full of photocopied guides to card-counting, most of them transparently bogus. It smells of dead cigars.

The city smells of dead cigars. The sign outside the shop reads 'Drug-free zone next 500 metres', which has the air of a consumer warning: drought ahead.

Outside, it seems like the election may as well be happening in Estonia. Nothing will ever reach Atlantic City, because it is a conspiracy of the doomed who kinda like the feel of that. Back in the room, it is C-SPAN and CNN and MSNBC and the whole thing is hysteria.

Some people may say I should be out on the road for the last two weeks, and I will be there on the frontline in Ohio, or wherever, listening to McCain say, again, 'I will make the earmarkers famous, you will know their names', and Sarah Palin say, 'Joe the Plumber said that sharing the wealth sounded like socialism', and Barack Obama say, 'Let's rally around a staged redistribution of selective benefits in order to grow the economy – are you with me?', and Joe Biden say, 'Barack is from the planet Zargoz 7 – elves told me so'.

But the candidates are on a final circuit now, doing pretty much what they have to do, which is to simply keep going. Polls show that 7 per cent of voters are still undecided, which makes people from all parties want to hunt them down and slap them and say 'What the fuck is wrong with you, are you just stupid?'.

But of course, that means that another 10–20 per cent may be persuadable, and that – whichever way it runs – is the election. For McCain and Palin, the endless stumps are a mixed blessing. The crowds turning up for McCain solo are just pitiful, which means they have to do a certain amount of campaigning together, which limits effectiveness.

But they also have the problem that the demands of their live audience are very different from those of the moderates and independents they need to convince. Most of these shindigs are now broadcast on cable, yet doing anything less than howling at the moon about 'socialism' gets tepid applause . . . What's a Republican to do?

For Obama, well, there ain't no problems. He had 100 000 people – a record – at a rally in St Louis the other day, and what he says to them is exactly the same thing he's saying to the whole of America. Though the oracular, prophetic Obama is long-ago replaced by a cautious Third Way politician, people still flock to him, for the simple reason that calm good sense, in post-crash America, is prophetic and oracular.

Anyone suggesting that reflection and cautious action might be a good way to go is prophetic and oracular these days.

Obama's problem, of course, is good old Joe, his VP choice. Make no mistake about it, it was a good choice. Biden has been going around the backblocks, Pennsylvania and Ohio, old white guy union towns, *Deer Hunter* country, scooping up wayward working-class people who might still have reservations about voting for a *schwartze*. Obama's slowly rising lead in these states is partly attributable to Joe Biden.

But Christ, the bloke's a dickhead. He's an old-style polly, schooled in the discipline of 'keep talking'. Keep the show on the road, keep the meeting going. Speaking to fundraisers and clearly not thinking about the contemporary world of total surveillance, Biden spat out that stuff about Obama facing some sort of crisis, etcetera etcetera etcetera, in the first six months of his term. Why, why, why?

Simply put, he couldn't stop speaking. The old street corner type of politician, he's spent his whole life training himself to never stop speaking. Whereas the dominant political skill now is to be short, sharp and haiku-ish.

'Joe has rhetorical flourishes,' Obama said today, spinning the statement into a general observation about the dangers any president will face, etcetera. Coincidentally, McCain was doing a sit-down interview for CNN the same day, which allowed him to go into the 'Obama hasn't been tested – I've been tested. I was on the deck of an aircraft carrier with a target during the Cuban Missile Crisis', etcetera etcetera. Fair enough, though that hardly tested McCain, since he had no strategic role – he was just the monkey running the jet, one of the few he didn't wreck.

But the strange thing about McCain was that his responses to the question were simply a cut and paste of earlier responses, not anything that sounded authentic, honest or from the heart. It will cheer up the diehards but it won't persuade waverers, especially younger voters.

Nevertheless it was the Chequers speech compared to Sarah Palin. My God, that woman has been the greatest single disaster for the McCain campaign bar . . . anything. Anything. She is now, at around 40 per cent, the single greatest reason why independent voters will not vote for John McCain, way ahead of McCain's 'approach to the economy'. And that was before recent revelations that she had rorted government spending to get travel for her kids (including five days in a New York hotel for her daughter Bristol while Governor Palin was on a one-day visit to the city), and that the RNC had spent a hundred and fifty grand on clothes for her.

The $150 000 tells you all you need to know about the McCain campaign. Obviously a female candidate has to have a bit of money spent on her, and always look first-rate – but a hundred and fifty Gs? For eight weeks? Thirty, forty – more than a year's income for a quarter of the US population – yes. But 150 large is a measure of the standards of the sort of people McCain has surrounded himself with, the inner-circle Republicans who've never been able to craft a winning strategy because, deep down, they've never really understood how most Americans live.

You can see this every time their two key spokespeople come on. Tucker Bounds is a sort of Doogie Howser 14-year-old spinmeister, with a whiny little manner that has 'raped in prison' written all over it. He has that technique that UK politicians first developed, of trained circular breathing used by actors for Shakespeare monologues, which allows you to speak for a minute without a break.

The other one is Nancy Pfotenhauer, the sort of thin Beltway blonde who would cut a prole like Palin dead if she ever managed to get beyond the ropeline. Perpetually nervy, Pfotenhauer looks like a woman who spends a lot of time sobbing hysterically behind locked bathroom doors about something you didn't know you'd said, but man, she can dress. Thirty times I've seen her on cable at least and every outfit is a designer original.

That should have been a clue to the McCain campaign right there. Team Obama may have its shortcomings, on which I have dilated at length, but they look like a bunch of focused professionals in cheap suits and chain-store specials. (Obama spends $1500 on a suit, but it's the genius of the man that he makes it look much, much cheaper.) Why didn't McCain realise that he was surrounded by the Dartmouth valedictorian crowd?

Because, of course, McCain himself has always been part of that crowd. The fourth child of an admiralty family, had John Sidney McCain IV not been born to the purple he would never have got a pilot's commission after his disastrous Academy result – and would never have got a second plane after he crashed the first. Everything he's got today he owes to the Vietcong (and there are questions about his conduct while a POW, but these have been swept over).

Having returned to an ex-model wife disfigured by an auto accident, he dumped her for a beer heiress – a marriage of prestige and money that would have had Anthony Trollope shouting 'Oh, *come on*'. He's never had a private sector job, never been poor, never lived between pay cheques. His prison experience was testing, but it was extraordinary, garish even – the sort of thing people see at the Multiplex – and less impressive to a media-saturated society than the Republicans could wish. In a society where Jack Bauer is raised in presidential debates, real suffering ain't that impressive. 'Them VCs beat you, man? You shoulda seen what they did to Kiefer in Season Three!'

McCain drafted in the evil Karl Rove crowd – including the people who'd trashed his wife and daughter in the 2000 primaries – but it wasn't enough. The conservative movement has withered on the vine, so the only people left there are the blinkered careerists – the girls in pearls and boys in blue suits and red ties – who could never imagine why anyone would vote other than Republican, and don't play well with others. If half your team has first names that are surnames – Tyler Cantwell, Grover Norquist, Hobart Grierson . . . Guess which ones I made up.

The clothes thing and the kids' travel thing will simply serve to confirm to many people what they've thought for a while about Palin – that she's a fraud, a tundra Eve Harrington, denied a glittering TV career and finding politics a path to fame by other means. Having stood up to big Alaska corruption, she couldn't wait to take a cut of small Alaska corruption – the per diems taken while she was staying at her own house, the free travel, heavying the sister's ex-husband, etcetera etcetera.

It's pretty interesting that her support is lowest among Independent-aligned women – exactly the sort of Hillary-leaning crowd the GOP was trying to get in. They're a wake-up to her. Her base? Fundamentalists and young single men. Freaks for Jesus and *Maxim* readers, what a coalition.

Well, she was a spin of the wheel, Palin was, a real last-chance Atlantic City bet. Oh come on, that's a great call-back. She was like a last-chance coke deal to save a hooker with a kid. No hang on, that was Burt Lancaster. Everything is on the roll of a dice in America today, from the financial non-recovery to McCain's last stand in Pennsylvania. And the sense is that the country's going to change on the turn of a card, with the economy (the Dow down another 500 today, on its way to 5000) on the spin of a wheel. Bet it all on black, I would suggest, and if you're lucky enough to get a view of the ocean – the giant Trump sign throwing light over the whole benighted town – never order from room service, never forget where you came from, never forget what's forty storeys below.

ATLANTIC CITY: THURSDAY, 23 OCTOBER

Three a.m. at Joe's Diner – is everyone in this damn country named Joe? – and the nightshift pit crew at the Tropicana is in to unwind. The place is a dive, with a 24-hour breakfast and grease on the grill that's older than Obama's speechwriting team, and the croupiers are lounging on torn stools, their neckties askew, watching the MSNBC repeats on a portable TV on top of the soda fridge. There are long lines of early voters in Fayetteville, North Carolina, and an angry mob of McCain supporters protesting them. You know people think they're going to lose when they're protesting the very act of voting – a touch of the Zimbabwes about that.

There's a political consultant from Ohio being interviewed. He was hired to sort out the mess that resulted from inadequate voting systems in 2004. That had caused queues lasting up to five hours in the state, with possibly hundreds of thousands either walking away in frustration or never getting a chance to vote. His verdict: this year might be worse. Cut to another report, of voting machines where a vote for Obama was recorded as a vote for McCain. 'We fixed it eventually,' says a poll clerk. Oh, that's alright then.

'Man,' says one guy over a black coffee, 'if we ran things like that, we'd all be in prison'.

Indeed. Nothing more forcefully suggests that this is a failed state than its refusal to get the simple act of voting properly funded and working. You would think a country whose legitimacy depends on nothing other than its electoral process – no monarch, monoculture, etcetera, to bind it together – would decide, especially after 2000 and 2004, to ensure that whatever happened, the process was smooth and transparent.

Ha ha, not Americans. With the electoral process run by a hodgepodge of federal, state and local authorities; with electronic machines, mechanical machines and paper ballots; with different times, processes and hours; and, most of all, with a lack of the money needed to ensure that everyone gets to vote within five minutes of turning up at a polling place; they are heading for a national nightmare – a close result so murky that one section of the population will simply refuse to accept it. Why can't— ay yay yay yay . . .

Man, oh man. At this point, lest I come off sounding like a 19-year-old socialist alternative recruit, it's probably necessary that I offer the usual caveat and say there's a lot I like about America, from Southern friendliness, to Alaskan frontier spirit, from *The Wall Street Journal* to the first fifteen minutes of Letterman, casual conversations and bottomless coffee in small-town diners, Los Angeles art deco, Texas prairie, the energy of New York, the timeless grace of Savannah, and on and on. I like high-school graduations and homecoming ceremonies, the whole sense of ceremony around everyday life that marks them off as utterly different to Australians. I like science fairs and seeing thousands turn out to watch high-school football games on a Friday night, off-duty soldiers in airport bars and Portland girls with prison tattoos, rye whisky and Bud Light, A&W vanilla cream soda, chicken-fried chicken and tobaccoless joints, Jules Feiffer and Roy Acuff, *Wonkette* and the *National Review*, and much, much more. OK? Got that? There's a lot to like!

But even the most robotic Americophile would have to admit that there is something deeply dissociated and dysfunctional about a country that after one entirely botched election and one reasonably disputed one – a country whose political system is teetering far closer to the edge of losing popular legitimacy than many people suspect – that cannot, eight years and hundreds of millions of dollars later, organise an efficient and transparent system for voting in a president. It seems the ultimate proof of the argument that Thomas Frank has mounted in his recent book *The Wrecking Crew* – it is not that the Republicans, in control of Congress and the White House these past six years, wanted to create minimal but efficient government. They seem, to judge by their results, hell-bent on creating bloated and bad government, and the election mess is the ultimate upshot of that.

Really it's hard to know where to start. The first disaster is staggered voting, so that fully a third of people will have cast their ballot before 4 November. This is a recent innovation – really, until the '90s, the US shared the belief with other electoral systems that voting was ideally a single day on which the country came together and made a decision, with early and absentee voting as an exception for people who would otherwise be denied their say. Why has it so quickly become a standard alternative?

Firstly, because voting is on a workday, a Tuesday, and all attempts to move it to a Saturday, or guarantee a real right to leave your workplace and vote have failed. The result? People miss out, or the voting is crowded into the hours after 5 p.m., ensuring that some people never get to vote. Since this is usually people whose jobs are, erm, inflexible with regards to taking an hour off, its the Democrats who usually suffer.

Secondly, it seems to fit with an American illusion that a

community will continue to exist no matter how much it is deformed by individual choice. Voting used to be understood as a quasi-sacred act, part of the 'civic religion' of America, and Tuesday was chosen because it should be at the start of a week, but some people would need 24-hours' travel time (no travelling on the Sabbath) to get to a polling station. The slippage in the idea of a single day's voting has come with the idea of convenience, the internet, scattered lives and communities, the whole vast dissociation of collective life whose effects the country has not even begun to properly reflect upon.

Just as some of the Southern megachurches in recent years quietly began informing people that they wouldn't be having Christmas day services (because people stay local at Christmas, so who wants a service with a hundred people in a converted aircraft hangar meant for 20 000), and never twigged that this might, just might, indicate a problem with their style of worship, so the popularity of partial voting hasn't registered as some harbinger of a social system in which consent is so minimal that it is dipping below the radar.

The main problem of staggered voting is partial information. You never get perfect information about a candidate, of course, and things often emerge after an election, but we do understand an electoral process as being a period of scrutiny and judgement at the end of which we all make our individual choices TOGETHER. In the past few days, for example, we have had Barack Obama's statement that he wants to 'spread the wealth' around – he was talking about increasing the purchasing power of average Americans, but nevertheless – and the revelation that Sarah Palin rorted the expenses system to take her kids on official travel. Anyone who's already voted has done so without this knowledge and can reasonably say 'Had I known . . .'. The point of a single collective vote is that no one can kibitz, everyone's on the same page, and the result is thus binding. The more you fragment the vote, the less people have a sense they were part of a common experience. In revolutionary terms, there's an argument that the more fragmentation the better, but I presume that is not the intent.

The second problem is the underfunding of the electoral process, which is so mad as to beggar belief. You would think that a society based on the revolutionary idea of choosing your own leader would take pride in the process of doing so. Even though voting is handled on a county-by-county and state-by-state basis, it would be easy enough for Congress to vote for mandated funds that ensured as many people as necessary were trained and ready to work as required.

The counties, as I said, control much of the process, and this is the next problem. The county level is necessary because of the American process of simultaneously electing umpteen public officials – from judges to local water board supervisors. This is seen as some sort of essential attribute of American democracy going back to the blah blah in Boston. In fact, it dates from the turn of the 20th century, when the huge 'Populist' movement swamped both major parties, establishing the principal of referendums, primary elections and individual voter propositions by which voters can directly amend the Constitution or pass specific laws. Electronic machines were seen as a solution to the huge amount of different types of ballot that would have to be printed, but with the multiple failure of such machines, most county officials are also printing up paper ballots. Most machines are meant to print out a paper record to enable a recount, but in half-a-dozen states there is still no permanent recountable record of your individual vote.

Got that? In half-a-dozen states there is no possibility of an exhaustive recount of votes. How is it possible to continue down this path, after the last two elections, with equanimity?

The answer has got to be that, despite endless discussion of a thing called 'America' and what it is, a lot of people don't really believe in it or believe they live in it. They live in some characterless middle-space, some day-to-day struggle for everyday existence, with the actual lineaments of power and government so far away you may as well try and catch the wind. I honestly don't understand why people six months, a year ago, weren't occupying government offices, demanding that the thing be got right. God knows what will happen if this election is stuffed up or delivers an unclear result for either side, but I would suggest that the legitimacy of the entire American political system is in the balance here. And who knows? A total collapse of such may be just what the place needs.

On MSNBC, the polls are being discussed, the results calling it for Obama ranging from 14 per cent to 1 per cent.

'It's a crap shoot,' someone says.

'I watched craps for an hour yesterday, and I don't understand it,' I say.

'Pal,' he says, turning to me, 'I've worked the tables for five years and neither do I'.

SUNDAY, 26 OCTOBER

'I see Joe the Plumber, and Lindy the Teacher, and Greg . . . Greg the only Republican in my street,' Sarah Palin yelled from the podium at some rally last week. The signs were waving in the crowd, who had made themselves into a whole army of people from the 'real' America. In Florida, McCain himself had been hitting the idea hard earlier, asking a bunch of people who they were: 'Jill the Nurse', 'Gary the Carpenter'. And then he pointed the mic at an older woman who told him she was 'the land developer', at which point McCain wisely curtailed the routine. Last thing you want is someone from the real America telling you how their sub-prime business has gone to crap and that's why they're voting for . . .

Though the Republican campaign is more or less completely falling apart, 'Joe the Plumber' is still the main through-line in both GOP candidates' speeches, even though the whole thing has been complicated by the fact that Joe's support for McCain is clearly against his own economic interests. Nothing wrong with that per se, but that has made the incessant brandishing of 'Joe' by McCain/Palin a double-ended plunger – to one group of people it suggests a belief in certain values independent of circumstances, while to others, especially core groups of inde-pendents, he may appear to be a bit of a dope.

In any case, neither Joe the Plumber nor Lisa the Gift Shop Owner are truly representative of the largest social groups in the modern US. In old-skool terms, they're classical petit-bourgeois, with skilled trade or property to take some pride in, a strong sense of abstract values – fair day's work, etcetera – attached to patriotism, and a haunting fear of loss or failure, a fall through the floor. Yet of the 150 million people employed in the US, they're a minority, around 25 million tops. They're dwarfed by management, service and sales occupations, at around 90 mil-lion. These are the lumpenservitariat of the processed world and while the figures include a few people with interesting jobs, for the most part it's people who, as the saying goes, have their names on their shirt. The shadow world of American life – which is, in fact, the real world – is barely represented in the whole panoply of American mass culture. Indeed, the only show I can think of in the last twenty years, really, to be set where most people live was the first few series of *Roseanne*, which depicted her transition from a full-time manufacturing job into the patchwork world of fast-food service, the mall, etcetera.

That Roseanne Barr then completely lost her mind and turned the final series into one in which her family won the lottery and was fantastically wealthy does not invalidate the distinctiveness of the earlier series, which faithfully depicted borderline poverty perpetually lapping at the heels of a family perpetually in danger of fracturing under the pressure.

Indeed, the lottery-win development was some sort of depiction of the fantasy that makes hinterland American life (the world of 24-hour cheque-cashing stores and emergency room GP treatments) bearable for so many – the lottery ticket forever on the fridge, the build-you-a-home makeover shows, etcetera etcetera. Was Joe the Plumber's belief that the two-man operation he was part of, clearing ninety-five grand a year, would somehow fall under the hammer of Obama's tax increases on quarter-a-million-plus incomes, some sort of false identification between dreams and reality?

Who knows, but, leaving Atlantic City, it seemed to me that a more accurate reading could be got from people who spend so much time working with the delusional-by-definition – casino gamblers – that they are inured not to dreams (we'll be dreaming as we die) but to fantasy.

Atlantic City may not be typical Americana, but the city's sheer and obsessive focus on fauxstentatious glamour, mug punting, low-rent commercial sex, street drugs and not much else (there is not a single cinema or proper bookstore in the city limits), its profoundly mishandled renaissance makes it somehow emblematic. Three a.m. at the craps bar last week I had sketched out a chapter list for a book using AC as a focus for every mistake the US has made in transition to post-industrial society: demolishing the old resorts (which, had they been preserved, would have been hugely popular boutique hotels today), pushing taxes through the floor, and killing the city to oblige the casinos, only to have the 1987 Indian Casinos Supreme Court decision ruin the place's one selling point, leaving half-filled hotels and vacant blocks across the city. An idea so great, so obvious that damn, some fugger already did it for OUP in 2006.

Hennyway, the prismatic character of AC is not diminished by that. Take Mike the Bellboy, a figure unlikely to appear at a McCain rally, a man in his fifties, and also in the sort of uniform otherwise not seen except on monkeys chained to accordions.

'I used to work in Youngstown [Ohio] in auto parts,' he said, humping my one bag to the room, a service it was made clear was not optional. I'd tipped him first so he was willing to talk.

'I got an ex-wife, a wife and a girlfriend to support, plus a kid. The wife and kid are back home. AC's no place for a family. Obama and McCain – look, for me, they both supported NAFTA. That killed us. But the Dems, of course, the Democrats. Better or worse. What? This job. I could do with a job that didn't rely on tips.'

In that bizarre, final American service ritual, he showed me how to operate the light switch, flicking it back and forth until I peeled off a couple more ones from the roll in my palm.

'Why should I vote? It's Jersey. A dead guy would win for the Democrats. And has.' Miles, the croupier, his clip-on bow tie hanging off his white shirt collar, is smoking and eating at the filthiest diner in town, maybe the last place in the US where you can find that once distinctive sight – plates of half-eaten eggs with filter tips stubbed out in them.

'I been a croupier all my life. Born in Pleasantville [truly, a place about ten miles from AC]. My parents still live there. I went to casino school near here.'

'Casino school?'

'Place above the pharmacy. Big room with a roulette table, craps table, blackjack. You play play play all day, take turns being customers. Learn the rules, then learn the types, y'know, drunk, clueless novice, card counter. I'm a better actor than I am a croupier. Anyone can be a croupier.'

That was self-deprecating. I'd watched Miles run a craps table for three hours and it relied on a pretty fly ability to keep half-a-dozen different players separate in your head, as they ceaselessly shift, double and split their bets around, depending on the throw of each pair of dice. What's most striking, though, is the quasi-industrial nature of the process – the relentless crashing of the dice, the players never pausing, never really at play, in any ludic sense of the notion, the deep-green baize table more like a machine-bed surrounded by workers, the players as much as the croupiers.

'I've never voted. I just have zero interest. Man, we need a health system, though. Know what? I lost a friend in 9/11. Haddabeen me I would told them Taliban, you got three days to hand whoever over and if not . . . just plane the place. Just flat. You smoke?'

After ten hours of watching the random fluctuations of chance, Miles's head was like a giant craps table, ideas bouncing round like boxcars.

'He's not a Muslim.'

'He is a Muslim, I saw it on FOX News.'

'FOX News, whadda they know?'

'They're fair and balanced!'

Jersey being Jersey, getting at least a couple of McCain supporters as a sure bet seemed to rely on talking to gamblers. Rose and Ted, white-haired in a mix of khaki and plaid costing approximately one nine-billionth of Sarah Palin's September budget, were roosted on the five-dollar roulette table. I was hoping to God they'd been something in haberdashery, but he'd been a health industry employment agent. I was, however, spot-on in assessing their politics, which was a pure set of GOP talking points – 'He wants to spread the wealth', 'Yah, he got money from Ahmadinejad' – the only division being that Ted was the moderate, unwilling to believe that Obama was a secret Weatherman-Arab under deep cover.

'Put it on red,' Rose said, 'I always bet on red, hahaha.'

'What will you do if he wins?'

'Tchhh. America's not going to elect a black man,' she said, with the air of suggesting the obvious, and clattered more chips down as if to dismiss me.

Predictably enough, the only other Republican was a bar hooker at one of the Trump outfits. A survey of the street hookers up Atlantic Avenue had found support for Obama running three to zero, with two abstentions and one fuck off. A plan to investigate grassroots support among the crack-distribution sector up an alley succumbed to fear and vestigial good sense, but the street of row houses had three 'Change we can believe in' stickers in windows.

'Ashley' at the Horseshoe bar wasn't having any of it.

'Obama's going to win 'cause he is darling, but he'll be a disaster. Hell, I own four houses, I was aiming for six before I got out of this. Things keep up, I'll be back to three. You going to buy me another vodkatini?

'The mistake McCain made,' Ashley continued, stirring her outrageously priced drink with a toothpick, 'was not separating from Mr George W Bush earlier. That was his only chance. I thought he was gone June. Obama and Pelosi and Reid are going to drive us into a new depression. You sure I can't call your editor, personal like?'

But that was it for Straight Talk Express support in the Boardwalk City, unless the shouts of one street person ('Obama Osama, they got gin in the El Dorado, ha ha ha') counted as a poetic denunciation of talking to our enemies. Bus drivers, wait staff, motel night clerks – those who were willing to talk at all, were all Obama, all for change. They didn't need to say what that change was, because everyone knows what it is. Those who think these shazzam words 'hope' and 'change' signify nothing must think these people are idiots. The words don't need to be unpacked because they constitute a program – tax breaks flowing towards low-income earners, health insurance that works, education that gives a chance for some mobility, hope that resides somewhere else than in a lottery ticket on the fridge, or everything on 23 red.

What would McCain have had to do to get a slice of these people, the slice he would have needed, not for New Jersey – forget

Jersey – but Pennsylvania, Virginia, Nevada etcetera? He would have had to be the genuine Teddy Roosevelt Republican he claimed to be – effectively, audaciously outflank the Democrats on the left, with a progressive tax deal, direct credits for education and health, all wrapped in the language of 'busting the trusts', Wall Street etcetera. Had he stuck with that – he had, after all, rejected the Bush tax cuts as a Senator – he would have been perfectly placed when the financial crash hit.

Rejecting the bailout and supplying an alternative plan, he would have been free from the taint of the non-recovery that occurred in the bailout's wake. This strategy would have allowed him to maintain his foreign policy and social policies on abortion, etcetera. When it came to it, he really didn't have the guts to break with the Republican machine and their corporate backers, and strike out for the grassroots support that Obama summoned.

The final crack in McCain's campaign – the half-hearted Joe populism he plumbed – came with the announcement of Sarah Palin's clothing allowance, and then her $20 000 make-up artist bill. Increasingly seen as a dill, she now became a symbol of the opposite of what she had hoped to project to independents – the small-town mom was dealing in figures that were simply stratospheric . . . whole year's wages. The fault may not have been Palin's, but that simply indicated how out of touch the GOP staffers were.

Atlantic City as you leave it, the buses rolling in and out every fifteen minutes, wears a layer of fatigue, thick as fog. Fatigue of the lapdancers, summoning up a new smile every ten minutes, of the Gap clothing-store workers on their twelve-hour shift, of the passengers with their return tickets who will call someone collect from the bus stop to pick them up. Typical, what's typical? Joe from Ohio, dreaming of a business he'll never afford, or the flotsam and jetsam of the Jersey shore, who, if they have nothing else, have a better idea of the odds?

MONDAY, 27 OCTOBER

With two weeks to go until the election, the Republicans recently pulled another John McCain special – they announced, or let it be known, that they were pulling out of New Mexico, Colorado and Iowa, all running at around 7 per cent plus for Obama, with Iowa hitting an 11 per cent high. The three states together would give Obama 21 votes (5+9+7 respectively), which would be sufficient to win the presidency. What's their game?

It's Pennsylvania, apparently. Team McCain's game plan is to sacrifice the West, hold Florida and Ohio, and gain Pennsylvania, which will keep things at equilibrium, thus guaranteeing McCain the presidency. It also involves holding Missouri, North Carolina, Nevada and Virginia as well, though one of those – and only one – could be lost.

Given that Pennsylvania is running between 10–13 per cent ahead for Obama, it is a frankly desperate strategy and one wholly based on the veracity of 'the Bradley effect', the idea that white people are too ashamed to tell pollsters that they won't vote for Obama because he's black.

However, it may be that the principal purpose of the strategy is less to win but to take the one strategy that has a long, long shot of winning, but which in any case gives the candidate something to do, some sense that he is not wandering aimlessly round meetings near airports doing the same pointless rah rah to diminishing crowds.

Possibly it's also a cover for a Senate strategy. By now, many Republicans (David Frum is the most vocal) want McCain to admit the thing is lost and spend most of his time touring marginal Republican Senate seats, like New Hampshire and Georgia. McCain could say that he has a chance of winning NH and a chance of losing Georgia, so he needs to be there. Neither would be true, but it would give him cover to try and get these people over the line, and help avoid the Republican nightmare, which is that the Democrats would get a filibuster-proof majority in the Senate – sixty seats, a gain of ten to twelve on their current quota. Impossible three months ago, it is still a long shot but now within the bounds of possibility.

GOP professionals fear that the McCain team is throwing everything away and it confirms everything they thought about him (that everyone's always thought about him) – that he's a bit of a jerk, out for himself, even in the Hanoi Hilton.

Mind you, he has allies – the Democrats, e.g. Joe Biden, telling a group of fundraisers that Obama would face a testing international crisis within six months and arrgggggghhh . . . the worst of Biden, the garrulous boaster, the let-me-tell-how-it-is man, spouting off and forgetting there are THINGS SUCH

AS DICTAPHONES, JOE . . . Good for a day or two of making trouble.

It's been added to the 'spread the wealth' thing, which McCain will relentlessly hammer, while his rallies appear full of signs saying 'X the teacher', 'Y the dental hygienist', etcetera etcetera, all of which, if they are true, represent people who will benefit from Obama's tax plan more than McCain's.

Indeed, you can fill in a sign on the McCain site, and get the finished artwork sent to your email. I reserved 'Adolf the Housepainter', though the software would not accept 'Walnuts the Cunt'.

With these possibilities narrowing, people are starting to look at the actual election itself (though fully a third of people will vote before the date, which is nuts), and how it could go crazy. Already, in Ohio and Florida voting machines are screwing up, recording Obama votes as McCain votes – there are no paper trails, there are three-hour queues. Goddamit, eight years they've been wandering around in this voting system daze, about the same time they've been trying to rebuild at Ground Zero. It's hopeless. People from the modern world look on and despair.

That's, of course, if it is just sheer screw-ups. Or has the GOP always intended to have this mess? So they can try and steal the election and/or appeal a clean result if they lose? These are not people, after all. Lizards in white shirts and pearls. Flushed down toilets as pets, they are now reappearing, ready to slither up your orifice. That is their game.

TUESDAY, 28 OCTOBER

On FOX News, Shephard Smith, a burly man whose tragedy is that without even TV make-up, he perpetually appears to be wearing eyeliner, was clearly angry. Not the fake, frikked up anger that FOX anchors deploy on dippy liberals, but the real thing. The source of his ire? False attacks on the . . . Democrats?

'Well, Barack Obama has made it clear that he regards Israel as our greatest ally and a permanent friend,' he hammered in the wake of a rocky interview, with the air of Mr G defending *Funny Girl* against the claims of *Cabaret*, 'and there doesn't seem to be any evidence that that's not his true belief'.

Then he looked down the barrel and shook his head. 'It's crazy what's getting out there.'

That he was defending the sainted one on the Poor Unbalanced network was one thing – but what was truly strange was that the man he was defending him against was Joe the Plumber, doing a phone interview on foreign policy.

The McCain campaign, knowing that it has no choice but to keep upping the ante, had gone from using Joe as a talisman, to getting him on the road – he'll be appearing with Walnuts in a coupla rallies later in the week, and this morning he was doing a personal appearance at a 'patriotism' store, which sells mainly US flags, and lives, no doubt, on mail-order from the Bay Area Black Bloc anarchist collective ('First class post – Must be flammable'). Joe's role was to be the heartfelt, yet trusting voice of the average folks, speaking home-spun wisdom about the strange European ideas of the Democrats.

'Joe said Obama's plan sounded like socialism,' Palin has been saying in her rallies. Note the phrasing – it's the 'Joe don't know much, but he know what he know, and it's the wisdom of the ages' sort of thing.

Sadly, Joe's media training was even worse than Palin's, and when an old Zionist in the audience threw out the remark that 'Barack Obama means the death of Israel', instead of referring him back to the campaign, Joe said: 'Those were comments I would agree with . . . I think that's true.'

Whoever the questioner was knew his mark, knew Joe was just busting to say his piece on just about anything. And he's entitled to his opinion, but the principal effect of the moment was to make the McCain campaign look even more wildly undisciplined than it already has, which is damn hard.

McCain has known for ages that portraying Obama as a current radical leftist won't work, that every poll shows it turns people off the McCain campaign more than anything. Despite the shrieks of conservapundits to open up that front, he's stuck to the idea that Obama is naive, not Hamas, and tried to use that as a way of tarnishing the 'hope/change' rhetoric. The questioner clearly wanted to jam the campaign up and force it to the right.

Well, he got it half right. The McCain campaign had to release a statement saying they disagreed with 'Joe the Plumber' on Obama on Israel, thus destroying the magic bond that had existed between them. Joe went on to the FOX News interview to say, when asked what his evidence for the assertion was: 'I'm not a foreign policy guy . . . I'll just put it back on you guys to find out the truth.' And: 'Well, the guy who asked the question, he was from middle America, it was something he felt deeply about.'

Me, I suspect the guy was from Mossad, on deep cover as an old Columbus Ohio Jew, his beige casual wear expertly constructed in the Tel Aviv labs, given to him by his handler Mem to help blend him in. But anyway, it marked the point at which Joe began to cross from the asset to the liabilities column on the McCain–Palin balance sheet. Mark the moment that FOX News lost love for Joe the P when he said to Shepherd Smith: 'Listen, I know you wanna really get some answers on this one. I'm just not gonna help you out here, Shepherd.'

Cos, really, that's exactly what you want to hear when you're a midafternoon anchor with four hours to fill, your interviewee saying, 'Ha, suffer and die sucker, twist in the wind'. Shepherd had a tough time, but it's nothing compared to what the McCain team must be feeling, watching Joe the P rise from the primeval swamp of GOPolitics, like Godzilla, trampling all before him.

What's next? Fluoride? The Fabian society's role in such? Here's my bet and if I'm right, every reader has to buy me a drink if they ever run into me: by the end of the week, Joe the Plumber will be talking about central banking, Andrew Jackson, the gold standard and the whole megillah, and though it will be too late, the campaign will send him down the same lift shaft that Carly Fiorina and Joe the McCain Brother were sent.

Poor old Walnuts. You can see, in the most recent McCain–Palin joint interview, his deep loathing for Palin – indeed, there's a faked video mashup that has him reaching across and knocking her over as she goes into one of her 'You betcha' routines. McCain's a warrior-psycho, but he knows foreign policy in depth, and values deep thinking about it (in strategy, at least – ethics not so much), and having Palin and Joe as his running mates must be deeply galling to him.

Indeed, both Sarah Palin and Joe Wurzelbacher illustrate the desperate delusions and deep stupidity of populism, its interest in identity and emotion ('He's from middle America, he feels this deeply') above actual work and governance. Formal education is not necessary to political participation, but intellectual curiosity, a belief that knowledge is real, that argument matters, is. Among all the terrible, but hopefully self-defeating, campaigns Team McCain has won, this basic assault on reason and knowledge, this celebration of a smug dumbness, is the worst thing they have done to themselves and their nation. Country first, hah.

Nothing goes right for the McCain campaign at the moment, though their plugging away at this socialism stuff has undoubtedly got them closer to a possible win. Today, McCain ducked out of an open-air rally in Pennsylvania because of rain – while Obama spoke to 9000 people who braved a downpour, the candidate in a rain jacket, water streaming down his face, telling them that: 'This is too important – we've got to go out in rain and sleet and hail and . . .' The conviction of Senator Ted Stevens of Alaska could have helped the GOP, given Palin's (lateish) stand against him – save for Stevens' stubborn refusal to stand down from the ticket, giving the Republicans a convicted felon as a candidate and McCain–Palin a challenge they can't resolve. S'funny really, but also sad – Stevens succumbed to the temptation to get a bunch of free stuff for his house, and turn Alaskan politics into a dynastic succession, at the end of a decades-long tenure as 'the father of Alaska'.

Palin et al are piling in on him, yet it was Stevens who ensured that Alaskans get a royalty from their own oil (rather than Exxon etcetera having a free hand), supported the largest closed-shop in the US when the Trans pipeline was built in the '70s, and as a young lawyer in the 1940s – the 1940s! – won land rights for the Inuit in a decade-long campaign. People ain't forgotten it in 'the land to which the tide is tending' (the meaning of 'Alayeska' in Aleutian Inuit), and don't be surprised if this rogue state/nation sends the felon back to the Big House, not the big house. If they do, I think I surely will move there.

Third problem is the way the infighting in the McPalin campaign is spilling out into the open. That Palin is routinely ignoring her handlers is now open knowledge. She did a transcendentally weird joint appearance with Elisabeth Hasselbeck, who appears on the women's morning show *The View*, her claim to fame hitherto being a *Survivor* finalist, is a nervy blonde, and of course, a Republican. Hasselbeck introduced Palin at a rally, and then Palin went into an extended rave about the clothes issue and how 'Elisabeth said I should say . . .' and 'Elisabeth thinks. . . .', and man, it was strange. It was a goddam slumber party. Were ear piercings and a pillow fight far behind? There was something gleeful about it – it was an escape from the Law of the Father, of old Walnuts, grumbling about 'Why doncher read a briefing note for once in yer life', and 'You spend that much money on clothes, you could read the Constitution once in a while and find out what you would actually do!', and of course, 'You kids get off my lawn'.

It's for this that an unnamed McCain staffer said that Palin was not just a 'diva', but 'a whack job'. Of course she is, and it goes back to her profound incuriosity, her sense that she has a set of beliefs and why disturb them with facts that would just lead to confusion?

It's not that the Obama campaign has been without errors. After Joe Biden was subjected to, well, a whack job interview in which he was asked if Obama was a communist, the Obama team banned interviews with that station and then with the whole of ABC Florida. Wise? Maybe they needed to be as heavy as possible in a swing state, but it's an ugly and repressive way of treating something better laughed off.

But by and large the Obama campaign is disciplined and tight, and has a truly extraordinary movement on the ground, reaching millions of people a week – and now pushing McCain to buy advertising time in places like Montana (won by Bush with 20 per cent in '04), North Dakota (ditto) and West Virginia (you got a purty mouth, boy). If by some wild chance the polls were wrong, but happened to be wrong in Obama's favour, the GOP would be reduced to a dozen states, Texas their only big population base. The party might then be fully taken over by the religious right and unelectable for a generation. Well, a man can dream.

Tomorrow, Obama has his half-hour film ad on all networks (except ABC), including the Spanish networks and cable.
It's huge, a tens of millions of dollars buy, dwarfing McCain's
remaining funds. Will that put the lid on it? We will find out,
but it's fair to say that when FOX is getting pissed off with you
because your rough-trade pick-up is going crazy in the green
room, then you are in last days of Kurt Cobain territory. He
was an eyeliner sort of guy too.

HARRISBURG, PENNSYLVANIA: WEDNESDAY, 29 OCTOBER

Rebecca Someone is unloading groceries from a car. But not
too many, cos she's poor. Having moved to the country so she
could send her kids to private schools, her husband had some
sort of awful meniscus injury – can that be right? – and now
they're struggling.

'I just want things to be better,' she says to the camera. 'Just
an end to everyday life being chaos.'

We're in a bar in Harrisburg, Pennsylvania, the state capital, a town so boring that it had to stage the Three Mile Island
nuclear near-disaster to get someone to pay attention. It's an
all-black place, including myself, the bags under my eyes having now spread to cover my face. On the TV above the bar,
Barack Obama's half-hour message is just starting, on NBC,
CBS, MSNBC, Univision (Spanish) and a coupla others. It's on
before the World Series baseball final, and McCain has tried to
spin it that Obama is delaying the baseball. In fact, it's merely

replaced broadcast of the pre-game entertainment – so any grizzled grand final veteran will see the logic instantly. Anything,
anything that pre-empts that nadir of human existence, that
unlife, has got to be an improvement.

No one's watching, though. In Pennsylvania, to find a black
Republican . . . man, you'd have to find some guy at the McCain
office, too neat, in a three-piece suit, with a thin moustache.

'Why's he doing this?' someone asks.

'Hell if I know.'

'When's the game?'

We're into it, and there's the story of an old black couple
who were looking forward to retirement. He's playing a mean
blues guitar. Then the story: she got ill, the retirement wouldn't
cover it, he had to go back to work as a 'sales associate' – i.e. a
paper-bag stuffer in a supermarket, in a denim uniform meant
for a 16-year-old kid in his first job. The sense not merely of
poverty, but of humiliation, is raw and real.

After that, Obama went into a series of itemised proposals
about his budget. And then into stuff about his mum.

People are watching it now, the show draws you in. It's slick
beyond slick, quiet music, perfect shots, fantastic subtle cutting.
It's being called an informercial, but it's a real movie.

'She died really quickly from cancer. It was a shock . . . It
was a reminder that life is short.'

That's the argument he's using to explain his neophyte status – he had to run fast because he knows how short life is. From
that it jumps to a white couple in Ohio, the killing ground of

manufacture. They're queuing up at a cut-price diner, the stewed steak being slopped into a paper container, the David Lynchesque gleam on the gravy, the obscenity of reduced circumstances.

In the bar, people are watching. It's alluring, even if you're rusted on. No one's asked to change the channel.

We get various governors and senators praising him, and Joe Biden saying how impressed he was by the way he worked with Richard Lugar on a nuclear weapons bill, etcetera. Then more stories, and a bit, live, from the Florida speech he's giving tonight, before he speaks with Bill Clinton . . . and we're out.

Was it powerful? Not for these folks – no one in inner-city Philly needs to be told about deprivation. But it wasn't aimed at them, obviously. It was aimed at the last few waverers, at the crowd of undecideds who, on FOX earlier, Frank Luntz had practically yelled at: 'Make up your minds!'

Was it worth it? the pundits asked. The point for the Obama campaign is, it don't matter too much. They have so much money they couldn't even spend it all in the last week if they tried. At about seven million in fees, and I reckon a million in production costs, it is really aimed at 2 per cent of waverers, and maybe half a per cent, a quarter or so, of the undecideds. It's coming in at about ten grand a stray Florida voter. It's part of leaving nothing to chance.

That's why the Obama campaign is in Pennsylvania, duking it out, even though it seems like they're ten points clear. Don't be complacent, don't fail to cover the bases, don't be, don't be, don't be . . . Democrats.

Meanwhile the McCain campaigns – there's about three of them – are simultaneously running the idea that Obama is a dangerous subversive who shouldn't be near power and also that he should be president later. 'Barack Obama – not ready yet'. That is so desperate, my God.

It's like that terrible scene in *Very Bad Things* when the five white Vegas-visiting arseholes, having accidentally murdered a stripper, then have to kill the black security guard sent to investigate. Someone stabs him in the heart with a corkscrew and he bleeds to death in the bathroom, yelling, 'Pleeeeeeease . . . pleeeeeease'. Why not just yell, 'John McCain – pleeeeeeeease. Pleeaaaaaaase. Oh pleeeeeeeeeasssse'?

Meanwhile, Joe the Plumber has got a record deal and an agent, the new 'terrorist' they've associated Obama with – Rashid Khalidi – was given a half-million dollars by a committee chaired by, um, John McCain, and Sarah Palin says she's 'not in this for nothing' (i.e. it's lost, but sets her up for '12). And the McCain campaign is running ads in Arizona. His home state. Where his margin is down to 5 per cent. Five per cent. Five per cent.

Almost too weary to do it, I try a couple of vox pops along the bar – having attracted some attention in the ads, tapping the laptop, juiced off the Holiday Inn wifi next door.

And I'll spare you the chaff, but this:

'Voting this year?'

'Man, I hate this shit. I hate it.' [pause] 'I'm working for Obama all day Tuesday.'

An end to life being chaos?

It's all going ballistic . . .

On the TV, in the live broadcast at the end of Obama's half-hour presentation, Florida looked breezy and fresh and exciting. Downtown Harrisburg, where the Monarch Tavern sits? Not so much. Even the visit of a former president was taken in its stride.

'Man, Bill sure can talk,' says Errol, chuckling into his drink. 'They shoulda had the hook out for him right there.'

As part of the all-out effort in Pennsylvania, President Clinton, Slick Willie himself, has been out on the stump in the state, rounding up those stray supporters of Hillary, still grousing at her loss, those wavering about Obama's patriotism, and – let's face it – just plain racist whites, lifelong Democrats who may not be able to bring themselves to pull the handle for a *schwartze*.

Errol is one of those *schwartzes*, a print shop worker and fourth generation African–American Pennsylvanian. He finds no significant racism in day-to-day life ('Nothing like the South. You been to Mississippi? My wife's got people there. Man . . .') and he lives, works and drinks with whites and blacks, and . . . and . . .

'I just don't know. We'll see how that whole thing goes down.'

That whole thing is the now famous 'Bradley effect', which haunts this election and America's idea of itself in general – and it's a measure of the desperation and cynicism of the McCain campaign that it has put all its chips on this, the final bet. Their idea, their faint hope: that the Bradley effect writ large, will deliver them Pennsylvania, a state won by Democrats since 1988, and currently running 10–13 per cent in Obama's favour. With the same effect in operation in Ohio and Florida, the McCain campaign will offset near-certain losses in Iowa and New Mexico, and likely losses in Virginia or Colorado, and squeak through with a narrow electoral college victory. To call this an outside chance is to understate it somewhat – McCain is leading in his own state of Arizona by only 5 per cent, half of the most conservative estimate of Obama's margin in Pennsylvania. But is it right?

'That's the old Pennsylvania,' Steve, a union organiser from Pottsville, tells me. Short, wiry, with a grey pencil moustache, he's an organiser from the SEIU (the major service union). He's gathering up 'Obama' signs after a small protest outside a Sarah Palin rally. Fifty or sixty unionists and others turned out to make the point that Western Pennsylvania does not uniformly consent to Palin-worship, or her appeal to identity over policy in the choice of a candidate.

'I worked in Michigan, when there was work in Michigan,' he laughs ruefully. 'Became an organiser for the UAW [United Auto Workers], came down here. You know what? Murtha was right!'

He was referring to John Murtha, a no-nonsense Pennsylvania congressman who had given the Obama team one of its many migraines by referring to his own constituents as 'racists', before helpfully clarifying that they weren't racists, they were 'rednecks'.

'Hey, I spent most of the '80s trying to integrate my local [the union branch], not on paper, but really. But look, this is a different place. Half my members work at colleges.' He pauses, pulling a yard sign out of the lawn. 'They're cleaners but even so . . . Look, race? That stuff means less. It just means less now.'

There is no American heartland. What the revolutionary Samuel Adams first called the 'united states' (note the lower case) in the early 1770s is a half-dozen nations under a common flag, held together by the ruthlessness of an inexperienced Illinois politician named Abraham Lincoln, who illegally suspended the Constitution and the Bill of Rights in order to make war on half his own country, in a 'scorched earth' conflict that served as an eerie rehearsal for Vietnam. Had that not occurred, North America would now look like South America, with a northern USA, a Southern CSA (Confederate States of America), a Republic of Texas, a Spanish-speaking Southwest and California, and a northern republic of Oregon, stretching to Alaska.

That alternative history is vital to remember when you try and assess 'what America thinks', because there is no one thing that it does think. Even state by state, political and social cultures vary wildly. Vermont is a quasi-socialist republic (with a secessionist newspaper on sale in every 7-Eleven), with free health care, Ben & Jerry's, and a population that voted en masse to impeach Bush. Neighbouring New Hampshire thinks of itself as a libertarian state, with no state income taxes, and a willingness to accept mass poverty as a price of self-reliance. And so on.

Pennsylvania has become the cockpit of the 2008 election because of its contradictory character, its combination of social radicalism and cultural conservatism. Here, mines were dug in the 18th century and American expansion began (into the Ohio valley). As Gary Nash relates in *The Unknown American Revolution*, violent conflicts began here, decades before the War of Independence proper. Settled initially by the northern English and the Scots, Eastern European migrants determined its later character.

Here in the '20s and '30s, the Communist Party of the USA had a stronghold, many of its members and supporters combining their belief in revolution with Christianity, a phenomenon that went all the way down the Appalachians (one Kentucky hymn from the 1930s is titled 'God Bless Lenin and all of them').

'Look, I don't talk about politics . . . I'm kinda dumb.'

Dolly, in the diner near the bus station in Johnstown, won't answer my questions. Because her boss is listening? Because she's sussed me, from my half-British accent, as a European pointyhead? Because she doesn't want to confess about voting Obama, or not voting Obama? Who knows? But she's willing to talk about her wage.

'Why, I earn four dollars twenty an hour, plus tips.'

Four dollars. This woman is in her late forties.

She wears high-cushion trainers ('My nephew brought 'em for me') to stand the 12-hour shifts on her feet. Tips round out her wage, because most Americans know to add 20 per cent to any bill – tips are factored not only into wages but also into income tax assessment. Yes, every American service industry worker is assumed by the IRS, the income tax body, to earn a certain percentage of their income from tips and is taxed accordingly. If you wanted a better picture of the sustained war against the low-waged that American governance has become, you couldn't get much better than that.

Barack Obama's economic plan would give this woman a sufficient income credit, which would mean she could buy her own goddam shoes, his support of union legislation would make it easier for her to unionise her workplace – why, even out of earshot of a boss, is she diffident about her choice?

Well, one answer is the marble church steeple visible out the window. It was built on the site of a former workshop, an evangelical church, paid for with Southern money, and with a mini shopping mall and office complex attached. Its high gloss tone is totally out of character with the rest of the town, but that's the point. It turns its back to tradition, promises new life.

In recent years, Pennsylvania has become an unlikely centre of Southern-style evangelical religion. The evangelocals would say that that is the movement of God. The rest of us would suggest that when you deprive people of everything that gives them dignity and a sense of self, the religion-candy of fundamentalism is a shoo-in. In Pennsylvania, in the town of Dover, the 'intelligent design' movement had its Scopes Monkey trial when a decision by a local school board to put stickers on high-school biology textbooks saying that 'evolution was merely a theory' was defeated in the courts.

The primary mover of the 'sticker' movement was a Gulf War veteran with a Benzodiazapene addiction derived from post-traumatic stress disorder, which is as effective a critique of the culture wars as you could imagine.

'Dude, I just don't think we want to surrender,' Travis says, as we burn through the Pittsburgh suburbs. He's a college student, a McCain volunteer, who's volunteered to pick me up from the airport. In the 19th century, P-burgh was a steel town, its virtual king, Andrew Carnegie, more or less melting his workers down for profit in the forges. Later he gave his wealth away in the form of public libraries and universities, so he is now celebrated as a humanitarian.

It's a funny old world. In any case, his legacy turned this city into a centre of art and learning, and Travis is an example of that. He's studying 'design software management' whatever that is. A child of a realtor (i.e. estate agent) and a 'homemaker', he's mildly fundamentalist ('I believe in a Flood, but not literally') and utterly pro-McCain.

'I just don't think these Bill Ayers connections have been answered.'

For months the right have tried to make an issue of the connection, hamstrung by John McCain's reluctance to go there, an instinct nourished no doubt by his memory of the murderous bruisers he had to accommodate in support of the Nicaraguan contras, etcetera. When things got desperate and McCain went there, his instincts were justified – no one gave a rat's arse about Ayers, either because the '60s were as distant as the war of 1812, or because they remembered the times and how crazy they were.

But Travis is one of the true believers. I try to like the guy, but I can't – like every leading Australian supporter of the Iraq war, his military experience extends to a marine-style haircut. With US military recruiting running at 30 per cent below target, Travis – aiming for an NYC management position – will not swell their stop-loss numbers.

'But man, I gotta lotta respect for those dudes.'

Travis the Manager was one of the McCain army, their leading figure Joe the Plumber. What is distinctive about every McCain supporter I've met – aside from the rich – is that they are confused about their own interests. Joe earned forty grand a year and the business he worked for cleared a hundred grand. In subsequent radio interviews, he railed against the whole idea of debt, a sort of medieval anti-usury position that sat ill with the loan he'd need to buy the business. He opposed progressive income tax, and then told FOX News's visibly uncomfortable business reporter Neil Cavuto that it was wrong that a bond trader earned thirty million a year for doing nothing, and that something should be done about it.

He was, in other words, delivering a raw and contradictory cry of rage from the lower-middle class, from people who make their income from physical labour and watch others coin it hand over fist from . . . well, nothing at all. Bond trading. Showbiz. Journalism. Joe the Plumber's politics, insofar as they matched anything, were lined up with Peron, with Poujade, with Hanson.

'Look, it's a bad time to be a Republican,' Laura, a Republican operative, had told me months earlier at the closing night of the Republican Convention. She'd slid into a spare chair at the *Wonkette* table, her winsome figure and cowboy hat something she clearly thought would be an all-access pass, which of course it was. 'People want something to believe in.'

She was right about the election, but she completely misunderstood the nature of the politics. The Republicans simply had not understood how much the dream was slipping away from them, how illusory the comfort they offered was.

Much of the blame for this has to be taken by FOX News, the unashamedly 'conservative' network which sought to spruik for the McCain campaign. Early on, the FOX network focused on Obama's earlier associations, with Ayers and others. But, despite having a full broadcast network at their disposal, they never seemed to actually investigate the story that was obviously there.

It was the same complacency that had defined the conservative campaign from the start. As recent days made clear, they could have made a good case about Obama's connection with these radical leftist individuals, but they never really bothered to extend it to actual evidence.

The problem for McCain was that, generous and friendly

as he was, the idea of stumping for the Republicans was beyond Travis.

'Man, I got stuff to do.'

And that, of course, was the problem. Days later, Obama would appear at a speech in jeans and a windcheater, rain streaming down his face, and tell an audience that 'The future is more important than a bit of weather'. Channelling Martin Luther King, in a way far beyond the failed Navy pilot John McCain, he called out to people to 'Make history, take the day off work, get out the vote'. The right-wing media could only play catch-up.

IO

DOUBLE DOWN ON THE LAST BEST HOPE

The Vote, The Victory

SUNDAY, 2 NOVEMBER

Well, as we enter the final week of the campaign, there are no more vox pops to be done, no more speeches to watch. Everyone's been interviewed, every speech is identical. Nothing to do but to surrender to the televisual OxyContin of the three 24-hour news networks. Memories of an actual high are now distant – now it's just about keeping withdrawal symptoms at bay.

Give me Hannity and Colmes, give me Keith Olbermann, give me pundits, David Gergen, Donna Brazile, Nancy Pfotenhauer, give me soundbites and cheap shots, angles and magic maps, just keep talking.

As m'esteemed colleagues have noted, the myth of a tight race is being spruiked to sell newspapers and TV ads and to have something to say. But there is, of course, another reason for that sort of push, and that is the supreme importance of a sense of possibility in order to get the vote out.

For Australia, with compulsory voting, the ideal position

is to actually be in the lead but to give the appearance of being the underdog. There's some of that too in the US, but what you desperately don't want to do is let expectations dip below a certain level. Why? Because at some point, for true believers, the prospect of defeat gets too much, and you switch off the TV, black out the windows and get drunk on Advokaat or moonshine, the two dominant tipples of hardcore Republicans. Then you get the weird effect whereby you lose not because MOR voters don't turn out for you, but because your base doesn't. The sense of being still in the game is far more important than putting yourself in the underdog slot.

That explains the relentless upbeat spruik of the Republican operatives – the magical thinking of conservative heartlands, such as the *National Review*'s 'Corner' rolling blog, much less so. Last week they battened on to a one-day Zogby result that had McCain leading by 1 per cent, but which had yet to be added in to Zogby's three-day rolling poll. When the full Zogby poll came out, it was within the range of all other polls that have Obama leading by 5–7 per cent. 'What happened to the Zogby lead?' Katherine Jean Lopez wailed on the site. 'I hate to be paranoid but . . .' Well, uh, what happened is that the Zogby one-day result got folded in to the three-day average and the lead disappeared. Are these people stupid?

Yes, sadly, a lot of them are. The Republicans and conservative think tanks, etcetera, in general have suffered from the fact that so many of their foot soldiers are not only children of conservatives, but come through elite universities of a conservative mien – Dartmouth is the supreme example – straight into an easy master's degree on a friendly topic, and then slide into a research position in a think tank or similar. They know all the talking points, the received idea of American exceptionalism, neoclassical economics, etcetera, but nothing deeper. When stuff like the financial crisis comes along, they're all at sea.

Indeed, one great moment in the McCain campaign was an ad featuring a stormy ocean and stuff about Obama's inexperience in tough times, etcetera. The ad ran in New Mexico, a landlocked desert state. Thirty per cent of its residents have never seen the ocean. Wouldn't you run an ad in New Mexico which played more on local fears – rockslides, rattlesnakes, mirages, etcetera, rather than something alien to local experience? Not if you spent summers on the New England coast. Stormy weather occurs to you as a great metaphor for sudden hazard if your CV includes, under the hobbies list, YACHTING. You dummies.

Conservatives long ago trapped themselves in a circular logic that goes like this: 1) America is a centre-right country; 2) Barack Obama, an unashamed liberal, is doing better than previous Democrats; 3) The media is giving him a soft run because otherwise America, a centre-right country, would never vote for him.

The possibility that the country that gave us May Day, four FDR victories, the '60s and the civil rights movement, is *not* a centre-right country but, to oversimplify it somewhat, a populist-oriented place, where right and left compete for 'ownership' of that populist impulse, is genuinely not acknowledged.

Though some strands of conservatism have a critique of the market and its effect on social life, American conservatism, partly for political coalition reasons, has so long seen the market as morally neutral and uninvolved in the shaping of character and culture, that they've sold themselves the idea that most Americans still believe there is some real relationship between effort and reward.

Whatever illusions many had on that score, the last eight years have beaten it out of them. The Bush tax cuts, the radical rise in inequality, the free kicks given to health insurers, credit card companies, union-busting corporations, etcetera etcetera, have given tens of millions a feeling that they are simply prey to forces beyond their control. Their lives are thus not exercises in the expression of virtue, but simply matters of survival.

To get into the position is to be something less than human, so many people will simply be voting for the opportunity to emerge from the tunnels once again. There is a great cultural studies thesis to be not-written around how the rise of monster and creepy creature movies (*Cloverfield*, etcetera) are expressions of these anxieties in mythologised form, a sense of being crushed and hunted.

In the final days of a campaign, you do what you do, of course. But a lot of conservative outlets – FOX News among them – have been running this story for months, if not years. What happened in Australia in the last years of the Howard government – that false assumption that Howard somehow mystically represented the general will of the Australian people – has been repeated times umpteen here, and it has sapped the ability of the right to understand the nature of a changing nation and a changing world. Hence they never spotted the way in which hitherto solid states like Virginia and Colorado were sliding from underneath them.

Much of this goes back, of course, to Murdoch, and his late-stage strategy of staffing his outlets with people who are less flexible, and more psychologically cracked, than the be-jowled one. The theory is that the people best-placed to wage a phoney culture war are those who believe it's a real one, so FOX News – which has lost 60 per cent of its market share to left-leaning MSNBC over the past two years – is stuffed with the same sort of people as *The Australian*, that wall-padded redoubt of old Groupers, ultramontane Catholics and ex-Maoists.

Such people are no more capable of flexibility than a toaster is of flipping you an omelette. They do what they do, which is why they could never start the conversation conservatism needed to have a coupla years ago, about what it needed to become in order to preserve its viability as a movement.

So, after Tuesday . . . oh hang on, here comes the dis-claimer – are you ready for it? McCain can still win this. This vote could be a 'black swan' – an unknown unknown – whereby the most important result is less the election of a president than the revelation that polling decisively, utterly, completely, does not work, even when results are aggregated, averaged, weighted, woo hoo blablabla fifififififi.

But that's what it needs.

That, or a stolen election.

Why does McCain have such an eerie smile – even, on his recent, very funny, *SNL* appearance, an air of insouciance? Because he's pretty sure he's lost? Or because he's utterly certain he hasn't?

WASHINGTON, DC: TUESDAY, 4 NOVEMBER

Well, four in the afternoon here and the strange vacuum that obtains on polling day is sucking everyone in. Though both Obama and McCain have foregone the traditional practice of not campaigning on polling day – always an odd one, I've thought, in a place of voluntary voting – and are holding rallies and doing phone bank appearances, etcetera, there ain't that much for the poor sods on the networks to talk about. There are no exit polls until late in the day and they're hopelessly sloppy in any case.

So we have endless photos of the long polling queues and stories about voting irregularities, all designed to scare people into a lather. Two jokers dressed in the uniform of the New Black Panther Party hung around outside a Philly polling station, and since it was more interesting than anything else on tape, it's been playing across the networks all day.

There are all sorts of minor stories about ballots getting wet in Virginia, misdelivered voter registration rolls in Missouri, etcetera etcetera. No reports so far of voting machines jumping votes from one column to another, but plenty of other stuff. Preemptive lawsuits have already begun – the GOP suing against restrictions on their polling place staff in New Hampshire, the NAACP in Virginia suing against the lack of polling places in minority areas. Get your bids in early.

You can't, as you watch queues half-a-mile long snaking out of places with machines designed by slot machine manufacturers, do anything but recall that moment in *Life of Brian* when the Roman soldiers watch the Judean People's Front trying to get their crap together, and slowly shake their heads . . . Really, can't these guys even vote right . . . ?

With around 30–40 per cent of votes already cast in some states – in places like Colorado it appears to be as high as 60–70 per cent – the election seems to be on the way to a century-high turnout, beating, I think, 1936, when FDR took 46 of 48 states, with around 63 per cent.

If it is heading towards those levels, you would have to conclude that McCain is toast. The states to watch will be Florida and Virginia, which close first (Indiana closes earlier but it has weird systems of counting and staggered closing times, and it must be said, some very dodgy practices in Gary, one of the bigger and heavy Dem cities), and if both of those go to Obama, it's good night, Vienna.

If Obama somehow loses both, and also Pennsylvania, then it will be a long and arduous night, hanging on promised high margins in the 'new West' – Colorado, New Mexico and Nevada. I don't think it will be a long night, but we'll see.

In the Senate, the races to watch are North Carolina, Alaska, Minnesota, Oregon and Mississippi – all of which were reasonably safe Republican ones until about ten weeks ago. But in Carolina, incumbent Elizabeth Dole, with the Democrats breathing down her neck, released an ad accusing her opponent (a church warden) of being godless – and saw her own numbers plummet.

In Minnesota, ex-*SNL* comedian Al Franken has fought incumbent Norm Coleman inch by inch for six months, and slowly got within striking distance – even with an independent splitting the Democratic vote. Alaska would, in all other situations, seem a shoo-in, since Ted Stevens, incumbent, will soon be going to jail. But hey, Mac, it's Alaska. In Oregon, the Republican incumbent has been running on a campaign of how well he works with Obama, but has lost 18 per cent of his lead to the Dems. And in Kentucky, Republican Senate leader Mitch McConnell may lose his seat, to really complete the rout.

If those five go, or even four of them, plus another three or four near-certain losses (New Hampshire, etcetera), then the magic sixty supermajority will be very close. Even if they don't get that, there'll be three or four Republicans – one or two of whom may simply change their party allegiance – who'll help them over the filibuster-proof line, in return for some nice fat pork.

One of the many Congressional races to watch is in Connecticut, where Chris Shays is the last Republican in the whole of New England – effectively marking the disappearance of the party in that region, a measure of the deep political-cultural crisis the GOP is in.

Of the manifold, not always nutty, propositions on the ballot, the first of the two key ones is Proposition 8 in California – an attempt to put a gay marriage ban in the State Constitution. If that loses, then gay marriage is effectively legal in the US, since anyone can come to California and get their marriage legally recognised. There will then be a decade of lawsuits to force other states to honour California's statutes.

In Colorado, Prop 48 is trying to define personhood beginning at conception, a new strategy to get an abortion ban in through the backdoor. This would criminalise standard IVF procedures, and make any woman who miscarried without even knowing she was pregnant potentially guilty of criminally negligent homicide if she had been to the gym or somesuch after conceiving.

The thing is deeply unconstitutional, but its success would mean the enshrinement of a new strategy for the anti-choice crowd. Its defeat would be a further blow to them in a period in which they are meeting increasing resistance.

So eyes down for a full house. Erewegoerewegoerewego . . .

8.30 p.m. DC in full party mode out the window, people walking the streets in old Halloween costumes dressed as political operatives, men in spy overcoats, girls in scary boots . . . Oh no – actually those are real people.

My desk is out of the FSN news services bureau, where talking heads are speaking to Asia from the desk next to me, and the TVs are buzzing with virtually useless knowledge.

The way it looks at the moment: Indiana is running neck and neck as the counting continues, 51 to 48 in favour of McCain, but without the huge votes from Gary, Indiana, which should swing it for Obama.

Virginia is running well ahead for McCain but this is purely on the basis of a bunch of southern counties – the northern areas are still to report, because they've got more votes to count.

The crucial finding everyone is pivoting on is the exit polls for Pennsylvania, where each demographic shows an Obama win – including the non-college educated white men who were the bedrock of McCain's strategy to swing the keystone state (so called because it sounds like keister, and the place is an arsehole). The cable news are already calling that as a loss for McCain, which, if true, is most likely the ballgame – but there is still nothing solid to base any sort of judgment on.

In the Senate races, there's more bad news for the GOP, with Elizabeth Dole said to have definitively lost in North Carolina. Mitch McConnell, Republican Senate leader, is struggling in Kentucky, which is real, real bad news for them. It means the water's up to the neck level.

The Dems also appear to have won the New Hampshire Senate seat, also Virginia – both seen as slum dunks for them – and they're leading in Minnesota and Georgia, so that filibuster bust is looking very, very possible.

But everyone's still running on fumes at the moment; nothing has really slammed down decisively.

McCain appeared on TV just now talking to the campaign

reporters on his plane, sounding tired and defeated, beyond getting any sort of energy out. He's done.

It wouldn't have helped that his 96-year-old aunt told reporters that McCain's mother really didn't care if he won or not – thanks, Mom. Even at seventy-two, you're still just a naughty boy.

And Palin bizarrely refused to tell reporters how she voted – a last gamine moment? Who knows? Crazy lady?

ABC and NBC have called Pennsylvania for McCain. But it will take another hour or two . . .

Tens of thousands streaming into Grant Park Chicago for the Obamathon.

Whooping outside, noise from the bars across the street.

Chinese food's arrived. America is in decline. China is near. I can smell it . . .

Grant Park is swarming with thousands, flashes going off like the proverbial thousand points of light, a diamond sea. Outside in the streets of DC, block parties are starting all over, including one outside the White House.

'America, if you ever doubted that anything was possible here . . . the answer has been spoken by rich and poor, young and old, black and white. We are and always will be the United States of America.'

Here in the newsroom, three TVs are playing this on different time delays, turning it into an echo chamber, a prism of oratory.

At 11 p.m. in Chicago on 4 November, Barack Obama claimed the Presidency of the United States of America.

Half an hour earlier, there had been a more subdued appearance in Phoenix.

'My friends, no, no . . .'

It was those hands again, the gesture. John McCain was conceding and congratulating Barack Obama and those assembled on the lawn of the Phoenix Biltmore Hotel were booing.

It was disappointment speaking, but it was on the edge of ugly.

'My friends . . .'

And the best he got out of them for the most part was a sullen silence. He spoke of the ugliness that had disfigured the country and how it had denied a section of its own people the opportunities to be American.

Still not much. Tepid applause.

He spoke of Obama's grandmother who had died the day before and talked of how both he and Obama believed she had returned to her Creator.

That seemed to get some sort of fellow feeling aroused, but it was hard yards.

Back in Chicago a half-hour later, Barack Obama went through the thank yous – Biden, Michelle, campaign heads Davids Plouffe and Axelrod, and then into the general campaign:

'This campaign was built in the backyards and living rooms, in the dollar donations, in millions of people volunteering and organising . . .

'We know the challenges to come, to live up to the best of this country . . . We may not get there in the first year, or the first term, but I promise you, we, as a people, will get there.'

He refers back to Lincoln, the other Illinois politician who came to the White House: our differences must strain but never break, the bonds that hold us together.

He goes into the story of a 106-year-old woman, Anne Nixon Cooper, through all the people who told her we couldn't – yes we can.

This is the old Obama of the primaries, the prophet, getting the audience calling back: 'Yes we can!'

The news crew set up in front of me waiting to do a live cross after the speech are clearing their throats, trying to look professional as they choke up . . . just something in my eye . . .

'We will respond to all those who say we can't solve the problems of the world – We say, yes we can. God Bless America and etcetera . . .' And then he was engulfed in cheering.

In Phoenix, not so much. Even on the TV you could feel a lingering air of bitterness. Still, you have to have some sympathy. Obama's lead in the popular vote is currently three million out of a hundred million votes cast. When the west coast comes in that may extend to five million, but it's not like an overwhelming will of the people thing. Nevertheless President Obama will have a pliant House and Senate, and any sense that he won't remake the US in a liberal image will depend on the genuineness of his promise that there will be no red- and blue-state America. I suspect that he will pleasantly surprise his enemies and disappoint his liberal supporters.

The provisional result would appear to be Obama 334 EC votes, to McCain 157. There's been a five-seat Senate pick-up so far, with another three possible, which would be close to the filibuster bust. So far there's been a 13-seat pick-up in the House, with another five in the offing.

In Colorado, Proposition 48 – personhood beginning at conception – was defeated 75 to 25.

But Proposition 8 – banning gay marriage in California – is leading 56 to 44, albeit with a low vote count.

That's it for the moment. I am now going to join the crowds outside the White House, to dissolve for an hour or so into History. Whatever and whenever it will be necessary to challenge the Obama Doctrine in the years that lie ahead, whatever the sense of symbolism and identity politics, this victory was built on millions of small donations, on tens of millions of foot miles, of leaflets, of meetings, of privilege and assumption surrounded and subjected by possibility. Whatever is to come may subtract from this moment, but can never dissolve it. Not even close.

Ya es de dia.

WASHINGTON, DC: WEDNESDAY, 5 NOVEMBER

These are the days of tears and laughter. Up midafternoon, after filing for UK media at 7 a.m., light pushing past the curtains. After the result was declared last night and Barack Obama gave his speech, we all headed down to the White House, where a street party had been brewing since McCain had commenced his concession speech. The city that had given Obama a 93 per cent to 7 per cent victory was going wild. Along the broad avenues – spokes in a wheel, an expression of the enlightenment worship of the pure form of the circle, written down in town planning – people were hanging out of cars, shouting, sounding their horns. Cops stood at each intersection, inscrutable.

People hugged each other spontaneously in the street, shook hands, slapped palms, black and white and brown and yellow. Everyone was gentle with each other, everyone was kind. Even the occasional disconsolate Republican – you could see them, the young men and women who work at think tanks, the boys in blue suits and red ties, the girls in black dresses and pearls, walking, no— marching, hand-in-hand, eyes fixed ahead, desperate for a cab to levitate them out of this hell-hole.

If they had any sense they've already put together the survival kit – the stack of DVDs, a half-dozen big books you wanted to read, the single malt and the smooth merlot, a few lines of China white, maybe a holiday in some awful all-in resort at Hilton Head. Pull the cable out the back of the TV, smack the laptop sharply against the wall, and swim into the embracing waters of the timeless imaginary. Emerge a week or two later when President-elect Obama – PRESIDENT-ELECT OBAMA, PRESIDENT-ELECT OBAMA, PRESIDENT-ELECT OBAMA! – has already announced his core staff, outlined a bunch of policies, set the course for the next year. A fortnight or so of chasing the dragon and *Lord of the Rings* and *World of*

Warcraft, and you can emerge at least partially restored to face at least the next four years ahead.

God knows, the left has done it often enough.

Outside the White House the crowd was several thousand strong by midnight – there were the young, there were old black women in pan-Africa scarfs and Sunday-best hats dancing a war-jig, there were old hippies, activists and tourists, straights in suits, white gangstas and the blinged-up, there were gay couples holding each other singing 'The Star Spangled Banner', there were drums and songs, and a sign hung on the wire fence with a photo of the Obamas' daughters, saying 'mali and sasha, welcome home' – and think about that for a while and what it means.

'Pack your stuff and go, pack your stuff and go!'

At 2 a.m. I ran into Alex Kelly, an old comrade I'd first met at S11, that moment in 2000 when Melbourne rose up and confronted the World Economic Forum, the most-effective challenge to these series of slick elite meetings to date in the anti-globalisation movement, Seattle included. S11 – September 11, 2000 – was swallowed in history by what happened a year later. But it felt like a direct line from there to here. When the anti-globalisation movement had, as it always would, fallen apart, I had gone west to London, and Alex had gone north and taken up the harder yards of working in, with and at the frontier of Indigenous Australia, out of, I think, a sense of absolute responsibility to battles close to home, battles most of us simply couldn't hack.

Seeing her there felt like the completion of a passage through dangerous waters, over a decade, and I hugged her tight enough to break her ribcage. It was the relief of possibility, of renewed hope.

On TV, in the streets, people kept breaking into tears. In a TV interview, Colin Powell could barely continue, and Jack Cafferty, an old newsman on CNN who lost his wife eight weeks ago, had to turn his face sideways and spit out a conclusion to his segment before he fell apart. Condoleezza Rice teared up. Even Dubya, in a White House lawn speech, seemed struck by the moment.

I lost it this morning, after filing the last article and radio interview and staggering down to the lobby for a coffee and some ice. DeShaya, a young black woman who'd been on the desk when I'd checked in, was on there for the graveyard shift. We'd traded insults over my routinely screwed-up reservation – this is the US, after all – and then bitched together about the inadequacies of the booking company. She was at the end of her twelve-hour shift, because that's how you work in Bush's America – and I was at the end of it all. And mutually wreathed in exhaustion and relief, we just held hands and wept for a minute or so, in happiness, in relief, in the victory of something larger than both of us, that contained both of us.

But I wouldn't mention it if it were unusual. All over the city, the Rome of the 20th century, the Capitol Monument and the Dome on the horizon, wherever you look, people were doing the same.

Tears and smiles in the street, in the Starbucks, in the metro station. No one is ashamed of their emotions, of this release, of this vulnerability to others in a city where, othertimes and even now, you would want to watch your back.

Let's be clear about what this victory means, and why it means so much. It is not simply the victory of a black man as president. A Colin Powell becoming the new Republican Eisenhower of 2008 would not arouse a hundredth of this enthusiasm. Nor is it a victory of the left. A Dennis Kucinich, by some bizarre cosmic accident, becoming president would not arouse this level of passion.

What makes it powerful is that it is a victory of the global left in the incarnation of a black American; that it is a double blow to power and skin-privilege. Will President Obama be a programmatically radical leader? Of course not. But will he be a shivering neurotic Jesus-freak sycophant like Tony Blair? No, equally.

His achievement before anything has occurred is this: that every vector of power – money, race, media – has been defeated in the US, the declining but still regnant capital of the world. That what won was the idea of wisdom, judgement, intelligence, prudence and audacity, conservatism and radicalism, a measuring up to the demands of the world. That, as opposed to past Democratic campaigns, this was not a party machine insider – a Tennessee grandee or a billionairess's husband – presenting themselves as the least worst option.

It was someone who, by his own account, had come through the world of the radical left, of radical black action, to the realisation that any change in America had to come not against its traditions, but within them, and who therefore drew on the strengths of every residual radical and progressive notion of this one-time revolutionary society. It was an achievement, but it was also a channelling in to a deeper moment of historical shift.

In the USA this has been greeted, even by conservatives, as a historic transcendent moment. Why? I am reminded of the Jorge Luis Borges essay about Buenos Aires during 1940, when it looked like the Nazis – who had a lot of support in Argentina out of hatred of British imperialism – would win. Borges, a resolute anti-Nazi, was visited by an Axis supporter. 'France has fallen,' he said. 'Nothing can stop them now!' And then Borges notes, 'I realised he was as terrified as I was'.

In other words – and am I not breaking Godwin's law – there are moments in politics when, on one side, no one really wants to win. That was the curse of the McCain campaign. Deep down they knew that McCain's moment was 2000, and that it had passed. But they kept going, against a historical moment which, deep, deep down, most of them – and that may well include John McCain himself – wanted to happen, and, deep, deep down, most did not want to stand in the way of.

For those of us who committed ourselves to the left – whatever that means – these are great days not because of what Obama will do, but because of what he will not do. Because he will normalise progressive, moderate, multilateral, modernised politics in the US and in the Western world, and that is the context in which we will work.

If you want to see some graciousness in that moment, read (sections of) the US conservative press. If you want to read bitterness and incomprehension about it, read Albrechtsen and Sheridan in the *Oz*.

For the rest of us, it is tears and laughter, laughter and tears. For all the people I've marched with, argued with, whatever, this is a moment. I have no compunction at all about feeling part of this in however distant a manner. For the right, globally, you will have to reinvent yourselves. You are the Whigs in the 1850s. You are about to cease to exist.

Tears and laughter and laughter and tears.

II

CODA

Slow Days in the Havre de Grace

HAVRE DE GRACE, MARYLAND: SUNDAY, 9 NOVEMBER

'Hey, can you tell me which college Obama attended first?'

'Occidental, in California.'

'Well done – you get a free extra espresso shot!'

'Would you have given it to me if I'd got it wrong?'

'Of course!'

How long is this going to go on? I wondered, staggering away from Caribou Coffee to DC Union Station, a supercharged Americano in hand. Nearly a week later and no one's stopped smiling, and this sense of freedom, of release, of possibility, seems to spread outward and inward. Whatever happens, there's a sense that policy arguments and discussion of ideas might be conducted in some rational manner, not as a baiting process, or some combination of free-market mantras and religious fundamentalism . . .

On the train out to a cheaper hotel in a harbour town on the Chesapeake coast – and seriously, what better place to sail into now than the 'harbour of grace'? Even better, the locals pronounce it with a longer 'a'.

'Are you going to Have-er, de Grace?' the cab driver asked.

Oh yes, mate, I'll have the grace, thanks. Straight up with an extra shot.

Tim, the cabbie, was a skinny white kid with an eight-day growth that doesn't seem to have the strength in it to make it to a beard. He was the only cab at the station, and I'd offered it to a soldier behind (what is *happening* to me?), but Tim had forgotten to renew his military base pass.

'I can't go on the proving grounds,' he said.

'They're called the proving grounds?'

'Ya-ahh.'

The Proving Grounds. Is everything intending to symbolise of itself today, like the mystical rose of Andalusia, which grows with the sutras of the Q'ran inscribed in its folds?

'Here on holiday?'

'In Have-er de Grace? No, I've got to finish a book off. I've been covering the election.'

'You like the result?'

How did he say it? I wondered to myself. Did I hear a slowing of the voice there, a tentativeness? Would I be taken to the Proving Grounds, pass or no pass? This kid looked like the 'before' shot in a crystal meth prevention campaign. Or the 'after' shot in a crystal meth prevention campaign in Oklahoma. I took a chance.

'Yeah, pretty much . . .'

'Yeah!' he whooped. 'Wasn't it great?'

Turns out Tim had a brother in Iraq. Or out of Iraq. Did two tours, having signed on for one and one only. Blown up, fucked up, in the second of these.

'How is he now?'

'He's . . . not good.' That lacuna needs another thirty stops or so. 'I was never much interested in politics till he went to the war. I still don't even know why we went. This is the first time I voted.'

And with that, the 'Bradley effect' passed to the status of a Trivial Pursuit question.

Now I guess I understand how people felt in the days after the Bastille, in October 1917, in England in 1945, when the Attlee Government swept to power. The bodily relief that is something more than merely physical and more than individual, the sense of possibility that keeps generating new thoughts. On the train through Baltimore and out to the harbour of grace, we passed one of those new prisons that have become the stock-in-trade of US regional economies.

They all look the same. Textured brick, well-shaped, an absence of towers or yards. Nothing would suggest it was other than a mall or convention centre, save for the slit brick windows, too small for escape. And suddenly you think, could they, could they? Could they wind down this mad, existentially sadistic living death of two million, most in 23-hours a day lock-down, banged up with a steel toilet bowl and time passing away?

What makes this moment different, different to Clinton,

different to Blair, is that whatever President Obama might do, especially in the field of foreign affairs, I have every confidence that he understands what a crime and a tragedy the American penal system is . . . and the health system, and social security etcetera. And that, however gradually it may have to occur, something will be done, through or by him. And that is not something I would ever have felt about Blair or Clinton, those Tweedledum/dee global narcissistic Tarzans, forever swinging on a vine into somewhere foreign to make a bad situation worse.

Cowards will flinch and traitors will sneer, but that belief in Obama is not the hope that he's some secret socialist Santa (Satan? Santana?) about to pull off the mask and make Bill Ayers his Secretary of Education (though it would be a great pick). The belief is that he's someone who has been through the left of the '80s and '90s and come to some conclusions about what is possible in 21st century America – not in terms of simple centrism or compromise, but in terms of a dynamic combination of the radical and conservative, the prudent and the audacious.

Though Tony Blair appropriated the idea, he quickly abandoned it to sign on to the global neocon narrative, abandoning any real attempt to reconstruct British society. Barack Obama is eight times smarter than Blair and has the advantage of being a real person, not a prototype of CNN's election-night holograms, and he has also been to the proving grounds, tested a few ideas against reality. There ain't nothing occidental about all of this.

That is my take, in any case, on Obama's first big staff pick, Rahm Emanuel, for Chief-of-Staff. There are many aspects of

Emanuel that will not be good cheer to the Democratic left. This is a guy, after all, who volunteered for the IDF during the first Gulf War, and is expressive of what my good friend Philip Frazer noted as the great unspoken truth of American politics – that a core group of the elite effectively hold dual citizenship and dual loyalties, and that any attempt to talk about this gets the 'anti-Semitism' airhorn in your ear.

In any case, it won't be a big story on FOX News. My thoughts are that Emanuel is a great choice for the job – he's inherited his father's skills as an enforcer; that it is specifically not a foreign policy job, but a discipline job; and he's a helluva lot better than Clinton's chaotic choices. Gonna take a lot more than that to kill my Obama buzz, dude.

Meanwhile, like the clown show after the history play in Elizabethan theatre, the Palin material just banks up. Apparently she thought Africa was a single country – well, hell, you can't see it from Wasilla – and that RNC lawyers are on their way to Alaska to get some of those clothes back. Marvellous.

But all that is an extra, really. The thing is what it is. And God knows what this book will look like to me, to anyone, in a year's time, after Guantanamo Bay swells with new inmates from President Obama's invasion of Pakistan, the week before he adopted a less-generous version of John McCain's health plan. Nothing in me believes this to be the case, but throughout these reports I've veered wildly between thinking of Obama as a transformational candidate with a centrist politics, to being an unelectable indulgence whose cautious policies did not warrant the risk for the Democrats of choosing him over a more sellable Hillary Clinton.

A more synthetised version of this book would make less of a foolish, passionate man, but it would also replicate the hedge-betting deadness that passes for much foreign policy commentary and coverage in the Australian media today.

The tumultuous year of Barack Obama's campaign mirrored my own radical uncertainty – and that felt by many people across the world – of what was possible for a global progressive movement, however broadly defined. Was it possible to be optimistic about what could be done in the heartland of empire as we face the years ahead, some process by which common ground could be reached on the problems and opportunities that face humanity?

Or would the election confirm our worst fears – that the American people would rather retreat, once again, into the comforting myths of exceptionalism and heroism, of the 'last best hope of man', of the snarling and childish incomprehension of a changing planet? Because if we were going into all of that, well, bring it on – but it meant facing the likelihood of a dark struggle and the necessity of some hideous alliances and choices. If the United States was going to go deeper into its own worst and most self-defeating traditions – and it still may – then the most likely vista of the 21st century was all-encompassing war, a conflict which would make the 20th century look like a curtain-raiser.

For the world, 'hope' is that there would now be someone in the White House who looked out at the changing, brawling, struggling, developing world, and understood that its multitudes were not simply people halfway along the track to an inevitable Hotel Terminus at the Extended Stay Suites, but were making their own history, finding their own path to a future not defined by a narrow American formulation of the idea of 'freedom'.

That is the 'hope' of the Obama T-shirt. The right never understood why those two words – 'hope' and 'change' – could command such power, could push millions to be out putting leaflets in letterboxes on cold March mornings in Billings, Montana. They mocked those who brandished such motifs, never realising that it was they who could not understand the deep meaning of those two single syllables, that their incomprehension was a measure of their own killing cynicism. Given a time machine, I would, of course, go back to the start of the primary process and sign-on – figuratively and perhaps literally – to the Obama campaign from the get-go. To be honest, my thinking for several months of it corresponded to Hillary Clinton's advisor Mark Penn, whose internal notes to his candidate suggested that the whole rainbow politics thing was an illusion – 'save it for 2050'.

But man, I've never been so happy to be wrong. Never been so happy to have my own sense of what is possible revised upwards. I came here to cover the thing with a cheap metaphor and it quickly became clear that reality was outstripping any easy way of framing it. So forget the crossroads. Now, we are out of the proving grounds and, at least for a while, we have grace, have grace, have entered the harbour of grace . . .

Acknowledgements

In some sort of chronological mash-up, thanks are due to: Kerry, Pete and Pearl at the Hurst, Shropshire, for the safe house; David and Julie in Ilfracombe for the rehab; Oskar, Linda, Moa, Sabina and many others in Uppsala; Philip Frazer and Kate Veitch for repeated bouts of hospitality in New York; Jim Hightower, Rick Hertzberg, Rick Perlstein, Ken Layne and Jim Newell at Wonkette; Lisa and Simon for past hospitality in Baltimore; Charles Richardson, our man in Montana; Karyn and Chad in Richmond; Nick, Chantay, Kip and Gloria at various Obama offices; Emma, Amy, Travis and some anonymous benefactors at McCain offices; Helen Searls and everyone at FSN in Washington; Gloria, Jim and others at Netroots Nation; Aliciya in Portland; State Senator Bill Wielechowski in Anchorage; Elizabeth in Fairbanks; Midge in Wasilla; Anonymous 1 through 3 in Juneau; Michael Veitch for the trip into deepest Vermont; Lizabeth in Savannah; V in Santa Fe; Alex K in DC; Justine and Kimchi in St Paul; Wendy, Sheila Dowd, Susan Gleason and Reinhard in Denver; Gary Nemeth in Vegas; Colin at TMZ; Morus at PoliticalBetting; and to Joe and Mike, *Crikey* competition winners in DC and, related to that, Melissa and two others at *The Monocle*.

Felicitations and thanks to James Norman, co-conspirator in the doomed video wing of the project; to Gay Alcorn and especially Amanda Dunn at *The Sunday Age* for putting up with hair-raising deadline deliveries; Rohan Barwick at ABC Radio Alice Springs; Laura Bailey and Richard Glover; Philip Adams and the *Late Night Live* team; to Brendan O'Neill, Nathalie Rothschild and Rob Lyons, and all at *Spiked Online*, for judicious cutting; to Alison, Grazyna, Valerie and all at *Arena Magazine*; and last and most thanks to all at Crikey/Private Media – Sophie B, Sarah S, Leigh J, Marika, First Dog on the Moon, Jane N, Eric and Diana – and above all, thanks beyond measure to Jonathan Green, editor extraordinaire, for putting me here, and for putting up with crack-ups and crazed ideas beyond measure, and for his unstinting support. Also to Michael Nolan at Penguin for wrangling this into shape amid sprawling chaos. And thanks to S, where she is, whoever she is now. Apologies to anyone I've forgotten along the way.

The bulk of this material appeared in an earlier form as daily reports in *Crikey.com.au*. Other material has been heavily adapted from articles in *Arena Magazine*, *Spiked Online*, and *The Sunday Age*. Thanks are due to all editors.